ARCHAEOLOGY IN THE HOLY LAND

By

KATHLEEN M. KENYON

THIRD EDITION

LONDON
ERNEST BENN LIMITED

FIRST EDITION PUBLISHED 1960 BY ERNEST BENN LIMITED

BOUVERIE HOUSE · FLEET STREET · LONDON · EC4

SECOND EDITION 1965

THIRD EDITION 1970

DISTRIBUTED IN CANADA BY

THE GENERAL PUBLISHING COMPANY LIMITED, TORONTO

© Kathleen M. Kenyon 1960, 1965, 1970

PRINTED IN GREAT BRITAIN

510-03301-6

510-03302-4 P/B

Preface to Third Edition

ARCHAEOLOGICAL WORK has been proceeding at an accelerating rate since the Preface to the Second Edition was written in 1964. Some of the new evidence is additional, some adds clarification, some requires amendments in quite substantial respects to the picture presented in the First Edition. A re-writing to incorporate all this new material would have been a major undertaking, which would have involved an interruption in what I think would be regarded as a more urgent requirement, to proceed as rapidly as possible with the publication of one's own excavations. The present edition is therefore a compromise. The Second Edition is sold out and there appears to be a continuing demand. A simple reprinting that ignored all the archaeological results since 1964, and many of those since 1960, could not be contemplated. I have therefore tried to bring the book up to date by a few amendments to the text, but basically by Addenda related to the original chapters and by adding to the Appendix on the sites. If the need arises for a Fourth Edition, I hope to be able to incorporate all these in the text.

1969   K. M. K.

Preface to Second Edition

Much important archaeological work has been in progress in Palestine since the writing of this book was completed in 1959. To incorporate all the results would have involved very considerable additions and alterations. All that has been attempted is to take note of outstanding new discoveries and make alterations where new evidence requires a considerably different interpretation or has confirmed or disproved tentative suggestions.

1964   K. M. K.

Preface

THE EMPHASIS in this book is on the first word in its title, archaeology. It does not claim to be a complete history, for in the historical period literary evidence can give a much more detailed political, religious and economic picture than has here been attempted. But nevertheless, a story of Palestine is the framework of the book, with the emphasis upon the contribution that archaeology can make. Down to *c.* 3000 B.C., archaeology alone can write the story. As the story is gradually merged into history, archaeology still plays a very large part. Only in the first millennium B.C. can history provide a reasonably consecutive story, and even then it would remain a one-sided, unbalanced story without the help of archaeology. This book therefore aims at showing the evidence that writes the story for the prehistoric period and in the historic periods concentrates on the evidence which supplements the written record, using this only as a background for the archaeological material.

An excellent book has already been written by Professor Albright on the archaeology of Palestine. But this appeared in 1949, and gave the picture provided by pre-war archaeology, for active field archaeology was virtually at a standstill between 1936 and 1952. Since then much has happened, for Palestinian archaeology in both Jordan and Israel is an extremely live affair, as all branches of archaeology should be. The great modifications and amplifications for which fresh discoveries have provided the evidence is the justification for a new book.

In any book of this sort, it is inevitable that the centre of the author's thought and reasoning should be those sites of which he has first-hand experience. This is my justification that Jericho, and to a lesser extent Samaria, bulks rather large in the Index, just as Tell Beit Mirsim did in Professor Albright's book. My further

3

excuse is that Jericho has broken fresh ground by plunging back into the dim period of the first beginnings of settled life. It is a literal fact that at the time of writing Jericho stands by itself in these periods between the eighth and fifth millennia B.C. This is undoubtedly illusory; other excavations will fill in the picture and show that Jericho was a part only of a whole stage of progress, though possibly an important part.

The progress of exploration is in fact so rapid at the moment that already by the time this book is in proof, new discoveries have been made which supplement (though not as far as I know disprove) the statements and theories that have been advanced, for instance, discoveries by Dr. Yadin at Megiddo confirming in the main the suggestions here put forward as the dating of Stratum IV. But if one waited to incorporate all the latest research, a book of this sort would never be published. It has been revised often enough as it is, since it was first begun some twelve years ago.

It is hoped that this book will be of interest to the wide general public which regards the Bible as the greatest literary document in the world, and which likes to be able to understand it as the record of an actual people against a factual background. An attempt has been made to provide this background. But at the same time I have had in mind more professional students of Palestinian archaeology, for whom no up-to-date consecutive account of the findings of archaeology in Palestine exists. Much of the basic archaeological material consists of dry stuff such as pottery forms and burial customs, and I have felt compelled to include some of this for the benefit of these students, as a guide to their studies of the much drier material of excavation reports. I hope that in an effort to provide something of interest both to the general public and to the student, I have not fallen between two stools.

K. M. K.

March 1960

Contents

6 CONTENTS

List of Plates

[All are inserted between pages 220 and 221]

7

List of Illustrations in Text

List of Acknowledgements

ACKNOWLEDGEMENTS for kind permission to reproduce illustrations is made to the following bodies, to whom the copyright of the illustrations belongs:

Oxford University Press: PLS. 1, 2a, 2b, 2c.

Jericho Excavation Fund: PLS. 4, 5a, 5b, 6a, 6b, 7, 8, 9a, 9b, 10, 11, 12a, 12b, 12c, 13, 14a, 14b, 16, 20, 21, 26, 27, 29, 30, 31, 35, 36a, 36b, 37, 38, 39, 40, 42. FIGS. 3, 4, 5.

Israel Exploration Journal: PLS. 17, 18.

University of Liverpool: PL. 15.

Ecole Biblique et Archéologique de St. Etienne, Jerusalem: 22a, 50b.

Oriental Institute, Chicago: PLS. 19b, 22b, 23, 28a, 28b, 45, 46a, 46b, 47b, 48, 49, 54. FIG. 59.

British School of Archaeology in Egypt: PL. 19a, 47a.

University of Philadelphia: PL. 24.

Trustees of the late Sir Henry Wellcome: PLS. 25, 32, 41, 44, 55, 56

James de Rothschild Hazor Expedition: PLS. 33, 50a.

American Schools of Oriental Research: PLS. 34a, 34b, 43.

Palestine Exploration Fund: PLS. 51a, 52, 53a, 53b. FIGS. 61, 62.

Palestine Exploration Fund and Messrs. Harrap: PL. 51b.

Gressmann, Altorientalische Bilder zum alten Testamentum: FIG. 53.

Institute of Archaeology, University of London, FIGS. 16, 36, 54, 55, 56.

A number of line blocks has been prepared from published material, by way of selection of pottery or other objects or by

15

simplification of plans to enable them to be reproduced at the requisite size.

The source and copyright of the originals is gratefully acknowledged as follows:

Pontifical Biblical Institute (*Ghassul*): FIGS. 6, 7, 8, 9.
Ecole Biblique et Archéologique de St. Etienne (*Revue Biblique*): FIGS. 10, 13, 60.
Jérusalem de l'Ancien Testament: FIGS. 58, 65.
Les Fouilles de 'Ay: FIGS. 12, 13.
Israel Exploration Fund: FIG. 14
University of Pennsylvania: FIG. 20.
Oriental Institute, Chicago: FIGS. 24, 30, 31, 37, 46, 47, 48, 51, 57.
American Schools of Oriental Research: FIGS. 44, 50.
Trustees of the Late Sir Henry Wellcome: FIGS. 28, 29, 49, 66.
Department of Antiquities of Palestine: FIG. 36.
Palestine Exploration Fund: FIGS. 63, 64.
Jericho Excavation Fund: FIGS. 11, 17, 18, 19, 21, 22, 25, 26, 32, 33 39, 40, 41, 42, 43.
University of Liverpool: FIG. 45.

CHAPTER ONE

★

Introduction:
The Setting of Palestine in the
History of the Near East

WHEN the Palestine Exploration Fund was founded in 1865 its aims were defined as "the accurate and systematic investigation of the archaeology, the topography, the geology and physical geography, the manners and customs of the Holy Land, for biblical illustration." The essence is in the last two words. In the mid-19th century there was in England a great awakening of interest in the ancient history of the Near East. From Mesopotamia and Egypt were coming spectacular finds that demonstrated that these countries must be placed beside Greece and Rome as the homes of major ancient civilisations. But to God-fearing Victorian England, the Land of the Bible was a potential source of interest exceeding the still rather shadowy empires of Assur-bani-pal and Sargon or Thothmes and Rameses. The Palestine Exploration Fund was indeed the first of the societies to be formed for the study of the ancient past overseas, older by nearly twenty years than the Egypt Exploration Society and by fourteen years than the Society for Hellenic Studies.

The study of the background of the Bible was therefore the motive force behind the earliest exploration of Palestine. In the ensuing hundred years, many great discoveries have been made in the course of this exploration, and much patient work has supplemented the more spectacular finds. As a result, a connected history of Palestine for the period covered by the books of the

Bible can now be written. But while this work has been going on, the study of the ancient history of the other countries of the eastern Mediterranean and western Asia has made enormous strides. It would be true to say that early in the 19th century the Jews were the one nation in the ancient Near East with which the European was familiar. Now, partly owing to the decipherment of their texts and partly from the excavation of their cities and shrines, the history of the Egyptians, the Sumerians and other inhabitants of modern Iraq, the Hittites, the Ḫurrians and others is almost equally well known, and the position of the little Jewish kingdoms can be seen in a much better perspective as part of the whole great civilisation of the Near East.

This is one aspect of our present understanding of Palestinian history and archaeology. The other is equally far-reaching. In Palestine and in the rest of the Near East, archaeology has pushed back our knowledge of places and people to thousands of years before the beginnings of written history. The decipherment of the Rosetta stone in the 1820s and of the Behistun inscription in the 1850s had given the key to the reading of the many documents of, respectively, Egypt and the Mesopotamian empires, which has carried back the beginnings of written history into the fourth millennium B.C. Pure archaeology without any help from documents provides our evidence for what went before.

Though the earliest interest in the archaeology of Palestine was in any association which could be established with the Bible, and though the interest in Egypt and Mesopotamia was in the spectacular monuments and written documents of their great periods of civilisation, the earlier periods can now be seen to be of equally compelling interest, for this area is recognised to be the ultimate cradle of all European civilisation. It is generally agreed that it was in the Near East that took place the first steps in the long process by which man ceased to be a savage, a hunter and collector of wild foods, and became the inhabitant of a civilised community. We can now say that Palestine was at least one of the places in which some of these first steps were made. In order to appreciate the significance of the finds in Palestine, and to see in

perspective the story that is told in the following chapters, a brief
outline must now be given of what is known or deduced of the
early steps in man's progress towards civilisation, and thus of
Palestine's setting in the general background of Near Eastern
history.

Our earliest human ancestors, the first representatives of *Homo
sapiens*, as well as those other species of man that for some
reason died out in the evolutionary struggle, lived in what is
known as the Palaeolithic stage. When the 19th century archaeologists were trying to introduce some system of classification
into the remains of ancient man, they used for the purpose the
artifacts believed to be typical of the different stages, giving a
primary classification of Stone, Bronze and Iron Ages. The Stone
Age was subdivided into the Old Stone Age, the Palaeolithic, in
which implements were mainly made by a chipping technique,
and the New Stone Age, the Neolithic, characterised by polished
stone axes. These distinctions were broadly valid for the area,
Western Europe, on the material of which the classification was
made. Nowadays our knowledge of man's way of life in the
various stages has enormously increased. As a result, when we
now speak of the Palaeolithic stage, we mean not only, and even
not necessarily, that the typical implements are chipped stone
hand-axes, but that the men of the period were dependent for
their existence on the food they could gather by hunting, fishing
and other natural sources; they were food-gatherers. This stage is
roughly co-terminous with the later stages of the Ice Age of
Europe. Between the Palaeolithic and the Neolithic it is now
recognised that there was an intermediate stage, the Mesolithic, in
Europe belonging to a time when the Ice Cap had receded, and
men were having to adapt their food-gathering methods to new
environmental conditions.

The great development from the Palaeolithic and ensuing
Mesolithic came when man started to produce food instead of
gathering it. The importance of this is that it made it possible for
him to settle down on one spot. The food-gatherers had to move
about following their sources of food, the seasonal movement of

the animals or the periods of growth of the herbs and grasses, and the resources of these foods meant that only a limited population could be supported in one area. Men lived, therefore, in nomadic family groups. The discovery of the possibility of cultivating wild grains, and thus of greatly increasing their yield, and of domesticating wild animals, and of thus keeping them within their owners' control, is basic to further progress. The cultivators of fields were not only enabled to settle in one spot because the yield of crops was sufficient to support them there, but they were in fact tied to that spot for at least part of the year while they waited for their crops to ripen.

This great step forward is believed to have taken place in the Near East, where are found wild the grains that man in due course cultivated and the animals he domesticated. This is well illustrated by the work of Professor Gordon Childe. He was primarily a European archaeologist. But his work on the origins of European civilisation led him to the lands of the eastern Mediterranean and western Asia, and as a result he wrote by far the best books so far written on the systematisation, and popularisation, of the early stages of progress in the Near East. For progress was a rapidly accelerating phenomenon once agriculture appears. The Palaeolithic stage, from man's first emergence from the beasts, may have lasted half a million years, the Neolithic some five thousand, the Bronze Age two thousand, and the Iron Age only five hundred or so before the Mediterranean classical civilisations emerge. Once man is settled in one spot, the rest follows. He has leisure to develop skills, and a sedentary life means that he can burden his household with their products, with the results of his handicrafts and his arts. A community life grows up, which is the basis of civilisation. It is no longer a case of one family group against nature, including other family groups; man gains the security of living in an increasingly large group, and in the give and take of group life he sacrifices some of his primitive freedoms in return for this security; the give and take becomes systematised into the regulation of customs and ultimately laws, and a communal organisation emerges.[1]

[1] For Addenda pp. 20–2, see p. 329.

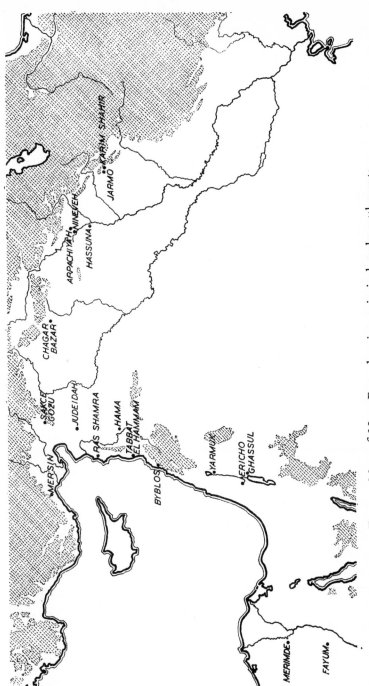

Fig. 1   Map of Near East, showing principal early settlements

The investigation of the process of this transition of man as a savage to man as a member of a civilised community is thus of fascinating interest even to people living as far away as England from its first centres in the Near East. As will be seen, one at least of the centres in which the transition took place was Palestine. But our knowledge of the process is still of extremely recent origin, much of it gained since the Second World War, and even now it is only in the first stages. A few landmarks are beginning to appear, but the general landscape is still covered in mist. It is becoming increasingly clear that progress did not derive from a single centre; parallel, though not necessarily contemporary, steps forward took place in different areas. One suspects that progress was uneven, in some places gradual, in some places a great spurt forward and then a slackening, but a clear understanding must await a very much wider knowledge gained from excavation. Excavation is the only basis of knowledge for these very ancient periods, and excavators in the Near East have barely begun to interest themselves in the predecessors of the great civilisations of the historic period.

Over the years between the two world wars, our knowledge was accumulating of a number of Neolithic villages in the Near East. Nothing was known of the way they had developed from the preceding Mesolithic stage, of which in fact there was only very slight evidence in this area. But the character of villages such as Byblos, Ras Shamra, Mersin and Hassuna was emerging. It appeared that they represented a phase of small self-sufficient communities, each providing its own food, and from materials locally available making its own tools, weapons, utensils and clothes. Flint or other local stone forms the material for the tools and weapons. One of the features taken to be especially characteristic of these western Asiatic villages and of their descendants in Europe was the manufacture of vessels of hand-made pottery. Other vessels were no doubt made of wood and skin, which have not survived. Clothes could have been made from skin or woven, the products of the herds and of hunting. This self-sufficiency may never have been quite complete, for there seems often to have been trade which carried for some distance objects like sea-shells for ornaments or amulets, malachite for eye decoration, and even especially good flint or obsidian for tools and weapons, but nevertheless it is basically true.

The evidence produced by archaeology in this period of the 1920s and 1930s suggested that these Neolithic communities were small in size. The villages seem to have spread over an area of only 2 to 3 acres. This seemed reasonable. One might presume that Neolithic agriculture would be primitive, producing but scanty crops, and therefore capable of supporting only a limited population. Excess population would have to form secondary groups, hiving off from the mother settlement. Moreover, primitive agriculture would tend to exhaust the land, and the original settlement must often have had to move, in order to obtain virgin fields to cultivate. It is believed that it was in this way that the Neolithic way of life was gradually diffused from its first centres, first over a wide field in the Near East, and ulti-mately across Europe. The picture that emerged was of this process taking place in the Near East in the fifth millennium B.C., with a slow spread until it reached the British Isles in the third millennium B.C., or even, in their ultimate extremities, the second millennium. In the last ten years, parts of the picture have required considerable redrawing, for, as will be seen, the finds at Jericho gave the first indication of much more remarkable developments in the Neolithic, and excavations elsewhere are starting to show the same thing.

The main area in which the Neolithic settlements emerged was the Fertile Crescent, running from the Nile valley in the west to the valleys of the Tigris and Euphrates in the east by way of the coastal strip of Palestine and Syria and the fertile steppe lying between the mountains of Asia Minor and the Arabian Desert. To this area recent finds have shown that the Anatolian uplands must be added. These areas saw the birth of a settled way of life, and in the Fertile Crescent arose the first great civilisations of the Western Hemisphere.

One of the stimuli that caused communities to develop beyond the Neolithic stage was the discovery of the uses of materials, chief among them copper, which could not be provided by each group for itself. As the advantages of copper over stone for tools and weapons became apparent, communities had to enter into trade to secure it, and therefore had to produce extra foodstuffs or other natural products to pay the traders and also the smiths who made the implements, and who, as specialists, no longer had the time to provide their own food. Thus the self-sufficiency of the small units began to break down, and the complex structure of civilised communities began to develop.

Up to this stage there was apparently more or less parallel development over much of the Fertile Crescent, including, as we shall see, Palestine. But in subsequent stages, dating from approximately the beginning of the fourth millennium B.C., the two tips of the Crescent began to outstrip the rest. The reason for this was the opportunity provided by the great rivers which watered the two valleys. The rivers provided the fertility that rendered possible the accumulation of surpluses of food which could be traded for other goods, and at the same time the necessity of controlling irrigation and flooding called forth the development of organisation and leadership. Also, the river valleys lacked stone for making tools or for building, so the communities early had to develop the enterprise necessary to obtain these materials. Thus the villages of the river valleys began to outstrip others less favourably situated, and in the course of the fourth millennium proceeded to develop into towns and city states. Early in the third millennium the process was in each case completed by one of the city states taking the lead, and uniting the rest into an empire. Connections between these two river valleys had begun to be established by the end of the fourth millennium, and the interplay between the two empires was to be the main theme of Near Eastern history for the next three thousand years. From each end of the Fertile Crescent the influence of the developing civilisations spread back into the rest of the Crescent, stimulating the more backward areas, and the rivalry between the two empires, later supplemented by other great Powers in Asia Minor and its fringes,

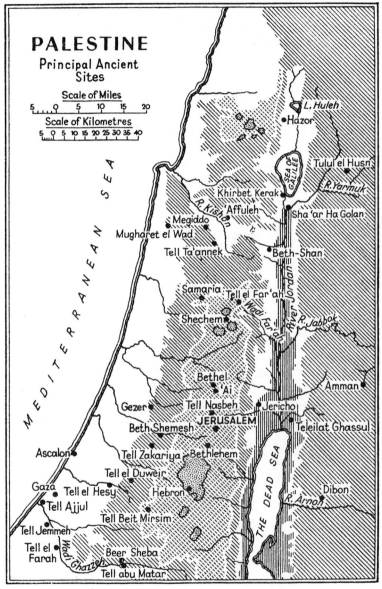

FIG. 2 Map of Palestine, showing principal ancient sites

25

inevitably affected continually the fate of countries such as Palestine which lay on the connecting route.

Such, in very brief outline, is the background against which the history of Palestine develops. Situated as it is towards the south-western end of the Fertile Crescent, it shared in the development towards civilisation of the people of the Crescent. When the great empires at the extremities of the Crescent began to assert themselves, it absorbed influences from them, primarily of course from its nearer neighbour Egypt, but Mesopotamian contacts can also be traced; it fell under their sway at times of their political expansion, and it formed the route they traversed in warfare against each other.

The degree to which different parts of Palestine were influenced by her neighbours was largely modified by the geography of the country itself. Like Syria to the north, which forms a physical unit with it, Palestine is divided into four sharply distinguishable belts running north and south: first, the Coastal Plain, secondly the Central Range, running down from the Lebanon through Galilee and the mountains of Samaria and Judaea, and then dropping to the table-land of the Negeb, thirdly the Jordan Valley, with its continuation the Wadi 'Arabah stretching down to the Gulf of Aqaba, and finally the Eastern Range running down through the Hauran and the mountains of Gilead and Moab to Edom, while to the east it slopes away into the plateau of the Arabian Desert. The Central Range rises fairly gradually from the Coastal Plain, by way of the Shephelah or low hill-country, but to the east, from an average height of 2,400 feet above sea level in the mountains of Judaea, it drops abruptly to the Jordan Valley, which at the Dead Sea lies 1,290 feet below sea level, and the Eastern Range rises almost as abruptly to about 2,000 feet.

This physical conformation has had two important historical results. In the first place, the easiest lines of communication are inevitably north and south, and among these routes the Coastal Plain provides the principal. Connected with the Coastal Plain is another physical feature of historical importance, the Plain of Esdraelon, which breaks across the Central Range and forms a connection between the Coastal Plain, the Jordan Valley and the uplands of Transjordan. This provided in fact the principal route between the extremities of the Fertile Crescent, for in Syria the Coastal Plain is much constricted and inconvenient, and it was by this Esdraelon route that passed the great armies of Egypt and her enemies. The Coastal Plain was also naturally open to influences from the sea, though its harbours were few and poor. Thus the flat country along the coast and the Plain of Esdraelon were especially affected by foreign influences and its cities were liable to destruction by foreign enemies.

On the other hand, the uplands of the Central Range, though by no means inaccessible even from the east, tend to lie to one side of the main currents. Foreign influences penetrate slowly, while foreign armies may pass by without affecting it, unless they are bent on subduing the country and not merely using it as a route.

But though most of the civilising influences throughout its history have come to Palestine along the Fertile Crescent, another equally important influence must not be forgotten. The Fertile Crescent encloses the plateau of the Arabian Desert, which from the dawn of history has served as a vast reservoir of nomadic raiders upon the riches of the surrounding Crescent. The history of each of the countries of the Crescent has been profoundly modified by a whole series of incursions of these nomads, sometimes raiding and returning, but more often overrunning and settling down. These nomads each in their turn destroyed much of the pre-existing civilisation, but also absorbed much, and, by the introduction of new blood, revitalised the population and in their turn produced a new civilisation. A study of the archaeology of Palestine will show evidence of a succession of waves of newcomers, many no doubt originating from the desert. Of these waves, two, those of the Hebrews and the Arabs, are well known to us, but they are only two among many.

Though Palestine is the home of the most famous book in the world, our knowledge of by far the greater part of its story, in terms of time, is dependent upon archaeology. Written history, or at least written documents upon which history can be based, are available at a date some fifteen hundred years earlier in the valleys of the Nile and Tigris–Euphrates, but even in these areas archaeology both carries the story back into earlier millennia and does much to supplement it even after the periods from which written documents survive in considerable numbers. Since much of the story to be told in the following chapters is based wholly or in part on archaeology, it is desirable at this stage to consider what archaeology can do, and what are its limitations.

Given reasonably favourable conditions, archaeology can recover from a site on which man lived those structures and those objects which have survived the passage of time. That is the first major limitation. Many materials, for instance wood, textiles, basketry, in fact almost all untreated organic materials, do not survive the passage of time, and one has only to consider one's own surroundings to see how incomplete the picture would be if all objects of organic materials had disappeared. Even solid structures, when abandoned, comparatively soon start to crumble under the effects of time and weather. One can see the process going on in abandoned crofters' houses in the Highlands of Scotland. The roofless walls stand up from heaps of débris derived from the collapsed roof and crumbling superstructure, and each year more stones from the walls add to the débris, until nothing but a mound remains, and vegetation completes its burial. The archaeologist would be able to recover the plan of the house from the stumps of the walls, and from the objects left behind by the inhabitants, as being not worth taking away when they evacuated, he would gain some impression, but a one-sided one, of their culture. From the traces of their outbuildings, he might obtain an impression of the area of land they cultivated and how they cultivated it. From stray coins, or from objects which could be associated with a particular period, say part of a bicycle, or a muzzle-loading fire-arm, he could make an estimate of when the building was first occupied and when abandoned.

In some cases, of course, conditions are more favourable. If a building, or a town, is overwhelmed by a great catastrophe, and the inhabitants have to leave all their possessions behind, there is much more to tell the archaeologist how they lived, particularly if the nature of the catastrophe is such as to preserve large portions of the buildings. The supreme examples of this are Pompeii and Herculaneum, where volcanic dust and mud respectively buried the houses to a great depth, so that sometimes even their upper storeys are preserved.

This then is the basic material upon which an archaeologist examining a house or town site has to work, the plans of the structures (and of course the architecture if there is enough preserved) and their contents. Sometimes these contents will include objects of art; sometimes only common household goods. Sometimes they will include written material, a dedicatory inscription of a Roman temple, or a centurial stone commemorating the building of a military structure, with attendant details of the Emperor and the responsible officials, while in western Asia archives or literary documents written on clay tablets may survive. In these cases, the association of the structures with known history, within a chronological framework, is easy.

In the excavation of a single, one-period building, or of a village or town of short duration, the archaeologist's *problem* is a relatively simple one, though considerable manual skill may be required to recover delicate objects. He has merely to trace the buildings and find and preserve (and of course interpret) the objects. But very often even a single building may have a complex history of rebuildings and alterations. In order to discover the full history of the building, these must be recognised and interpreted, and the objects found associated with the correct phase. Sometimes the interpretation may be relatively easy. To return to our example of the crofter's homestead. If after the original homestead had crumbled into a mound a second crofter had come and built his house on top of the mound, the two houses would be separated by the débris derived from the earlier. There should not be much difficulty in differentiating between the objects belonging to the two periods, except that the foundations of the later walls might have been cut down some distance into the earlier débris. More often, however, the position is much more complex. An original nucleus may have a whole series of additions made to it, converting a simple cottage into an elaborate farm or even mansion. Successive houses may have cut into earlier ones, on almost the same level, or even terraced down below the absolute level of the earlier floors. If the picture of the social and economic development is to be correctly interpreted, one must be able to say which objects are to be associated with which stage; otherwise one might date the original building much too late, or, if the evidence seemed to point clearly to its being of a certain period, one might ascribe objects erroneously believed to be associated with it to too early a date. One might, for instance, say that one had evidence that bicycles were in use in the Highlands in A.D.1800, because one found a bicycle frame outside the front door of a homestead dated by coins to that date, whereas really it was in the cellar of an overlying homestead built in A.D. 1910.

The position in the Near East is usually much more complicated. For one thing, settled life has been going on there for far longer than it has in the West. Moreover, the tendency is for villages and towns to remain on the same site for hundreds or even thousands of years, usually because the site is favourable either for military or for economic reasons, such as proximity to a good water supply. From natural decay or from destruction by enemies, by earthquakes, or by accidental fires, houses and public buildings have succeeded one another time and time again. Each has risen on the ruins of its predecessor, sometimes a few inches higher only, sometimes upon feet of débris. Though deliberate cutting down or terracing into earlier buildings has sometimes taken place, the general tendency has been for the town level to rise. Much of the Near East is therefore covered by mounds marking the site of ancient towns or villages, sometimes with a modern settlement on top, sometimes abandoned. In the Arabic-speaking areas these artificial mounds are known as *tells*. Ancient Jericho is thus Tell es Sultan, Megiddo Tell el Mutesellim, and the central mound of Ur Tell el Muqayyar. The growth of these tells is particularly characteristic of those areas in which the local building material was mud-brick, for a destroyed building of mud-brick disintegrates into mud again, which cannot be used again in the same way that stone from a stone building can be. The growth of the tell is therefore more rapid. The job of the archaeologist is to excavate these tells in such a way that from the surviving remains he can reconstruct their history.

This is completely dependent on recognising the different layers in the soil and correctly associating them with the successive buildings. In this way, one knows which objects are on, or in, the floors of a building, and which belong to the débris of the building underneath. As long ago as 1890, Sir Flinders Petrie established for Near Eastern archaeology the main principle of the succession of building levels in his excavation of Tell Hesi in southern Palestine. But the full refinement of this stratigraphical excavation is a product of western European archaeology, especially British, German, Scandinavian and Dutch. The remains of ancient structures in these countries are mainly so slight, and the finds so relatively scanty and commonplace, that the development of refinements in excavation technique was essential to extract any information at all. Excavation in the Near East had big potential prizes—temples, palaces and royal archives—and also a large and cheap labour force available, and therefore minutiae of archaeological observation were ignored. In Palestine the greater part of results of the major excavations before the First World War on sites such as Gezer, Samaria and Jericho cannot be relied upon, and much revision is required of the results of the excavations between the two wars, though improvements in technique did result in sufficient information being provided for the necessary reinterpretation. Reference to some of these reinterpretations will be made in the following chapters.

By the proper technique, therefore, the archaeologist should be able to produce the story of the sequence of events and cultures of the site with which he is concerned. But this is only the beginning. The site must be fitted into a regional and a chronological framework. Even at very early periods, in the Palaeolithic stage, fashions of technique in the making of stone implements provide evidence of regional cultures, and their succession provides a broad chronological framework, which can be tied in with phases in the Ice Age and the geological features connected with it. In the early post-glacial phases, flint techniques, and also techniques in making bone implements, are still the basis of establishing cultural relationships. But once the manufacture of pottery becomes common, this becomes much the most important means of diagnosis. The usefulness of pottery vessels ensures their presence in every household, their comparative fragility ensures the presence of great numbers of potsherds on all occupied sites, and the practical indestructibility of a potsherd ensures for the benefit of archaeologists the survival of evidence of what kind of pottery was in use. Moreover, conservatism and imitativeness as human characteristics have resulted in the widespread use of similar forms of vessel among allied peoples, and of the almost contemporary spread of newly introduced types. We can therefore say that groups of people in, say, Early Bronze Age Palestine, using the same types of pottery, are approximately contemporary, and that the appearance of a new type on different sites marks a definite chronological point. By stratigraphical excavation we can associate this same chronological point with a structural phase in the history of the different sites. Other objects also can be shown to have regional and chronological significance, for instance types of bronze daggers and pins, but pottery is relatively so much more common that its importance transcends all other finds.

Between the two wars a reasonably complete and accurate knowledge of the sequence of the pottery forms of Palestine was built up. But a sequence is not a chronology. Chronology in Palestine cannot stand on its own feet until one is dealing with a relatively late epoch. Until the first millennium B.C. it must rely on links with neighbouring countries. Earlier in this chapter mention was made that by the end of the fourth millennium the towns of the great river valleys of the Nile and Tigris–Euphrates began to outstrip the settlements of the rest of the Fertile Crescent. The increasing complexities of town and state organisation involved, among other things, the working out of a calendar. The first true calendar was established in Egypt, perhaps as early

as *c.* 3000 B.C., and a combination of literary sources and archaeological evidence makes it possible to date dynasties and phases
in Egypt and Mesopotamia reasonably accurately back to about
that date. We have no early literary sources or king-lists for
Palestine. Even in the period covered by the biblical record the
genealogical evidence is not reliable (a point which is discussed in
a later chapter) until the period of David, *c.* 1000 B.C., and no
true calendar is used at all. Events are recorded as taking place,
for example, "in the thirty and first year of Asa King of Judah,"
and though the chronology of the various kings of Judah and
Israel can now be fixed within close limits this is only because
their reigns can at certain points be linked with Egypt.

Archaeological remains, however, must still be linked with the
reigns of these biblical kings, and it has so happened that there is
very seldom much direct evidence for this. An exception is
Samaria. It was founded by Omri on a virgin site in the sixth year
after his accession, which can be fixed, ultimately by links with
the Egyptian calendar, to 880 B.C. The destruction of Samaria in
720 B.C. by the Assyrians, and of other cities, such as Lachish, by
the Babylonians in 596 and 588 B.C., can also be fixed, and be
associated with archaeological levels. Otherwise, even in these
comparatively late periods, it is mainly a matter of establishing a
sequence and fitting it in as closely as possible with known events.
It is true that a certain amount of epigraphic material of the period
of Hebrew kingdoms has been found. None in itself, however,
provides dating for a phase in the history of a site, for it so happens
that none providing exact chronological data has been found *in situ*
on a site,[1] and the knowledge of ancient Hebrew epigraphy is
not yet exact; the epigraphic material has to be dated from its
find-spot, and not vice versa.

For the earlier periods, both those preceding the biblical period

[1] The Siloam inscription, which can reasonably be associated with the work
of King Hezekiah (see pp. 287-9), dates the Siloam tunnel, but not any phase in
the history of the town of Jerusalem itself. The Moabite stone was a casual
discovery. The Samaria ostraca by the regnal years of the king provide limits
for the reigns of the king to which they refer, but their find-spot was not
accurately recorded with reference to the structural phases of the town.

and those for the period in which the biblical record is in the form of a traditional account rather than of a contemporary chronicle, the archaeological sequence is the only framework, and this can only be given a broad chronological significance by relation to Egypt and, occasionally, to Mesopotamia. In the late fourth and third millennium there were occasional imports into Palestine which serve to tie in the Palestinian periods with those of those countries that had already entered the historic period. Moreover, it is clear that the fortunes of the Palestinian and Syrian littoral became broadly linked with those of Egypt once the Old Empire was established c. 3200 B.C.[1] Under the Old Empire, and even earlier, contacts were established at least as far north as Byblos, just north of Beirut, and some control may have been exercised over the coastal lands. In Palestine such links as we have provide reasonable evidence that the period of settled and urban development of the Early Bronze Age is approximately contemporary with the Old Empire. The Intermediate Early Bronze–Middle Bronze period in Palestine, marked by nomadic invasions, corresponds with the interruption of civilisation of the First Intermediate of Egypt, due to the same reason and possibly to the same groups of people. The restoration of civilisation in the Middle Bronze Age of Palestine corresponds with the Middle Empire of Egypt, and numerous imports reflect a close connection. The evidence of the Hyksos invasion of Egypt c. 1730 B.C. can be traced in Palestine, as can the events when the first kings of the Eighteenth Dynasty in Egypt threw the Hyksos back into Palestine c. 1560 B.C. The archaeological sequence in Palestine from c. 3000 B.C. can thus broadly be linked with the fixed chronology of Egypt, but only broadly, and any attempt to assign exact dates in years within these broad limits can be guesswork only.

A chronology based on an ancient calendar, however, can take us no farther back than c. 3000 B.C. Until very recently, that was all that we had. Anything earlier was a sequence only and dates in

[1] Egyptian chronology itself is still not quite firmly fixed for these early dates, and different authorities suggest initial dates for Dynasty I between c. 3200 B.C. and c. 2900 B.C. The revised C.A.H. favours 3100 B.C.

years assigned to any phase were also only guesswork. Since 1944, however, a new method, first developed by Dr. Libby in Chicago, has been introduced. This is usually known as the Carbon-14, or radio-active carbon, method. It is based on the fact that all living organisms, human beings and other animals, trees and plants, absorb radio-activity while they are alive, and after they are dead give it up at a rate which can be established. The surviving amount can be measured in organic materials recovered on archaeological sites. For various technical reasons charcoal, and to a lesser extent shell, is the most satisfactory material. By comparison of the surviving amount of radio-activity and the established annual rate of loss, the date at which the organism died, for instance the date at which the tree was cut down, can be established. The method is not yet absolutely reliable, but a series of consistent results, including ones which can be checked against evidence from other sources, makes it probable that it can be of much use to archaeologists. There is, however, always a standard margin of deviation, usually of about a hundred and fifty to two hundred years on either side of a central date. Therefore for the periods after c. 3000 B.C., the Carbon-14 method is unlikely to give as exact a result as evidence based on other archaeological grounds. But for the earlier periods it is our only source. As will be seen, we already have dates going back to c. 9000 B.C., and as evidence accumulates from additional observations we shall both gain assurance whether or not these comparatively isolated results are reliable, and be able to fit other phases and cultures into the general scheme.

CHAPTER TWO

★

The Beginnings of Settled Life

ON THE seaward slopes of Mount Carmel are a number of caves
that have provided evidence of human occupation covering
tens of thousands of years during the Palaeolithic period (Pl. 1).
Hunters, resembling those of Europe both in physical type and in
the implements they used, made these caves their headquarters.
Overlying these Palaeolithic levels are others belonging to the
Mesolithic, the period in which in Europe the Ice Cap was
retreating, and in which the descendants of the hunters of the
Palaeolithic were adapting themselves to their changed environ-
ment. In the Mount Carmel caves, there is evidence that in
Palestine too man adopted a new way of life.

Above the layers containing Palaeolithic implements is the
evidence of the appearance of a new group. The flint industry
does not seem to be derived directly from any Upper Palaeolithic
culture, and its ancestry has not yet been traced. It seems, however, to have been an indigenous Palestinian culture, found only
as far north as the mid-Lebanon, and in the south there is an
outlier at Helouan in Egypt. The name Natufian has been given
to this culture, after the Wadi en-Natuf where it was first found.
Like the Mesolithic industry in Europe, the flints include great
numbers of microliths, small flakes of various shapes, many of
them probably used as part of composite tools. Most characteristic
of all are the lunates, very fine little flakes with a straight edge
and a crescent-shaped back. Over four thousand of these were
found in one of the Mount Carmel caves (Pl. 3B).

The Natufians of Mount Carmel, and of rock-shelters on the
eastern and western slopes of the Judaean hills, lived mainly by

hunting. In the Mount Carmel caves were found enormous quantities of gazelle bones. Gazelles live in open country and fairly dry conditions, indicating that as conditions in Europe were changing as the Ice Cap receded, so in the Mediterranean area the contemporary pluvial period was passing away. Fishing was also a means of subsistence, for both bone harpoon-points and bone fish-hooks are found.

One type of implement among the equipment of the Natufians is of special interest. This is a sickle. Large numbers of sections of blades were found with the cutting edge showing a broad band of lustre from use, and with, as a rule, the back trimmed to a ridge to fit into a V-shaped groove in a haft. Portions of bone hafts with flints still in position have been found, and also two complete hafts, each of which has an animal head or figure carved on the end of the handle (Pls. 2A, 3A).

The presence of sickles is not a proof that agriculture was practised, for the sickles might be used for gathering wild grains. Many authorities do, however, accept the view that the Natufians of Mount Carmel had begun to cultivate grain. Some claim that wild grasses cannot be harvested with such sickles, since the heads are too brittle and the seeds would be lost. It is also compellingly argued that since so much care was lavished on the fashioning of the sickles and since such a high proportion of sickle blades was found, they represented something of considerable importance in the life of the community. Certainly, too, the Natufian group inhabited the Mount Carmel area for a very long time, so something probably tied them to the spot. A case can therefore be made out for some first experiments in agriculture in Palestine in the transitional stage following the end of the Ice Age.

The other main point of interest about the Natufian people is their burial practices. The dead were buried beneath the area inhabited by the living. At the Mughâret el Wad, on Mount Carmel, more than sixty individuals were buried in the cave or on the terrace in front of it. The earlier burials seem to have been communal, with the bodies tightly flexed, the later individual, with the bodies less tightly flexed. The communal burials in particular give evidence of the taste of the Natufians for personal ornament. In each group one skeleton, presumably that of the most important member of the family, has a quite elaborate adornment of shells and pendants. The most common ornaments were made up of *dentalia* shells, little tubes which can be picked up on the shore of Palestine today. These would of course be readily accessible to the inhabitants of the Mount Carmel caves, but they are also found on sites on the eastern slopes of the Judaean hills, showing that objects even at this early date could be collected or traded from an appreciable distance. The most elaborate use of these shells for adornment was in a head-dress consisting of a fan-shaped arrangement on either side of the head (Pl. 2B). The bodies also had necklaces of pendants, made of pierced teeth or the toe-bones of gazelle, or carved in bone and arranged in pairs rather like opposed heads of wooden golf-clubs (Pl. 2C).

The burial of the dead was apparently a matter of some ceremony. At the Mugharet el Wad, a wall, pavement, and some basins hollowed out of the rock were apparently associated with a group burial, and at Erq el Ahmar a similar group was also covered by a pavement. At 'Ain Mallaha, on the shores of Lake Huleh in the Jordan Valley, a burial closely resembling that of Mount Carmel, with a crown of *dentalia* shells, was made in a pit lined with plaster, covered by a pavement above which was an arrangement of stones in circles.

In the period following the end of the Ice Age, Palestine therefore was inhabited by a group of which the way of life resembled that of Mesolithic groups in Europe in many ways, particularly in its reliance on hunting and fishing and in its use of microlithic implements. The ornaments worn are peculiar to the group, but neither these nor the carvings in bone and stone would be out of place among similar European communities. It is in the probability that these people were experimenting in agriculture that they are unique. The finds from Mount Carmel are the earliest suggestion of the cultivation of food that have so far been found.

The Natufian on Mount Carmel and other sites had a long life.

A Middle and Upper Natufian can be identified from developments of the types of implements. On the whole, these represent deterioration, particularly in the bone implements made. A new introduction in the Upper Natufian is a recognisable arrowhead. A claim that there is evidence in a Middle Natufian level for the domestication of dogs has recently been queried.

But it now becomes probable that the sequence from Lower Natufian to a Middle and Upper Natufian of a similar but poorer character is not the only line of development. In 1957 Professor Dorothy Garrod could say "there is no trace of Natufian occupation at the base of any of the Palestinian tells."[1] This position has now been changed by the latest finds at Jericho.

Ancient Jericho is today represented by a mound about 10 acres in extent and about 70 feet high, on the outskirts of the oasis of modern Jericho. It owes its existence, as indeed does modern Jericho, to the magnificent perennial stream that wells up at its foot. The stream must draw its source from some underground reservoir fed by the rains on the uplands of Judaea, and it is vital to the life of Jericho. Rainfall in the Jordan Valley may be violent in winter, but in summer the great heat of this area, at Jericho c. 900 feet below sea level, dries everything up. Only in areas within reach of the waters of some permanent source such as that of the spring of Ain es Sultan at Jericho can the rich soil of the valley be made truly productive.

The mound of ancient Jericho (Pl. 4) is an emphatic witness to the importance of the spring. The whole of its 70 feet is the result of human occupation, covering a period of over seven thousand years. The spring today emerges at the eastern side of the tell, forcing its way out of the ground over a fairly wide area. The original source, perhaps a cave in the limestone, must lie buried beneath the débris of occupation, and has not been found. But it is clear from the evidence of the various areas excavated to bedrock that before there was any human occupation the surface of the rock sloped gently down from the west, from the ultimate foothills of the cliff-wall bounding the Jordan Valley, and that

[1] *Proc. of the British Academy*, XVIII, p. 214.

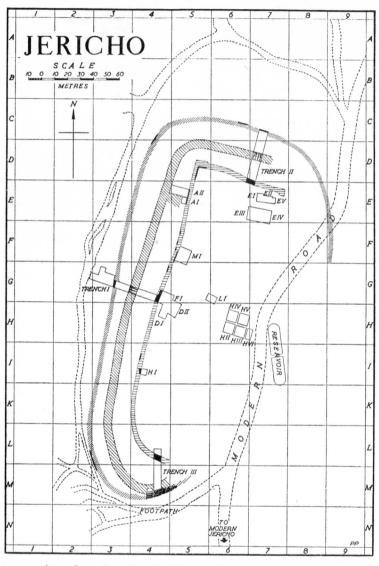

FIG. 3 Plan of Jericho, showing Bronze Age walls and excavated areas

40

the spring must have broken out to the surface just at the point at which the hill slopes flatten off into the alluvial plain of the valley-bed.

Hunters may have visited the spring from the very earliest stages of the Palaeolithic, as no doubt did the animals they hunted. One Palaeolithic hand-axe was indeed found in a Neolithic level, but there is no means of telling whether it was derived from the vicinity or from farther afield. The first definite evidence on the site concerns the Mesolithic period. On bed-rock towards the north end of the tell (Site E on Fig. 3) excavations in 1958 revealed a curious structure. In this area the basic limestone was in its natural state covered by a layer of clay about a foot thick. Over most of the area excavated this clay had been removed by man, and the surface of the limestone exposed. But at the south end of the excavated area, a rectangle of the clay, 3·50 metres broad and more than 6·50 metres long, had been left, and had been enclosed by a substantial wall of stones, with wooden posts set in the wall at intervals. This structure was quite unlike any dwelling-house found on the site. Moreover there were two other noteworthy features. Built into the wall were two large stone blocks, which had had holes bored right through them, the total depth of the holes being about 2 feet 6 inches. They had obviously been intended to hold posts, and from their resemblance to flag-pole sockets, one is tempted to suggest that they held totem-poles, the primitive equivalent to flag-poles. Secondly, though the adjacent rock surface was covered with débris and rubbish, the surface of the clay platform had been kept scrupulously clean throughout the time it was in use. It is therefore possible that this curious structure was a sanctuary or some kind of holy place.

The interpretation of the structure is hypothetical, but its cultural setting is certain. From the associated débris were recovered a collection of objects which are certainly Natufian. Among the numerous microliths was a beautiful little lunate, and, most characteristic of all, there was a bone harpoon head (Pl. 9A). This is particularly important, since at Mount Carmel harpoon heads were found only in the Lower Natufian levels. Therefore it

is certain that the first structure at Jericho was built by people allied
to the first Mesolithic group in the Mount Carmel caves. Thus
one can reasonably interpret it as a sanctuary established by
Mesolithic hunters beside the source of the Jericho spring. Water
sources have been held sacred by primitive people throughout the
ages. Beautiful little votive objects have been found at the source
of the Seine; many fine Romano-British objects have been found
in the well of Coventina on the Roman Wall in Britain; and
even today, in the Orient, rags will be attached to a tree beside a
spring as a propitiation of the spirit of the spring.

Most fortunately for archaeologists, this structure was eventually burnt down. The surrounding area was covered by charcoal
from the beams that had been incorporated in it. This charcoal
has provided a Carbon-14 dating of 7800 B.C. ± 210. Even though,
in our present state of knowledge, one must use Carbon-14 dating
with caution, for its reliability has still to stand up to the test of
full experience, this dating has for the first time given us a
relatively fixed point for the transitional stage in man's development into a civilised being.[1]

The general background of the Mesolithic builders of this
structure is certainly that of hunters and food-gatherers. But as
we have seen, the inhabitants of the caves on Mount Carmel may
have already been experimenting in agriculture, the prerequisite
of any full settled occupation. The finds at Jericho show that these
experiments laid the basis of success. Towards the centre of the
tell (Site M on Fig. 3) a highly significant discovery was made.
Here was found a series of the Neolithic structures which are
described below. But between them and bed-rock was a deposit
of 13 feet which produced no traces of any solid structure. A
close study showed that this 13 feet was made up of innumerable
floors bounded by slight humps which were all that remained of
slight, hut-like structures. Therefore, for a very considerable
length of time, people were living beside the spring of Jericho;
living on the same spot, but still living in the sort of habitation
suited to a nomadic, hunting type of life. Only after a length of
time which, judging from the number of floors which went to

[1] Addenda pp. 330–31.

the building up of this nucleus of the tell of 13 feet, was consider-able, did they start to build solid structures.

Ultimately some genius led the way in building a solid house, and one can say that the first Palestinian architecture appears. These first houses have an obvious derivation from the primitive shelters, for they are round or curvilinear in plan, and the inwards-inclination of the surviving portions of the walls suggests that they had domed roofs (Pl. 5B). They are a translation into a solid medium of the impermanent huts of a nomadic population. Each has a projecting porch, in which is a stepped or sloping entrance leading down from a higher external level (Pl. 6B). The walls are constructed with hand-moulded bricks, of the type known as plano-convex, with a flat base and a curved top, which often has a hog-backed silhouette. Sometimes wooden posts and wattling are incorporated in the walls.

The extent of the transitional, or Proto-Neolithic, settlement which produced the 13 feet of deposit without any substantial structure was apparently not large, for the deposit was found only in the one area. But the stage in which solid architecture was evolved was followed by a major expansion. The round houses have been found from end to end of the tell, covering an area which may be estimated at about 10 acres.[1]

The great interest of this development is that it derived directly from the first visits of the Natufian, Mesolithic hunters, which may be inferred from the Mesolithic structure. The same flint and bone industry (Pl. 9A), allied to the Natufian of Mount Carmel, runs right through the transitional Proto-Neolithic stage to the large-scale settlement to which the designation Pre-Pottery Neolithic A has been given (Pls. 9B, 10). Jericho has therefore provided evidence of the process for which archaeologists have long been looking, of the transition from man as a hunter to man as a member of a settled community.

After the settlement had expanded to its full size, it was surrounded by massive defences, and assumes an urban character.

---

[1] This can only be an estimate, since the limits on the east side are uncertain, owing to the encroachment of the modern road.

The town wall was a solid, free-standing, stone affair 6 feet 6 inches wide. At the north and south ends as found it had been destroyed to its lower courses, but on the west side it was preserved to a height of 12 feet. At this point the excavated area coincided with the position of a great stone tower built against the inside of the wall, still surviving to a height of 30 feet (Pl. 7). It is to be presumed that it was for the purpose of defence, and provision was made for manning the top by a passage entering from the eastern side, and leading to a steep flight of twenty-two steps climbing up to the top of the tower. The whole comprises an amazing bit of architecture.

The tower and defences had a long history. Three main building phases in the tower and town wall can be traced. With the second town wall goes a rock-cut ditch, 27 feet wide and 9 feet deep. The third and final stage of the town wall is that shown in Pl. 8. By the time it was built, the internal level had risen considerably, and on its inner side its lower part was not free-standing, but built against a fill. It still survives to a height of 25 feet. Subsequently a series of houses, of the usual curvilinear plan, was built against the tower and wall. The third in succession of these houses was burnt down, and the charcoal timbers lying on its floor provided material that gave a Carbon-14 dating of 6850 B.C. ± 210. This date of course comes late in the history of the tower and defences, which must date back to c. 7000 B.C.[1]

The descendants of the Mesolithic hunters who had established their sanctuary by the spring at Jericho had therefore made remarkable progress. In the course of a period which Carbon-14 evidence suggests is about a thousand years, they had made the full transition from a wandering to a settled existence in what must have been a community of considerable complexity, for the imposing defences are evidence of an efficient communal organisation. When these finds were made at Jericho, the earliest villages known elsewhere were dated more than two thousand years later, and the pyramids of Egypt, the first great stone buildings of the Nile Valley, are four thousand years younger than the great tower

[1] Addenda p. 331.

of Jericho. The reasons for this development are obviously of great interest.

It may be inferred with a high degree of probability that this Pre-Pottery Neolithic A settlement of Jericho was based on a successful system of agriculture. Actual evidence of this is not yet available, as the samples which it is hoped will provide information about grain have not yet been examined.[1] The inference can be made from the size of the settlement. A closely built-up area of about 10 acres might, by modern oriental standards, house a population of about two thousand people, and such a population could not have been supported on supplies of wild grain and wild animals obtainable within reach of the settlement. At a stage in the occupation of the site, which one may presume to be coincidental with the development of the nucleus-tell of 13 feet of deposit, the first experiments in agriculture, ascribed to their cave-dwelling predecessors on Mount Carmel and elsewhere, were developed by the Natufians at Jericho into the practice of regular food production. This produced sufficiently reliable supplies of food to enable them to settle permanently on the site and build the long succession of hut-like shelters. But the waters of the spring in its natural state would only have reached a limited area. Today, the widespread oasis is based on an elaborate system of irrigation. A further inference on the economy of Pre-Pottery Neolithic A Jericho can therefore be made. At a stage when the expanding population required a large area of fields, irrigation channels must have been constructed to carry the waters of the spring farther afield.

This inference has important implications. The successful practice of irrigation involves an elaborate control system. A system of main channels feeds subsidiary channels watering the fields when the necessary sluice-gate is closed. Therefore the channels must be planned, the length of time each farmer may take water by closing the sluice-gates must be established, and there must be some sanction to be used against those who contravene the regulations. The implications therefore are that there must be some central communal organisation and the beginnings of a code

[1] Addenda p. 331.

of laws which the organisation enforces. It has long been recognised that a major influence in the development of the villages of the valleys of the Nile and the Tigris–Euphrates into towns and states was their dependence on irrigation, which both brought them great wealth and stimulated the evolution of urban characteristics.

The inference is that something of the same sort developed at Jericho. As regards evidence of the actual irrigation, it can never be more than inference, for all the area concerned is now covered by modern fields and irrigation channels. But the evidence that there was an efficient communal organisation is to be seen in the great defensive system. The visual evidence that this provides links with the chain of reasoning based on the size of the settlement. The expansion of the settlement precedes the building of the defences, and thus the need for irrigation had called into being the organisation of which the defences are evidence.[1]

There were thus the greatest possible contrasts between the urban Natufian settlement at Jericho and the other settlements in which evidence of the stages developed from the Lower Natufian have been found. It looks as though there were two lines of development. One Lower Natufian group settled down at Jericho, and it is surely to be presumed that other groups established settlements in comparable positions. It is difficult to believe that Pre-Pottery Neolithic A Jericho developed in isolation; there must be comparable sites, but they have escaped observation, perhaps because they are not so large. But the cousins of the settled groups, living mainly in the hills, in areas less favourable for agriculture, continued in a Mesolithic way of life, still living as hunters and food-gatherers. The caves and shelters in which they lived have produced the implements which have been classified as Middle and Upper Natufian.

One of these sites, El Khiam near Bethlehem, is claimed to show a further transition. The flint industry which has for long been accepted as the classic Neolithic industry of Palestine is called the Tahunian. At El Khiam it is claimed that this develops out of the latest Natufian industry. This would therefore derive the

[1] Addenda p. 331.

Natufian groups from the descendants of the cousins of the settlers at Jericho. Not all authorities accept this derivation, and the alternative suggestion is that the Tahunian is superimposed on the Natufian. In this case we must bring the Tahunians in from outside, from a source not yet traced.

But though it is thus possible that the Tahunians are the descendants of the Natufians who long continued their nomadic way of life, they are certainly not the descendants of the settlers at Jericho. The Tahunians appear there, but only after a complete break. Wherever the Pre-Pottery Neolithic A town of Jericho has been examined along the edge of the mound, the layers have suffered considerable erosion. In Trench I, on the west side of the tell, it is clear that the upper part of the town wall ultimately collapsed. The layers representing the successive houses built up against its inner side were eroded, as was the top of the tower, and the resultant débris filled up the ditch and piled up against the base of the town wall. By the time the débris had reached its angle of rest, the town wall was completely covered. In Site E, towards the north end of the site, a corresponding phase of erosion is represented by a stream bed, which cut down into the house levels in three successive phases before it finally silted up. Elsewhere the evidence is similar.

It is impossible to tell how long a period of time is covered by this phase of erosion. It may have taken place very quickly, or it may have covered a period of years or centuries. What is quite clear is that it marks the end of the occupation of the Pre-Pottery Neolithic A people. They may have been driven out, and their town destroyed, by their successors, or some disaster, such as an earthquake temporarily diverting the water supply and destroying the irrigation system, may have caused them to abandon the site.

These successors were an entirely different group, to which the name Pre-Pottery Neolithic B is given, and their flint industry is Tahunian. Almost all their other equipment also was different, for instance even the shape of the querns and of the grinding stones used with them. But most striking of all is the difference in architecture, which is described below, with large, many-roomed houses of rectilinear plan.

Historically, the most important point is that the newcomers arrived with this architecture already fully developed. Immediately above the layers of erosion appear houses of a remarkably stereotyped plan which lasts throughout the Pre-Pottery Neolithic B period at Jericho. This means that the newcomers had already behind them a sufficiently long period of settled occupation to develop an architecture, and even a detailed house plan, which was to serve their needs for a thousand years or more at Jericho. They were not, therefore, the immediate descendants of the Tahunians who lived at El Khiam, but of groups that had developed their own way of settled life. One might guess that their settlements were not far away, and that it was against them that the Pre-Pottery Neolithic A people had fortified their settlement, but here one enters the realms of hypothesis.

The houses of the Pre-Pottery Neolithic B phase are of very surprising architectural development. The rooms were mostly large, with wide doorways, sometimes flanked by timber posts. The plan of these rooms was rectangular, with slightly rounded corners, and the walls were straight and solid (Pl. 11). The bricks of which the walls were constructed (Pl. 12A) were made by hand (not in moulds as is usual later), in shape rather like a flattened cigar, with the surface impressed with a herringbone pattern by pairs of prints of the brick-maker's thumbs, thus giving a keying for the mortar such as is provided by the hollow in modern bricks. Such bricks again are entirely different from those used by the A people. The floors were covered with a hard lime-plaster, often reddish or cream-coloured, carried also up the walls, with its surface finished with a high burnish. The main rooms were flanked by small chambers, some of them apparently used for storage, and rain-water was conserved in plastered vats built against the walls. The houses were built round courtyards, in which most of the cooking seems to have taken place, for the floors were found covered with thick charcoal layers.

The only utensils belonging to these people which have survived are stone bowls of various forms, the majority in a white limestone, finely worked and carefully finished. These vessels no doubt would have been supplemented by others of materials which have perished, probably of skin, and possibly of wood, though it is a curious fact that the tools found included very few suitable for heavy woodworking. The tools (Pl. 12B) are mainly of flint or chert. The great majority are blades formed from flakes, which would have served as knives of all varieties and sizes. Some of the blades have been given fine serrated edges, and from the characteristic gloss that most of them bear it is clear that they were used as sickles to cut corn or grass; most are short sections which would have been set in a wooden haft; longer ones may have been provided with handles in the same manner as a knife. Other implements are borers and scrapers for use on skins. But, again in contrast to the A group, there are hardly any heavy tools which could have been used as axes, adzes or hoes, and it is difficult to see what implements were used to cut down trees; the use of some timber is attested by the sockets of posts in the walls, but it seems probable that wood was not extensively used. In addition to the cutting implements, there are innumerable hammer stones, pestles and polishing stones of all sizes (Pl. 12C).

Evidence of agriculture is provided by the sickles already mentioned, by the find of large numbers of querns and rubbers (Pl. 12C), and by the find of actual grain. The querns are of a standardised form, sub-rectangular, with a wide, flat rim round three sides, and the grinding hollow running out to the edge at one end. Cultivation of the ground was probably carried out by digging-sticks, pointed sticks weighted by stones, of which the evidence survives in the form of heavy stones pierced by a hole.

The implements found include arrowheads, some of them finely worked, but they do not form a high proportion of the total. Hunting therefore was an element in the economy of the inhabitants, but probably not an important element. Large numbers of animal bones found on the site, however, show that they were certainly meat-eaters. The only animal of which the skeletal remains suggest, in Professor Zeuner's opinion,[1] evidence of domestication is the goat. However, in addition to this, there are great numbers of bones of pig, sheep and cow. These can be described as potentially domesticable breeds, and not enough is yet known about the effect of domestication as revealed in the bones to decide whether they were still wild or were already herded. There are also great numbers of gazelle bones; these may have been hunted, but Professor Zeuner[2] suggests that even they may have been herded, so as to keep them under control. The question of to what degree these Jerichoans were pastoralists, therefore, cannot be answered, but the scarcity of arrowheads in comparison with the great number of animal bones (and of other flint implements) suggests that they were.[3]

The economy so far revealed is that typical of a Neolithic community, consisting of self-sufficient farmers, with some domesticated animals, but still obtaining some of their food supply by hunting. The self-sufficiency was not quite complete, for a few of the tools were made of obsidian, which was probably obtained from Anatolia. Some small lumps of turquoise matrix have also been found, which must have come from the Sinai Peninsula, and cowrie shells may have come from the Mediterranean. Such exceptions are quite usual in many Neolithic communities, for even in those early times a few luxury articles seem to have been obtained from distant sources.

The evidence of agriculture, the elaborate architecture, and the comparatively lavish equipment (even though it did not include pottery) show that these early inhabitants of Jericho formed a prosperous and highly organised community. There is also some evidence as to their spiritual and aesthetic development.

The principal concern of such a community would no doubt be the fertility of their fields and flocks. A number of little clay figurines of animals have been found, which were probably votive offerings to a supernatural power which was believed to control these things. More striking is a figurine of a woman, only some 2 inches high, an elegant little lady with flowing

[1] P.E.Q., 1955.   [2] P.E.Q., 1955.   [3] Addenda p. 332.

gown gathered at the waist, her arms akimbo and her hands beneath her breasts; unfortunately her head is missing. In attitude, the figure is typical of representations of the Mother Goddess common in much later cultures, and it is evidence that our early inhabitants already imagined a personified deity.

Another aspect of their approach to the deity is provided by a small shrine in a private house. The shrine was formed by blocking openings in the walls of one of the large rooms. In one of the walls of the small room so formed was a semicircular niche, at the base of which was set a rough stone to serve as a pedestal. In the débris of the house, not far away, was found a remarkable stone which exactly fitted the niche. It was of volcanic rock from the neighbourhood of the Dead Sea. It had been elaborately flaked into a pillar of pointed oval section 1 foot 6 inches high. The unusualness of this object, and its probable association with the niche, strongly suggest that it had a cult significance, probably as a representation of the deity. It thus foreshadows the *mazzeboth* of the Canaanite religion of many centuries later, the stone pillars which are found on the sites of so many Semitic sanctuaries.

Another structure that might serve a religious purpose was a building with a central room 20 feet long and more than 12 feet wide, in the centre of which was a carefully plastered and moulded rectangular basin. At each end of the main room were annexes with rounded walls. The size, elaborateness, unusual plan, and central basin all suggest some ceremonial use.

The most remarkable finds of all at Jericho have implications both for the religion and the artistic capabilities of the Neolithic inhabitants. In 1952 a find was made which suggested that special reverence was paid to human skulls. This could be deduced from the skull of an elderly man which had been set carefully upright beneath the floor of one of the rooms, in the angle of two walls. The find suggested that his spirit was intended to remain in the house, and his wisdom to be preserved for its inhabitants. In 1953 a find was made which gave even greater evidence on the importance attached to skulls.

In the débris beneath the floor of one of the houses of the Pre-Pottery B stage there came to light a deposit of seven human skulls. Later two other similar skulls were found in another room of the same house. The lower part of these skulls had been covered with plaster, moulded into the likeness of human features. Each head has a most individual character, and one cannot escape the impression that one is looking at real portraits. The eyes are inset in shells. In the case of six of the heads, the eyes are made of ordinary bivalve shells, with a vertical slit between two sections giving the appearance of the pupil. The seventh head has cowrie shells, and the horizontal opening of the shells gives him a distinctly sleepy expression. The moulding of the features, mouth, nose, ears and eyelids is fine and delicate, giving the impression that the people whose portraits we here see had small and well-fashioned features. The top of the skull is always left uncovered, though in one case the skull is painted with broad bands of dark paint, perhaps to represent a head-dress. One curious fact is that in only one instance is the lower jaw present. In the rest, the chin is moulded over the upper teeth, and the heads have therefore a somewhat squat appearance (Pls. 13, 14A).

These heads give an amazing impression of the technical skill and artistic powers of their creators, totally unexpected at such an early date. They are not the oldest representations of the human form, nor even possibly the oldest portraits, for representations exist in Palaeolithic and Mesolithic art. But they are far more lifelike than any earlier examples. Moreover, it can be claimed that they are the earliest human portraits directly ancestral to modern art. The art of the earlier epochs is divided by a gap of some thousands of years from subsequent developments, whereas from the Neolithic period onwards civilisation develops in an unbroken line, and the line of artistic achievement through the ancient Sumerian and Egyptian leads on to the Hellenic and so to the modern world.

The artistic importance of these heads is clear. But their cultural significance is more obscure. When found, the original seven were in a tumbled pile, obviously discarded when the house in which they had been treasured was ruined and succeeded by the next, beneath the floor of which they were buried. There was nothing in the part of the lower house that was uncovered to show whether they had been set in a shrine, or simply preserved in a dwelling house. But what was discovered was the source from which the skulls themselves must have been derived.

Beneath the floor of the lower house was found a large number of burials. Burial beneath the floors of the houses seems to have been the normal practice. What was exceptional was the very large number of individuals in the particular place, some forty or more within quite a small area. In some cases the skeletons were intact. In others the skull had been removed, leaving the lower jaw behind. In still others, the disturbance was much greater, but again hardly any skulls were found, and it looked as if a pile of partly decayed bodies had been searched through for the particular purpose of removing the skulls. The nine plastered heads did not account for by any means all the missing skulls, but the fact that the skulls had been carefully removed from the burials showed that they received special treatment, and almost certainly this is the source from which the nine skulls came.

Modern anthropological parallels would suggest that the heads preserved were either those of venerated ancestors or of enemies, kept as trophies. The only possible light on this is that such a mass of burials suggests some disaster. When the bodies were buried, there was at the same time built the first of the town walls belonging to the Pre-Pottery Neolithic B period; previous to this the town of the B people had apparently not been defended. This might suggest that a massacre by enemies had shown the necessity of providing defences. The heads, on which too much loving care had been spent for it to be likely that they were enemies, might be those of important people killed in a massacre. But the evidence is slender, and is not borne out by any signs of injuries on the skeletons.

In 1958 another plastered skull was found far away at the north end of the tell. Moreover, as successive layers were excavated in all the different areas, skeletons were found from which the cranium had been removed. Though a corresponding number of plastered skulls was not found, it is clear that the removal of crania from burials was a regular practice; it is possible that they were removed to some central repository or shrine, which has not been located. It is therefore clear that the Jericho skulls are those of venerated ancestors and are not trophies.

From this practice of making portrait heads with an actual skull as a basis, there seems to have been a stylistic development. In the 1930–36 excavations, a very different kind of human representation was found. This consisted apparently of three almost life-sized figures of plaster, but of them only the head of one could be preserved. This head (Pl. 15) resembles the plastered skulls in the use of shells to represent the eyes, but in almost nothing else. The head in profile is a flat disk, and is thus a very stylised representation. There was some uncertainty as to whether these figures came from the Pre-Pottery Neolithic B levels or the succeeding Pottery Neolithic levels. Finds in 1958 make it probable that they belonged to the Pre-Pottery phase, for the 1959 finds represent a further degree of stylisation, and they came from the very top of the Pre-Pottery levels. They also may have been representations of complete, life-size figures, for many fragments were found. But the only one of which a substantial portion could be recovered extended only as far as the bust (Pl. 14B). The head (and numerous other fragments of heads) is now completely stylised, a spade-shaped disk without any attempt to render any features, and painted completely schematically. The shoulders and bust, however, are moulded comparatively realistically. The three types of figures are most interesting evidence on the developments of primitive art.

The first Pre-Pottery Neolithic B settlement at Jericho was apparently not defended. The houses extended well down the slopes of the mound which the earlier settlement had already built up to a height of about 24 feet above the plain, and in Trench I, where the sequence could best be studied, there was a succession of ten house levels without any trace of an enclosure wall. The need then apparently arose for defence. It may be of

significance that this immediately followed the multiple burials
already referred to (p. 53), but, as is there pointed out, the
skeletons did not provide any evidence of wounds which would
prove death at the hands of enemies. The defensive wall which
was then built was a massive affair, not so regularly built as the
Pre-Pottery Neolithic A walls, nor surviving to so great a height
as the final wall of that phase, but employing much larger stones.
One, visible in Pl. 16, was a great orthostat nearly 5 feet by 3 feet
in surface dimensions, and one in what is probably the continuation of the wall 140 feet to the north (in Square M I), was nearly
10 feet by 6 feet. The wall was, to the height to which it survived,
free-standing only on the outer side. It was constructed by
cutting it back into the house levels on the inner side, removing
the corresponding levels on the outer side, and piling the soil so
derived on the inner side to form a terrace. On this terrace, houses
were built right up to the inner side of the wall.

This wall has been located only at the two places on the western
side already mentioned, Trench I and Square M I. In Trenches II
and III, at the north and south end of the tell respectively, the
houses of the period run to the extremities of the trenches, where
they are truncated by the great Middle Bronze Age revetment
(pp. 178-9). It therefore cannot be proved that it was a town wall
and not a citadel wall, but the contours of the tell suggest that
it was a town wall enclosing the whole area of the town, which
was therefore considerably greater than the area of the largest
Bronze Age town, for the Middle Bronze Age revetment was
the base of a band of defences at least 130 feet wide, and the
dimensions of the Neolithic town exceeded those of the
Bronze Age town by at least that amount at the north and south
ends.

This wall may not have had a very long life. In Trench I it
seems to have collapsed, possibly owing to the weight of soil in
the terrace behind it, and to have been succeeded by a similar
wall about 40 feet in advance. There may even have been a third
stage, on the evidence of further advancement of the house levels,
but if so this has disappeared in subsequent denudation.

The Pre-Pottery Neolithic B settlement of Jericho has therefore all the urban characteristics of its predecessor in long-continued occupation, size and evidence of communal organisation. The possible temple in Trench I may be evidence also of the public buildings which are one of the features suggested as necessary[1] to support a claim to the title of a town. The domestic architecture, with its large and rectilinear plans, is obviously much more sophisticated than that of the A phase. Two Carbon-14 dates give some indication of the absolute chronology of the phase. In squares E I, II, V, nineteen successive building stages of the phase were traced; this is not, however, the complete sequence, since the uppermost stage in this area had been removed in the 1930–36 excavations. In the sixteenth phase from the bottom, material was obtained which gave a date of 6250 B.C. $\pm$ 200. In Trench I twenty-six building stages were traced, and material from the ninth stage from the bottom gave a date of 5850 B.C. $\pm$ 160. This material came from a stage immediately preceding the building of the first of the Pre-Pottery Neolithic B town walls.[2]

These developments at Jericho were unique in Palestine or elsewhere when they were found. The history of the development of settlement in Palestine has therefore so far been illustrated from Jericho alone. But it was always to be expected that these finds would stimulate the search for others. Jericho may have been the most important settlement in Palestine, but other sites, for instance Beidha near Petra, are now being investigated. In Anatolia too, the finds at Çatal Hüyük suggest a related culture of high attainments.

On the other hand, it is equally certain that not all groups of Neolithic people in Palestine shared in the remarkable developments shown at Jericho. Long before the excavations of 1935–36 first showed the association of the Tahunian industry with a firmly settled population, implements of this industry had been accepted as typical of a population living in caves, shelters and small settlements, showing only the very rudiments of a Neolithic economy. So, as in the case of the Natufians, there may have been

[1] V. G. Childe, *Antiquity*, March 1957.   [2] Addenda pp. 332–3.

two lines of development, one group advancing towards a status which one can claim at Jericho to be urban, another, possibly with a pastoral rather than an agricultural economy, and living in the hills rather than in the Jordan Valley, providing evidence of only very slight settlements. The more evidence that comes to light, the more complex the story becomes.

★

From the First Settlements to the Beginnings of Civilisation

PALESTINE, AS represented by Jericho, can therefore put forward a good claim to be one of the places in which there took place the transition from a nomadic way of life to the settled existence that is the prerequisite of all development towards civilisation. We must, however, be careful *not* to claim that it was the only area and the only site in which this development took place.

In the introductory chapter, a sketch was given of the stages in development which archaeological work over the last twenty years or so has shown to lead up to the emergence of the empires of the great river valleys in the third millennium B.C. One important stage in this development is that at which a series of villages stretched right round the northern part of the Fertile Crescent from the Iranian foothills to the Mediterranean coast (map, Fig. 1). These villages are by no means uniform in their culture or economy. Architecture and equipment vary considerably. All, however, appear to be fairly firmly settled groups of modest size. One feature that they have in common is the use of simple, hand-made pottery. At most of the sites this pottery is of more than one sort, but, fortunately for the needs of archaeological correlation, one type, a dark-faced burnished ware made in simple, bag-shaped forms, appears at a great number of sites. Its home seems to be the Syro-Cilician plains, and at Mersin and sites such as Judeidah in the Amuq valley it is the dominant type, while to the east as far as Hassuna and to the south as far as Byblos it becomes less common, until it is a minor element appearing with more typical local wares. All these sites were excavated at a date before the use of Carbon-14 for establishing an absolute chronology was available. A date in about the middle of the fifth millennium B.C. seemed to fit the stages which succeeded them down to the beginning of the historic period at the end of the fourth millennium.

In Iraq it seems possible to establish a series of preceding stages showing the development of these villages from the final food-gathering stage.[1] An industry known as the Zarzian is the latest found in caves, and may correspond in setting to the Natufian of Mount Carmel. Succeeding that are open settlements such as Karim Shahir, in which there is no trace of permanent habitations, but which may represent the stage of incipient agriculture. At Jarmo the earliest permanent village appears, covering an area of about 3 acres, with solid rectangular buildings. Jarmo shares the characteristic of the first stages of Jericho that no pottery is found, though the inhabitants certainly do not belong to either of the two Jericho groups, for the architecture and equipment is quite different. This is the stage which is considered to precede Hassuna, which takes its place in the spread of village communities described in the last paragraph. In this sequence in Iraq, no one site produced direct evidence of sequence, and there are certainly developmental gaps between each of the sites. The general range, however, corresponds to the more complete sequence in Palestine described in the last chapter.

Jarmo was one of the first sites in the Near East to be dated by Carbon-14. A series of six tests all gave dates of *c.* 4750 B.C. Some more recent tests have suggested an earlier date.[2] Two of these give dates in the tenth millennium, and three give dates ranging from 5990 B.C. to 7080 B.C. Professor Braidwood selects these last as likely to cover the correct range, with a life for Jarmo of about five hundred years centring on 6500 B.C. His arguments do not carry complete conviction,[3] and a date in the mid-fifth

---

[1] R. J. and L. Braidwood, *Journal of World History*, I, 1953.
[2] R. J. Braidwood, *Science*, Vol. 127, No. 3512.
[3] K. M. Kenyon, *Journal of the Royal Anthropological Institute*, 1959.

millennium for the spread of village settlements in the northern part of the Fertile Crescent still seems more probable.

The important point, however, is not so much the date as the evidence that there were a number of different lines of development. That in Palestine is clearly independent of that in Iraq. In northern Syria and Iraq there were probably also several different lines, for the resultant village communities varied so much in their architectural styles, and the mixture of pottery types found in most of them suggests a combination of earlier elements. This diverse background is confirmed by the stages in Palestine which succeed the Pre-Pottery Neolithic.

Like its predecessor, the Pre-Pottery Neolithic B town of Jericho comes to an abrupt end. Its destruction was much more disastrous to progress, for the succeeding occupation marks a great retrogression. The newcomers brought with them the use of pottery, but in every other respect they were much more primitive than their predecessors. As in the case of the end of the Pre-Pottery Neolithic A town, the destruction of the final B town is followed by a period of erosion, with the familiar wearing-away of the levels on the edges of the mound until the débris reached a natural angle of rest. Above these ruins, again after a time interval which it is impossible to estimate, appears the evidence of the newcomers. This evidence is of a very curious sort. Everywhere the first pottery appears in pits cut into the ruins of the earlier town. These pits literally honeycomb the mound wherever it has been excavated. In the earlier seasons of the excavations, it was thought that the pits were quarry pits to obtain materials to make mud-bricks, at a stage in which a camping existence was being succeeded by one with permanent structures. Further examination has shown that this was a mis-interpretation. The pits are really pit-dwellings. In them are a series of floors, and the edges of the pits are revetted by slight walls of pisée and stone. The newcomers were therefore almost troglo-dytes; wherever there appear to be layers belonging to the period which are not in pits, they consist of surfaces and hearths only, and no solid structures. Such a way of life is very surprising, but has

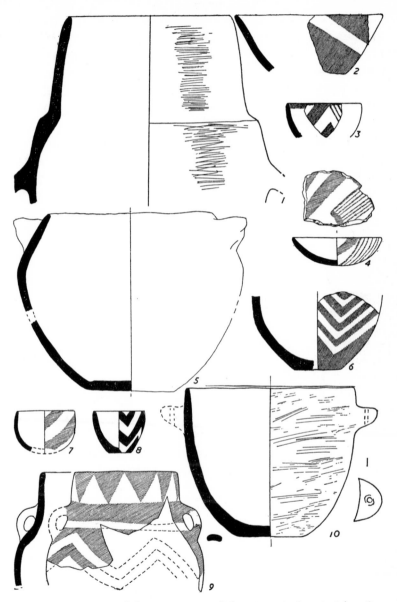

FIG. 4 Pottery of the Pottery Neolithic A period at Jericho. $\frac{1}{5}$

been made less so by the discovery of the subterranean settlement
of the Chalcolithic period near Beersheba (pp. 77 ff.).

The most notable product of the newcomers, the Pottery
Neolithic A people, is their pottery. They certainly arrived at the
site already possessing the art of making it. The vessels divide
themselves into two main classes, coarse ware and fine decorated
ware. The shapes in both classes are approximately the same, and
are simple and primitive (Fig. 4). The most common vessels are
saucer-bowls with flat base and splaying wall, of varying sizes.
There are also a few bowls with gently curved walls. The jar form
has a flattish base with globular body, slight shoulder, high neck
contracting upwards and no moulding on the rim. Usually there
are two small lug handles at the base of the neck; ledge and knob
handles, however, also occur both on jars and bowls.

The ware of the coarse vessels is crude in the extreme, and
certainly suggests that the craft of pot-making had not progressed
very far. It has many grits, perhaps derived from the clay
employed, and, to provide the necessary cohesion, straw has
been added in considerable quantities. The firing was obviously
at a low temperature, and as a result the ware is soft and crumbly.
The surface has often been smoothed over with a handful of grass.

The finer pottery is very different in appearance. It is still
friable and has considerable straw in it, but it is distinctly better
fired and of cleaner clay. But the chief difference is in the finish.
The surface is comparatively smooth, and is covered as a rule by a
cream-coloured slip. This slip in turn is partially covered by a red
slip, so that the reserved portions of the cream slip form a pattern,
usually in some combination of chevrons or triangles. To heighten
the contrast, the red slip is finely burnished with a beautifully
lustrous finish. Altogether, it is a most attractive ware and contrasts strongly with the coarse pottery.

Not only were the Pottery Neolithic A people distinguished
from their predecessors by their use of pottery, but their other
equipment was quite different. The fine grinding querns, pestles
and stone bowls disappear, and only crudely worked stone vessels
seem to have been used. The flint industry also was quite different,

the most notable change being the use of a sickle blade with a coarse denticulation instead of the finely serrated edge of the blades used in the Pre-Pottery B phase. This type of sickle blade continues in use in Palestine throughout the Early Bronze Age, and it is therefore probable that the descendants of this group formed one element of the Bronze Age population.

What the antecedents of these people were we do not yet know. This distinctive pottery has only rarely been found elsewhere, a single sherd from a cave at Tell Duweir in southern Palestine,[1] two sherds from the Wadi Rabah on the west slopes of the central upland zone, near the head-waters of the River Yarkon,[2] and a few probable sherds from the lowest levels at Megiddo.[3] Though these finds are scanty[4], their wide geographical distribution may be an indication that the Pottery Neolithic A people of Jericho will eventually be found to have been established in a considerable part of Palestine.

The pits containing this pottery are found all over the tell at Jericho, and the population was therefore numerous. But throughout their period of occupation at Jericho, the Pottery Neolithic A people seem to have built no solid, free-standing structures. They were succeeded by another group, the Pottery Neolithic B people, which, at least to begin with, seem to have been almost equally primitive, for they seem to have built their huts in the upper levels of the pits occupied by their predecessors. How sharp the break between the two groups was is not yet certain, for the evidence has not been fully worked out. At any rate, a new and considerably more sophisticated pottery appears, brought by newcomers who either superseded, or more probably mingled with, the A group. This pottery is much better fired, the ware is thinner and has not the large amount of straw in it that is found in the early sherds, and the forms are more advanced. Notable characteristics are jar forms with rims which are concave internally, to which the name "bow-rim" has been given, and jar handles which splay out at their attachment to the vessel. The

[1] *Lachish*, IV, Fig. (1) and p. 300, Cave 6019.   [2] *I.E.J.*, 8, Fig. 4.
[3] *M. II*, Pl. 2. 30, 31, 34-36.   [4] Some other finds have recently been made.

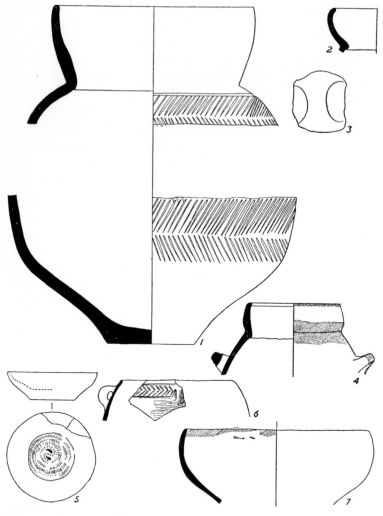

FIG. 5 Pottery of the Pottery Neolithic B period at Jericho. $\frac{1}{5}$

burnished, red-on-cream decoration of the earlier finer ware disappears, but many of the vessels are covered with a deep red slip, sometimes burnished, sometimes matt. The most characteristic decoration, found both on jars and bowls, is in bands of herringbone incisions. The bands are usually delineated by grooves, and very often they are covered by a band of cream slip, with the rest of the vessel covered by a red slip (Fig. 5).

The Pottery Neolithic B people do not seem to have brought the practice of solid architecture with them. But in due course they started to build free-standing houses. These have stone foundations, with a superstructure of mud-bricks. These bricks are still hand- and not mould-made, but they are quite different from those used in the Pre-Pottery phases. They are plano-convex, and can be described as bun-shaped, round in plan and humped on top. The structural remains that survive of the period are comparatively slight, for the levels suffered some denudation after the end of the period. Some of the buildings seem to have been rectilinear, while some of the walls were curved, but no complete house plan has been recovered. There were several building stages, and belonging to the second of them was a wall, 2·25 metres broad, which has been traced for a distance of 19 metres, which is certainly an enclosure wall, and might even have been a town wall. At a later stage, buildings with substantial, rectilinear stone walls were constructed, but again little of the plan survived.

The great importance of this stage is that at last it provides us with a link with other sites. Another site in the Jordan Valley has produced closely similar pottery. This is near a settlement called Sha'ar ha Golan, at the junction of the River Yarmuk with the Jordan, just south of the Sea of Galilee. The finds came not from an archaeological excavation but from the digging of an anti-tank ditch and subsequent agricultural cuttings. The material was derived from a layer of dark earth overlying river gravel with Palaeolithic implements. No structural features were recovered, but great quantities of pottery, flint implements and animal bones were found. The inhabitants of the settlement certainly harvested grain, but it is not clear whether this was wild or cultivated, and they apparently relied to a considerable degree on wild animals for food. The culture and economy of the group would not appear to have been of an advanced type. Some of the pottery is very close to that of Jericho Pottery Neolithic B, particularly vessels decorated with bands of herringbone incisions (Pl. 17). The total range of forms at the two sites, however, is not the same, so the groups are related but not of identical composition. A very distinctive class of find at Sha'ar ha Golan is the large number of very schematic figurines made from pebbles (Pl. 18); the pebbles from which these were made were, however, a natural feature of the area, whereas they do not occur in the neighbourhood of Jericho, so their absence at Jericho is not necessarily significant.

This connection between the Yarmuk site and Jericho is interesting, as for the first time Jericho ceases, in our present state of knowledge, to be in a state of solitary splendour. But more important is the fact that the pottery with the bands of herringbone incisions also occurs at Byblos. The ancient town of Byblos was one of the most famous of those on the Syrian coast. Its harbour was the principal route by which the natural resources of the Lebanon, especially its renowned cedarwood, were exported to the rest of the Mediterranean. This was of particular interest to treeless Egypt, and there is definite evidence that trade relations existed between Byblos and the Nile Valley in Predynastic times, that is to say, in the fourth millennium B.C. For many years the painstaking excavation of the mound by the beautiful little natural harbour has been in progress, and at the base two layers have been found, to which the description Éneolithic (or Chalcolithic) A and B has been given. The lowest, Éneolithic A, consists of a settlement of houses approximately rectangular in plan, with well-made plaster floors. These floors have a resemblance to the Pre-Pottery Neolithic B houses at Jericho in that their surface was polished, but the resemblance stops there. The superstructure of the houses was apparently flimsy in the extreme, possibly little more than a tent of branches,

covered with skins. The pottery from this level includes a surprisingly large number of quite different types of ware. Perhaps
this suggests that the population of Byblos was already cosmopolitan, and that a number of different groups had already been
attracted by the natural advantages of its position. One type of
ware with incised decoration, often in herringbone pattern, does
seem to have definite affinities to the ware of Sha'ar ha Golan and
the Pottery Neolithic B of Jericho. A further link is that at Byblos
the pebble figurines of Sha'ar ha Golan are also found, which
adds much weight to the pottery evidence.

One of the other groups of pottery at Byblos was the dark
burnished ware which has already been mentioned (p. 58) as
occurring in the Neolithic villages stretching right round the
northern part of the Fertile Crescent. This is a point of great
importance. For the first time an approximate chronological link,
independent of any question of Carbon-14 dating, can be established between Jericho and the rest of the northern Fertile
Crescent. It would seem that a way of life had grown up which
spread from the foothills of the Iranian plateau right round the
fringes of Anatolia and down into Palestine. It was a way of life
with comparatively simple characteristics, small villages, permanent but unelaborated structures and a modest agricultural
economy. The interesting thing is the divergencies and the links.
As has already been suggested, the divergencies indicate that the
route the ancestors of the village communities had traversed on
their journey from a nomadic to a settled existence had not been
a single one. But by a date probably in the mid-fifth millennium
(or possibly earlier if the most recent Carbon-14 datings are to be
accepted) the various routes had begun to come together. A
similar way of life was growing up, and the similarities were
stimulated by the contacts which the villagers apparently had with
each other.

This way of life was undoubtedly a retrogression as far as
Palestine, as represented by Jericho, was concerned. Nothing on
the scale of the Pre-Pottery Neolithic A and B towns of Jericho is
found. For some reason, the light of progress seems to flicker out.

It is possible that the town-dwellers had become decadent, and fell victims to more barbarous elements, descendants of their relatives who had continued to pursue a nomadic existence, or adventurers from the less progressive area to the north. Alternatively, something may have happened to upset their economy, a deterioration of climate to which they failed to adapt their agricultural methods, or at Jericho some interference with the course of the spring. At any rate, the drab villages which were the highest achievement to date of the rest of the Fertile Crescent succeed the far higher achievements of eighth to sixth millennium Jericho.

But though as far as Palestine is concerned this stage is a retrogression, it is nevertheless an interesting stage, just for the reason that all these various lines of progress towards a settled life were beginning to converge. Progress is also both competitive and imitative, and this growth of a generally similar way of life over a wide area was a stimulant to progress. The next stage was that of the Chalcolithic. The term Chalcolithic implies that a metal, copper, was being used as well as stone. The significance of this goes far deeper than the mere fact that more efficient tools and weapons were available. It lies in the fact that the sources of copper are geographically restricted. Regular trade to supply the new material gave a great stimulus to the breakdown of isolation and the spread of cultures and ideas. Side by side with it went the change in economy involved in the necessity of specialists to deal with the new material, which is referred to in Chapter 1.

The difficulty in deciding where to place the transition from the Neolithic to the Chalcolithic is reflected in the existing confusion in nomenclature. Sometimes the one and sometimes the other name is given to allied groups. The transition is in fact a gradual one. The dawn of the new era is not marked by the sudden appearance of copper implements on a site, but by the gradual breakdown of isolation and the resultant spreading of ideas and cultures over a considerable area. In Palestine, in fact, as far as our evidence goes, metal seems to have played a relatively small part among the materials employed until quite a late date, about the end of the third millennium. But in spite of this, the change in outlook is reflected in the gradual growth of widespread cultures, and the eventual amalgamation of isolated groups into a cultural whole.

In the northern part of the Fertile Crescent, this stage is marked by the appearance of a widespread culture, called Halafian, after Tell Halaf in northern Iraq where it was first found. Site after site, from Mesopotamia across to the Mediterranean coast, has shown that after the stage of the Neolithic villages with all their diverse ways of life, a remarkably similar economy appears, with, as a characteristic feature, a type of pottery with geometric decoration in red on a light background. This is usually dated to the late fifth millennium, and in Mesopotamia the phase is succeeded by the stages which lead up to the evolution of the city states to which the name "Proto-literate" has been given.

The Halafian culture does not extend as far south as Palestine. Twenty years ago one would have thought that there was nothing to correspond with it. But each year now is bringing new discoveries which have to be fitted in in the period between the Pottery Neolithic B of Jericho and the beginning of the Early Bronze Age. There is still much that is uncertain. We know a number of isolated facts, and we know that there are a number of communities with distinctive cultures, which have to be fitted in in this twilight of prehistory before we reach the dawn of history, with reasonable illuminated landmarks, round about 3000 B.C. In trying to fit into place the cultures these communities represent, we should learn a lesson from the progress of research in European prehistory. Earlier European scholars tried to place each culture observed into a regular sequence. Now it is recognised that many cultures represent regional developments, and several may have existed side by side. The older sequence-method tended to produce very inflated chronologies, which have had to be considerably reduced now that the picture has become more coherent. This we should bear in mind in trying to piece together the jig-saw puzzle which our present state of knowledge in Palestine represents, and in fact some of the new pieces of the jigsaw which almost every year emerge from the ground do suggest that the whole picture will eventually portray a number of groups of people living side by side each with their own distinctive culture, but with just enough links with other groups to suggest contemporaneity.

The first discovery of a group which seemed to belong to this period was at Teleilat Ghassul, which has given its name to the Ghassulian culture. The pottery on this site has some affinities with that of Jericho Pottery Neolithic B. A form of jar, of a simple, bag-like shape with incurved rim, called a hole-mouth jar, is found on both sites. At both the potters often made their vessels by setting them on a mat. A peculiar vessel found at Ghassul is shaped like an ice-cream cornet, and some fragments of these have been found at Jericho; and there are a few other similarities. But many highly individual forms found at Ghassul are not found at Jericho, and we do not yet know whether the reason is difference of period or difference of group. It may be that Ghassul belongs mainly to a period when there was a gap in occupation at Jericho, probably after the Pottery Neolithic B stage, or is the site of a settlement of a different group. The present weight of evidence does suggest that the Ghassulians were newcomers from outside Palestine, and the fact that near-by Jericho shows only slight evidence of connection with them may support the idea of a gap there covering most of the period of occupation at Ghassul.

Teleilat Ghassul, like Jericho, lies in the Jordan Valley, a little north-east of the Dead Sea and about 3 miles east of the Jordan. The site is not an impressive one. You can search for a long time through the scrub-covered sandy waste until you locate the low hillocks, only about 6 feet high, which mark the site. The district does not seem to be particularly inviting, for today most of the immediate neighbourhood is uncultivated, and the only signs of life are Bedouin encampments. But water is not far off, coming down from the precipitous hills of the east side of the Jordan Valley, and the excavated remains show that the resources of the

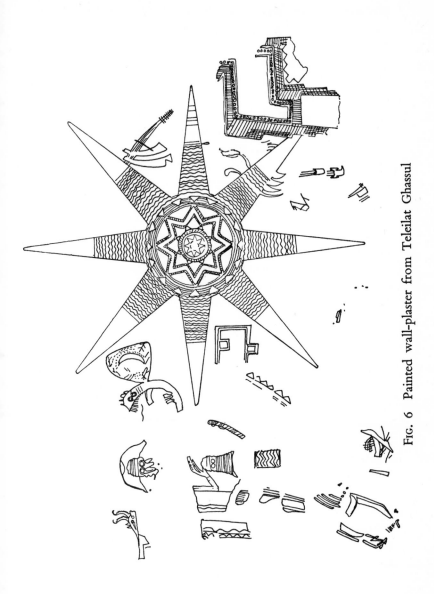

FIG. 6 Painted wall-plaster from Teleilat Ghassul

neighbourhood in antiquity were well able to support a settled population.

The excavations, carried out between 1930 and 1938 by the Pontifical Biblical Institute, revealed a settlement covering a total area of about 850 yards by 475 yards, but divided into three hamlets which each built up its own little mound during the period the site was inhabited. The excavation showed that there were four main layers of occupation, each marked by a rebuilding of the houses, apparently after a destruction by fire, and a raising of the level of the site on the ruins of the earlier houses.

Only the top layer of houses was excavated in any completeness. The evidence from this layer suggests that we have a firmly settled farming community. The houses are of moderate size and closely built, giving each the appearance of a closely knit unit, but there was no evidence of any enclosure wall. The houses are irregular in plan, and the rooms vary from approximately rectangular to trapezoidal. The walls have solidly built foundations of stone, with a superstructure of hand-moulded bricks or in some cases of *terre pisée*. One might perhaps think that the general appearance was of somewhat simple, crude structures, if it were not for the fact that some fragments of remarkable painted wall plaster were recovered. One fragment shows a spirited representation of a bird somewhat resembling a pheasant. Other fragments could be reassembled to form an extraordinary futuristic-looking composition with stylised human forms, sun-rays and an impression of some religious ritual (Fig. 6).

The equipment of the houses seems to be almost standardised. Each had well-built storage pits, large jars to hold grain or other food, flat paved spaces which may have been threshing-floors, and querns for grinding grain. Cooking was done both on open hearths and, which represents a considerable advance in the use of fire, in ovens heated by sunk combustion chambers. In the storage pits were found corn grains, and, even more important, date stones and olive stones. The importance of these is that the Ghassulians had access to orchards, which implies a necessarily very much more permanently settled occupation than the cultivation of grain, for the trees require long years to come to maturity. Today, the olive does not flourish in the Jordan Valley, though it can grow, and it may be that the olives were traded from some orchard-cultivating community in the hills, which would be an interesting inference of the breakdown of self-sufficiency. Date palms, of course, grow well in suitable irrigated areas of the valley.

The household goods, tools and weapons of the inhabitants of Ghassul differ greatly from those of any of the Jericho stages. Even the querns are different, for they are of the common saddle-quern type, a plain block of stone with a concave grinding surface, quite unlike those of Jericho described above. The few points of contact between the pottery of Ghassul and that of the Pottery Neolithic B of Jericho have already been mentioned, but in ware

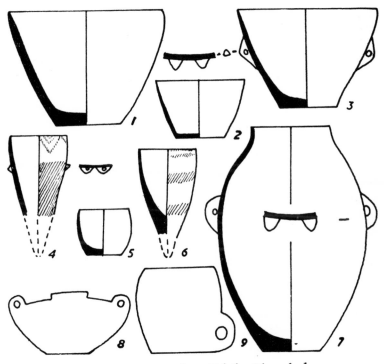

FIG. 7   Pottery from Teleilat Ghassul. $\frac{1}{5}$

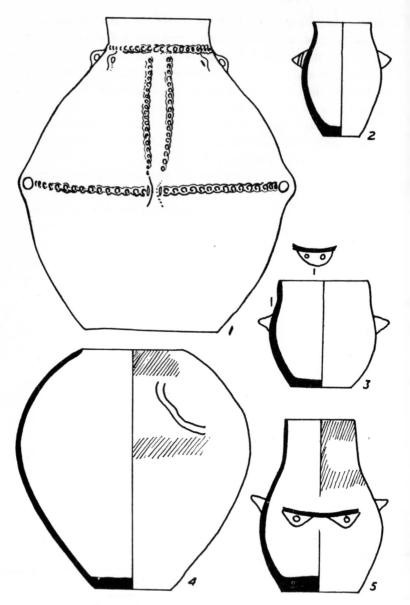

FIG. 8   Pottery from Teleilat Ghassul. $\frac{1}{5}$

and in varied repertory of forms the Ghassul pottery presents a much more advanced and sophisticated appearance. Many of the vessels are of quite hard, thin and well-fired ware. The forms are surprisingly elaborate. One vessel was given the name of the bird-jar. It had a handle at either end of a body which might remind one of a sitting hen, and a central neck, and for it the suggestion has been made, on the basis of modern Arab use, that it was a churn for making butter by suspension and rocking. Two types of decoration are found. There is a frequent use of applied bands, mainly decorated with crescentic impressions, sometimes in the form of snakes, and incisions on the body of the vessel are also common. The second class has painted decoration, of a dark colour, usually red, on a light background, cream or pink. The designs are simple and geometric.

The stone vessels are also elaborate. There are many finely ground stone saucers, and a remarkable type is a brazier-like vessel with a pierced conical base, the cutting of which out of a hard basalt must have been a skilled operation.

The flint industry is rich (Fig. 9). The most striking form is a fan-scraper, a large thin flake with one semicircular edge, struck from a block of tabular flint, so that the cortex (or outer crust) of the block is often left on the implement, and the semicircular edge then finely flaked. Knife blades and toothed sickle blades are common, as are also efficient-looking picks or adzes, which according to their varying sizes would have served as wood-working tools or hoes for agriculture. Only a few arrowheads were found, showing that hunting did not constitute an important part of the economy.

An interesting find was that of two copper axes of simple form, which would show that this culture is correctly assigned to the Chalcolithic phase, when metal was beginning to make its appearance.[1]

When the excavations of the Pontifical Biblical Institute first revealed the culture of the inhabitants of Ghassul, it appeared to represent an isolated phenomenon, which might be contemporary with one of the other main cultural phases, and the elaborateness

[1] Addenda p. 333–4.

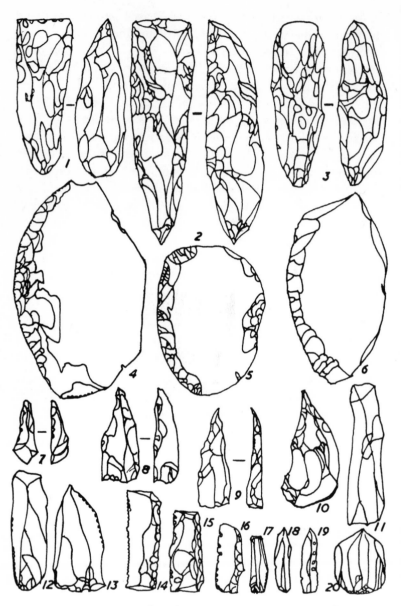

FIG. 9   Flints from Teleilat Ghassul. ½

of much of the equipment suggested that it might be as late as the Early Bronze Age in the third millennium. But subsequent discoveries, and the reassessment of some earlier ones, show that people sharing the culture were widespread over Palestine. Finds of the characteristic pottery have been made in places as far apart as a site near Jericho, at 'Affuleh in the Plain of Esdraelon, on the Coastal Plain, and in the neighbourhood of Beersheba in the south, to mention a few only. An interesting find at Ḥederah in the Coastal Plain, associated with Ghassulian pottery, was of a number of pottery ossuaries to hold the bones of the dead. Some were in the form of model houses, with either slightly rounded or gabled roofs, which give valuable evidence of the form of contemporary houses, and show that the dead were considered to need their dwellings as in lifetime.

A group of sites which are interesting for another reason lies in the Wadi Ghazzeh in southern Palestine, not far from Gaza. Here Sir Flinders Petrie excavated a number of sites. Many of the finds are almost identical with those at Ghassul. There are such specialised pot forms as the "bird vessel" or churn, the cornet and the same types of decoration. The stone vessels include the same elaborate brazier type, and the flint industries the fine fan-scrapers and the characteristic hoes. But these finds, instead of coming from a site with all the evidence of long-established settlement such as Ghassul, come from a number of settlements which give no evidence of substantial structures and are in fact clearly camping sites. We have here, therefore, to do with nomadic groups, possibly practising a seasonal agriculture which the sporadic rainfall of the area allows, but never settling long enough in one spot to find it worth while to build themselves permanent houses. With such a nomadic way of life, one difference between the equipment of these people and those of Ghassul, the presence of far more flint arrowheads, would fit in well.

The most recent find of a settlement related to that at Ghassul is at Tell Abu Matar, just south of Beersheba. This is a most remarkable affair. The site was a natural mound made up of a layer of alluvial loam and a layer of loess to a combined depth of

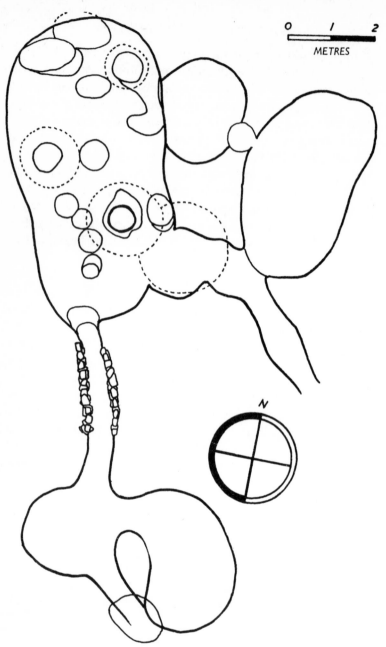

0   1   2
METRES

N

FIG. 10   Subterranean dwelling at Tell Abu Matar

about 14 feet above bed-rock. In these layers had been constructed a series of artificial cave-dwellings. Some were entered by horizontal passages from the edge of the mound, some by vertical pits, in the sides of which hand- and foot-holds were cut, giving on to horizontal galleries. The dwelling-caves were of an average size of about 14 feet by 10 feet, and they were connected by galleries into groups of five, six or seven chambers. Along the walls of the chambers were pits, some of them lined with plaster, presumably for water storage, and in the middle of the chambers, or in the connecting galleries, were bell-shaped silos with a capacity of 40 to 55 bushels. On the surface of the mound were associated pits and fireplaces. The main dwelling-chambers showed numerous occupation layers, with spreads of ash and occupation material separated by deposits of sand, and pits and silos could be assigned to the successive layers. There was also a succession of structural phases. The comparatively soft material into which the caves were cut tended to crumble and the roofs to collapse. The dwelling might then be superseded by another, or a new dwelling be established in the pit formed by the collapse of the cave, presumably with a superstructure partly above ground. Altogether, three main phases of subterranean dwellings could be traced. The fourth phase on the site represented a major change, for above the filled-in pits of the earlier stages were found rectilinear houses with walls built on stone foundations.

This curious troglodyte community, which the twenty houses found suggest might have numbered about two hundred persons, seems to have lived primarily by agriculture. Their flint industry included no arrowheads, and they were therefore not hunters, while the numerous silos show that they had abundant supplies of grain, in spite of the semi-arid neighbourhood. But the most striking thing about them was that they were copper-workers. Evidence of the whole process was found. The preliminary reduction was carried out in open fireplaces. Then the ore was smelted in specially constructed ovens, circular basins about a foot to 18 inches in diameter, with thick walls of earth mixed with straw; as found, the interior of these chambers was glazed from a combination of the melted metal, silica and residual matter. Then the ore was refined in crucibles, and finally it must have been cast in moulds, though these were not found. This represents the earliest undoubted impact of the metal age upon Palestine. The nearest source from which the ore could have been obtained is 60 miles away to the south; a regular trade in raw materials must therefore have existed, and the inhabitants of Tell Abu Matar must have been able to produce sufficient supplies of food material to finance expeditions to fetch it, or to buy it from itinerant merchants. Moreover, the working of the metal was a specialist's job, and he also had to be supported by the food production of the rest of the community. We have here, therefore, evidence of an important stage of transition from a self-sufficient Neolithic way of life to that of a complex community. But the evidence shows that the use of metal had not yet become a dominant factor. The tools and implements of the inhabitants of Tell Abu Matar were still of flint. The manufactured copper objects found were mace-heads (which probably had a ceremonial rather than a warlike significance), pins, rings, ornamental cylinders and handles. The metal was still regarded as far too precious for rough, everyday use.

There is no doubt that these people have some connection with the inhabitants of Ghassul. Their flint industry is not identical, since most of the implements were rough choppers made from pebbles locally available; there were only a very few of the fine fan-scrapers so common at Ghassul, but they did use the hump-backed Ghassulian picks. Their stone vessels included basalt bowls with brazier-like bases, which were very characteristic both of Ghassul and of the sites in the Wadi Ghazzeh. The pottery again is not identical, but includes a number of similar forms, especially the peculiar "bird-vessel" or churn.

It is suggested that the rectangular houses which were the final stage at Tell Abu Matar correspond to the houses at Ghassul, which belonged to the fourth stage at that site, and that in the lower levels at Ghassul, which have hardly been examined, there may be stages in which there were cave-dwellings corresponding to the earlier stages at the other site. This is a possibility, but not a certainty, for, as emphasised in the last paragraph, there are many differences between the two groups.

There are, in fact, three inferences that can be drawn from our present knowledge of the Ghassulian culture. The first is that it is intrusive and not indigenous in Palestine. Its highly developed and specialised pottery is not derived from anything which, as far as we know, went before in Palestine. The flint industry, especially at Ghassul itself, is also very individual. Attempts have been made to find parallels both for the pottery and the flint industry, but without any real success. Some parallels can be traced in Egypt, but they are so general that one must conclude that the group was not derived from that direction. The conclusion is that they must have come from the east or north-east, but there material of the period is almost unknown owing to lack of exploration.

The second inference is that there were a number of groups only rather loosely connected. There is no identity in equipment and way of life between the inhabitants of Ghassul, of the Wadi Ghazzeh and of Tell Abu Matar. It is suggested that these groups were all inhabiting marginal areas. But the potential fertility of the Jordan Valley, when water supplies are controlled by a settled population, is undoubted, and as one approaches the Beersheba neighbourhood from the south in spring one realises why the Israelites considered Palestine a land flowing with milk and honey. On the other hand the area of the Wadi Ghazzeh is the real desert-fringe (Pl. 19A). The contrast of economy between the settlements there and those of Ghassul and Tell Abu Matar is emphasised by the high proportion of arrowheads found in the former, while they are practically absent in the other two sites. Allied settlements are also found in the north, at 'Affuleh on the fringes of the Plain of Esdraelon and Ḥederah in the Plain of Sharon, comparatively rich agricultural areas. Immigrant groups therefore settled all over the country, though on present evidence more in the south than the north, and adapted their way of life to their environment.

The third inference is that though on the Tell Abu Matar evidence these groups had an economy which was transitional towards the great advances of the metal ages, they directly contributed surprisingly little to the ultimate civilisation of Palestine. So far, evidence of Ghassulian occupation has never been found in the lower levels of any of the sites which subsequently became a town. Their settlements seem simply to have died out. The recognisably Ghassulian forms of pottery and flint implements do not have their descendants in the forms of the Early Bronze Age. The origins of the town-builders of the Early Bronze Age must be sought elsewhere.

There is so far no direct evidence for the dating of the Ghassulian culture.[1] We are still dealing with a relatively early period; trade is growing, but still not, at least as far as Palestine is concerned, covering sufficient distances to provide certain links with Egypt or Mesopotamia, where the sequences are well established. It has been suggested that the decorated Ghassulian pottery, with its geometric patterns in red on a cream background, resembles the Halafian pottery of the widespread Chalcolithic culture of the northern Fertile Crescent; this, if one allows a time lag for the spread south, would suggest a date early in the fourth millennium. The forms of the pottery are, however, quite different, and the resemblances in decoration only very general, so the link is a doubtful one. The first half of the fourth millennium would, however, appear a probable period. There is a slight link with the Pottery Neolithic B at Jericho, in that cornet-shaped vessels are also found there, but other Ghassulian types are not; the main phase of Ghassul ought therefore to correspond with a gap in occupation at near-by Jericho. At the other end cornets provide a link with a site with which we shall soon be concerned, Tell el Far'ah, near Nablus, where they occur in the Middle Chalcolithic. The Upper Chalcolithic there, as we shall see, falls into the last third of the fourth millennium. The evidence on the whole, therefore, points to the first half of the fourth millennium as the period in which the Ghassulians were penetrating in Palestine.

They were, as has been stressed, undoubtedly immigrants. They certainly do not account for all the groups that exploration is

[1] Addenda p. 334.

gradually bringing to light, which must be fitted in between the Neolithic and the stages preceding the full Bronze Age. Some of these are probably to be regarded as indigenous descendants of the inhabitants of Sha'ar ha Golan and Pottery Neolithic B Jericho. The lowest levels at Beth-shan and Megiddo, and some so far unrelated deposits at Jericho suggest something of the sort, while a recent survey of the Jordan Valley shows that there are a number of ancient sites which must fall into the general period. Palestine in the early fourth millennium must be visualised as settled by a number of groups of diverse origins, living side by side.

Towards the end of the millennium we reach a period for which excavation has provided much clearer evidence. We reach the period in which many of the subsequent towns seem to have been founded. It has already been pointed out that occupation of a Ghassulian character has not so far been found at the base of a tell. The new material does occur in the lower levels of a number of important sites, and from it a direct succession to the full Bronze Age can be shown. We are therefore at the dawn of a new period.

★

CHAPTER FOUR

The Proto-Urban Period

THE NEW period is ushered in by the invasion of a number of new groups, that recurrent theme in Palestinian history. They arrive as migrant tribesmen, probably from different areas and with varying equipment, and they do not bring with them a ready-made urban civilisation. But, as was pointed out in the last chapter, the settlements they established grew into the city states of the Early Bronze Age. These invasions took place in the last third of the fourth millennium B.C. For reasons which will be discussed later, the best name for the phase in which they took place seems to be the Proto-Urban period.

The first evidence of the new groups comes from tombs. Their presence in some considerable numbers and over a wide area in the north and centre of the country is attested by their burials, but so far the evidence of their actual settlements is slight. On a number of sites which were subsequently to grow into towns, for instance Megiddo, Jericho, Beth-shan, Tell el Far'ah, pottery and occupation levels are found at the base of the layers of the city-mounds, but little in the way of structures. At other sites, for instance Tell Nasbeh, a few miles north of Jerusalem, and Samaria, traces of occupation are found, but the sites are subsequently deserted, in both cases until the Iron Age; the first village popula-tion was perhaps absorbed into a town elsewhere.

The appearance of the tombs is of interest in itself, and is strong additional evidence, over and above the new types of pottery, of the arrival of entirely new groups. For the first time in Palestine, tombs are cut in the rock, or natural caves are used, and in them multiple burials of up to three or four hundred individuals were made over a long space of time. At Jericho the contrast is very marked. In all the large area searched for tombs, not a single one has been found of an earlier period. The Pre-Pottery Neolithic people of both groups buried beneath the floor of their houses. There is no evidence as to how either of the Pottery Neolithic groups disposed of their dead; from this it can probably be deduced that they were not formally buried at all, but the bodies simply exposed, unless they were buried in simple graves, without grave goods, in the cultivated land to the east and south of the tell, which is not very likely. There is a suggestion that the Ghassulian burials are associated with megalithic monuments, but the evidence is not yet clear. With the newcomers in the last part of the fourth millennium comes the new practice of multiple tomb-burial, and, to the great benefit of archaeologists, this is associated with the practice of offerings to accompany the dead. Presumably the offerings were originally of food and drink, or perhaps scents and perfumes, but what survives is the containers of pottery. These vessels provide us with evidence to define the culture of the group that used the tomb. Since vessels found in tombs are often reasonably intact, whereas on occupation sites only broken sherds are found, the tomb deposits are a very important element in our knowledge of the pottery. It must, however, be remembered that not all types of vessel were placed in tombs (for instance cooking-pots are always rare), so there may be differences between finds in tombs and those from contemporary occupation deposits.

It is probable that the newcomers came from the north and east, for so far little evidence of their presence has been found in southern Palestine except at Gezer, easily approachable from the coastal plain; in this area it may be presumed that the descendants of the Ghassulian people continued to live side by side with them. To groups arriving from the east, Jericho would be a natural point of entry, and the evidence suggests that some of them did in fact come in that way.

Some half a dozen tombs at Jericho contain pottery of the same new types. The tombs are cut into the soft limestone of the slopes surrounding the settlement. The roofs of all the tombs of this period that have so far been discovered have disappeared, which is an indication that there has been a considerable subsequent erosion of the rock, a point which will be referred to later. What survives are the bases and walls of large chambers, about 4·50 metres by 3 metres, with the lower parts of the entrance shafts that gave access to them. In general construction they appear to have been similar to later tombs, which have a roughly circular vertical entrance shaft, from the base of which an entrance leads into a tomb chamber, at this period, judging from the surviving height of the walls, about 2 metres high.

The burial practices in these tombs were strange. They all contained the remains of a very large number of individuals, in one case of about a hundred and forty, in another of over four hundred. But though we can say that four hundred individuals are represented, we have nothing like the complete remains of four hundred bodies. The count is made on the skulls. These we find for the most part entirely separated from the bodies, and neatly ranged round the edge of the tomb. In the middle of the tomb is a jumble of the other bones, mostly completely disarranged, but sometimes one finds a complete limb, a leg or an arm, in articulation, though separated from the rest of the body. In one tomb these bones in the central area were cremated; a few of the nearest skulls round the edge were scorched, though not included in the cremation, but there was no sign of fire in the other tombs. Another remarkable fact is that there are not nearly enough long bones to go with all the skulls. All this points to the fact that the burials as we find them were secondary. That is to say, the bones were only placed in their present position after the flesh had largely decayed. It is very difficult to decide what were the first stages. Was the process a lengthy one, with continuous burials in each tomb, and, as the bodies decayed and new burials were made, the skulls placed round the edge and the rest of the bones left in the centre? Or, at intervals, were skeletons collected up, from other tombs or simply after exposure, and the skulls and some of the other bones placed in mass ossuary-tombs? On the

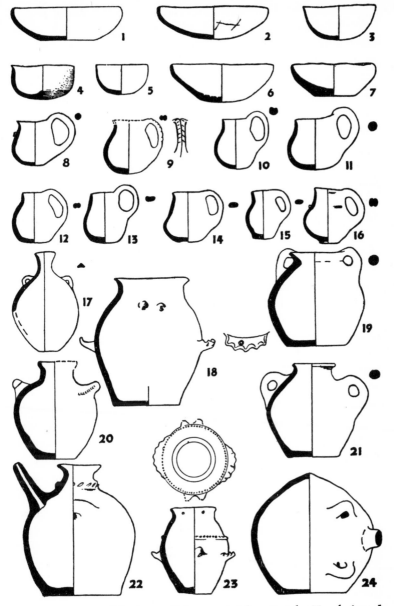

FIG. 11   Pottery of the Proto–Urban period from Jericho Tomb A94. ⅛

87

whole, the latter process seems the more probable, for if there had been prolonged continuous use it seems improbable that the earliest skulls would not have become crushed in the process, whereas some of them had still preserved the fragile bones of the face. On the other hand, in later tombs, of the Early Bronze Age, it seems fairly clear that burials were made of intact bodies, and that when space had to be made for subsequent burials many of the long bones were thrown out. There was not at this stage, however, the practice of the neat ranging of the skulls, so the process may not have been the same. The question must for the time being remain unanswered.[1]

The pottery vessels placed in these tombs did not cover a great range of forms. The vast majority consisted of shallow bowls with gently curved sides and little bag-shaped juglets with a relatively large handle, sometimes rising well above the rim of the vessel (Fig. 11.*10–11*); some, both of the bowls and of the jugs, have a very crude decoration in red or brown lines. In addition there were some jars with ledge handles, some jars with a high projecting spout, and in one tomb, A94, which may be taken as a representative of this group, a very odd vessel of beehive shape, with a spout and two handles on one side (Fig. 11.*24*).

This type of pottery is found in tombs at a number of other places. At Tell Nasbeh the range of forms in Tombs 32, 52 and 67 seems to have been very similar, and the same group of people may have pushed on from Jericho into the central uplands. But in another tomb at the same site, Cave Tomb 5–6, and at the site of 'Ai, not far from Tell Nasbeh, in Tombs B, C and G, the same pottery appears in conjunction with a quite distinct type, not found in Jericho Tomb A94 and the allied group. This type is characterised by decoration in fairly elaborate patterns of grouped bands, quite different from the crude drip-lines which are all that is found on the other group. The forms, with deep bowls, basket-handle vessels with vertical spouts, and round-based bottles, are also different.

The distinction is made more clear by the fact that in Jericho a single tomb, A13, was found in which, above lower levels

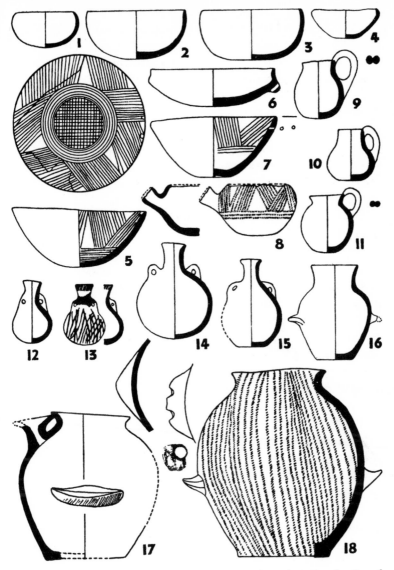

FIG. 12   Pottery of the Proto-Urban period from 'Ai Tombs G and
C(10).⅕

89

containing pottery like A94, this other pottery is found, unmixed with the A94 pottery. On the ceramic evidence, therefore, we have two groups of people, and we may label the A94 people Proto-Urban A and the A13 people Proto-Urban B. At Jericho and in some of the Tell Nasbeh tombs they are distinct, but they must have been living side by side, and on the evidence of Tell Nasbeh Cave Tomb 5-6 and of the 'Ai tomb they must in due course have mingled. The pottery of the B people is also found on Ophel, the spur south of the present city of Jerusalem which was the site of the earliest settlement, but it is not quite certain whether or not they were here mixed with the A people.

The Proto-Urban A people were also found further north. In 1946 the École Biblique of the Dominican Fathers in Jerusalem began the excavation of the imposing site of Tell el Far'ah. This site, not to be confused with the site of the same name (referred to in this book as Tell Fara for the sake of distinction, though this is an anglicised form) in southern Palestine, lies in the Wadi Far'ah, which is one of the main valleys that cut down into the west side of the Jordan Valley from near Nablus. It has a long history, though not without interruption, from the period we are now considering down to the Iron Age, when it has a position of especial importance in connection with biblical history (Chapter 11). Besides lying on this important route between the central highlands and the Jordan, the site has the advantage of two excellent springs at the foot of the hill on which the settlement was established.

Only quite a small area of the very large tell has been so far excavated to bed-rock. The first occupation is called by Père R. de Vaux, its excavator, Middle Chalcolithic. Above it is a level which he calls Upper Chalcolithic. The structural remains of this period are not very substantial, but indicate a firmly settled occupation. Most of the finds of the period come from tombs in large natural caves in the surrounding hill slopes. The tombs seem to be typical of the period in containing multiple burials, similar to those of Jericho, but they were much disturbed by subsequent re-use.

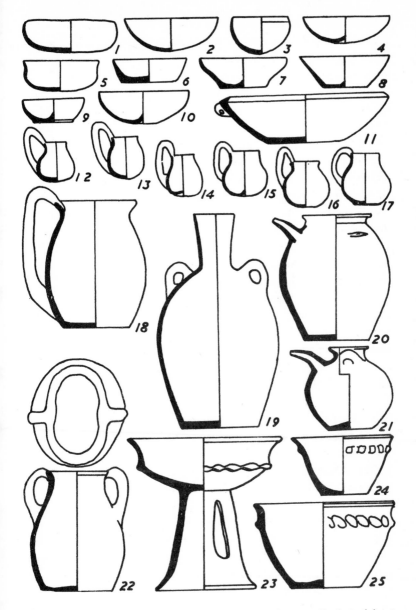

FIG. 13   Pottery of the Proto-Urban period from Tell el Far'ah. ⅕

91

These tombs contain pottery closely allied to that found in the Proto-Urban A tombs at Jericho. There are the same innumerable little bag-shaped juglets, the same shallow bowls with curved walls, the same jars with high curving spouts, and even an almost identical beehive-shaped jar with side spout. There are, however, some differences. The forms are rather more elaborate, the loop-handles of the juglets higher, some of the bowls have developed an odd conical knob in the centre, and there is a type of jar that has been compressed laterally at the mouth (Fig. 13.22). Another difference is that a fairly high proportion of the vessels have a burnished red slip, which is rare at Jericho; this may suggest that the Far'ah tombs are somewhat later, since it is a practice that becomes very common in the Early Bronze Age.

A final difference is more important. With the Proto-Urban A pottery is found a type that does not occur at Jericho nor in the central upland sites in which the Proto-Urban A and B groups occur. This is a type with distinctive forms (Fig. 13.23–25) and characterised by a highly burnished grey slip. It has been found on a number of sites in northern Palestine, and since it was first recognised in a group of sites in the Plain of Esdraelon, it is usually known as Esdraelon ware. At Tell el Far'ah all the tombs containing Proto-Urban A pottery contain Esdraelon ware as well, as do the Upper Chalcolithic levels on the tell; it was therefore presumed to belong to the same culture. The Jericho evidence shows that this is not necessarily so. We can therefore identify a third group, which we can designate Proto-Urban C.[1]

At this stage we first come to the great site of Megiddo, where the same combination of Proto-Urban A and C is found. The ancient city, several times mentioned in the Old Testament, today is represented by perhaps the most impressive tell in the whole of Palestine (Pl. 19B), a great oval mound looking out north-wards over the Plain of Esdraelon. In historic times its great importance lay in the fact that it guarded the pass that cut across the low neck between Mount Carmel, jutting out towards the sea, and the central mountain range. This pass formed part of the route of age-long historic importance between Egypt and Syria,

[1] Addenda p. 335.

and the interest of Egypt in the control of Megiddo recurs at many stages in the Egyptian archives. Excavation, however, has shown that the first occupation of the site dates back to well before the Egyptian Empire began to be interested in foreign contacts.

Megiddo, like Jericho, has been the subject of interest to more than one archaeological expedition. The most ambitious attempt to investigate was the excavations begun by the Oriental Institute of Chicago in 1925. The plan was to excavate it completely from top to bottom. But the mound of Megiddo covers at its summit 13 acres, and its depth in the centre of the mound is some 55 feet. The scheme proved beyond the powers even of the Oriental Institute. With the financial depression of the 1930s, a much reduced plan had to be adopted, and the base of the mound was, in the sequel, only investigated in a very limited area.

In this small area beneath the mound, and also on the slopes of the hill on which it is situated in an area which was cleared before the dumping on it of spoil, evidence was found of periods long before Megiddo became a walled town. The very earliest occupation of all was rather curious. It was found in a cave in the rock surface. The deposits contained only flint and bone implements, with no pottery at all. But the flints are of the same type which in the occupation on the surface of the rock are associated with pottery of, as we shall see, the second half of the fourth millennium, and are therefore probably not much earlier than this phase. By this time, of course, the fully pottery-using cultures just described were found widely spread over Palestine, and it seems strange that there was still a group at Megiddo in the pre-pottery stage. There may be an explanation in some specialist use made of the cave, or it may be a further illustration of the separate groups living in Palestine, each progressing towards civilisation at a different rate.

Though these earliest inhabitants at Megiddo apparently lived in caves, and though in the area excavated there are no structures that can be ascribed to them, they were by no means entirely primitive in their equipment. Among the flint or chert implements found were javelin heads, which showed that hunting

played a part in their economy, but there were also a number of
sickle blades, which suggests they were agriculturists. What were
apparently two complete sets of teeth of sickles showed that these
had cutting edges about 32 centimetres long. Still more interesting
are a number of long "wands" of bone, carefully shaved down
from the long bones of animals, which are pointed at one end
and pierced by a circular hole at the other. It is suggested that
these were used as needle shuttles for weaving, and also to beat
up the weft. The textile made must have been light, since the
tools are slender, and may have been of a material like flax.
Similar tools were found at Ghassul, where a fragment of textile
was probably of some plant fibre.

The succeeding people who lived in the surface of the rock had
still a distinctly primitive culture. All that survives in the way of
structures are some slight, irregular and disconnected foundations,
suggesting only flimsy buildings. Besides these there are a number
of pits cut into the rock, some of which no doubt correspond in
function as silos (storage pits) with the brick- or stone-lined pits
of Ghassul. Others may have served for some purpose such as
pressing olives for oil, for two adjacent pits are often joined by
channels. The occupation of this period must have been widespread, for the area in which it was found spreads well down the
slope of the hill.

The published material from the lowest levels of the tell proper
is a mixture,[1] for the stratigraphical deposits were not properly
analysed. It contains material allied to both Jericho Pottery
Neolithic A and B and Chalcolithic sherds with some contact
with Ghassulian. With this mixture, and also in the lowest layers
of the early occupation that spread down the slopes of the hill
before the later nucleated settlement was defined,[2] are published
(though they are certainly not truly associated) vessels of Esdraelon
ware and Proto-Urban A material. Some of the occupation of the
period was in caves, for in Tomb 903[3] and elsewhere the same
pottery is found in occupation levels underlying burials of a later
period.

[1] M. II, Pl. 1-2, 92-95.   [2] M. Stages, Stages VII-IV.   [3] M. Tombs, Pl. 3.

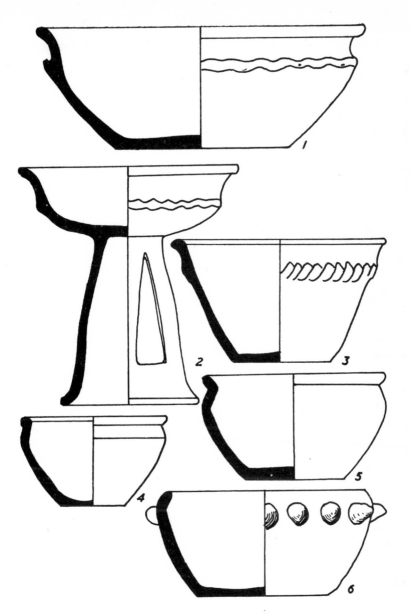

FIG. 14   Forms of Esdraelon ware vessels. $\frac{1}{5}$

Other sites in the Plain of Esdraelon at which the Proto-Urban
C ware is found are 'Affuleh and Beth-shan. At 'Affuleh the
evidence is slight, owing to the nature of the excavation. At
Beth-shan the lowest levels beneath the great tell, representing
the town that was to rival Megiddo in importance at a later date,
were only examined in a small sounding. The lowest levels,
deposits in pits and Level XVIII, contained material which may
be related to Jericho Pottery Neolithic B, and may represent the
indigenous Chalcolithic which probably existed side by side with
Ghassulian, and in which in the earliest stage pit-dwellings were
also customary. In Level XVII Esdraelon ware appears, and is
more common in XVI.[1] At this site, however, the published
material does not suggest any mixture with Proto-Urban A,
but rather with the preceding indigenous Chalcolithic. This is
an additional indication of the separate identity of the Proto-
Urban C group.

The Proto-Urban C ware is completely lacking at Jericho, both
in the tombs and on the tell. But curiously enough it is found in
appreciable quantities in a deposit beneath Herodian Jericho,
about a mile to the south of Tell es Sultan.[2] The published evidence
is not very clear, but none of the characteristic Proto-Urban A
forms are illustrated, and the accompanying material may again
belong to the indigenous Chalcolithic. Since the Tell el Far'ah
evidence shows that the two groups must have been approximately contemporary, the complete contrast between two sites
so close together may suggest hostility between them in this area.

The interlocking of the three Proto-Urban groups and of the
presumed indigenous Chalcolithic shows that a complex intermingling was going on. The process may of course have been a
slow one. G. E. Wright[3] has shown that it is very probable that
successive stages in the forms of the Esdraelon bowls may be
recognised: form 1 (Fig. 14.1) found at Beth-shan and only in one
tomb, 3, at Tell el Far'ah;[4] succeeded by form 2, found in the

---

[1] *Museum Journal*, Philadelphia, XXIV, Pl. III.
[2] *A.A.S.O.R.*, XXXII-XXXIII, Pl. 37.
[3] *Eretz Israel*, V, pp. 41* ff.   [4] *R.B.*, LVI, Fig. 2, 1-7.

rest of the tombs at Tell el Far‘ah; with forms 3 and 4, found at Megiddo,[1] coming later. It has already been suggested that the Tell el Far‘ah tombs may be later than the Proto-Urban A tomb at Jericho. As more material becomes available it may be possible to work out a complete sequence.

So far, we have mainly discussed the different elements in terms of different groups of pottery types. Accumulated archaeological experience has shown that a distinctive group of pottery types in fact is the evidence, sometimes the only evidence, which survives of a distinctive group of people. Therefore, we can translate our A, B and C pottery types into three groups of people who appear in Palestine at this time. They come in as independent groups, as the Jericho evidence shows, and as they penetrate into the country some of them intermingle. Perhaps, as the Jericho tombs show that there the A and B groups were separate, Jericho was actually the point of entry of these groups, indicating that they came from the east, as so many groups did in the later history of Palestine. Thence they may have penetrated almost due west into the highlands, where, at Tell en Nasbeh and ‘Ai, some of them settled down together. Others of the A group may have turned north up the Jordan Valley, and then west up the Wadi Far‘ah, where they met the C group. The latter almost certainly came from the north, either direct down from the Lebanon highland zone or perhaps from inland Syria to the north-east, crossing the Jordan Valley, near the Sea of Galilee, into the Plain of Esdraelon. Unfortunately, the homeland of none of these groups can be satisfactorily identified, since we cannot point to the same pottery elsewhere. But there is little doubt that eventually we shall be able to do so, when the lower levels of the great occupation sites in countries bordering on Palestine have been more fully examined. Until we know more about their homeland, we shall have to be content to leave them anonymously designated by letters of the alphabet.

So far nothing has been said as to the date of this phase. For the preceding one, that of the third stage of Jericho and Ghassul,

[1] e.g. M. Tombs, Pl. 3, 26 and 31.

the first half of the fourth millennium has been tentatively suggested. For this phase we have two more definite pieces of evidence. Charcoal from the Jericho Proto-Urban tomb in which some of the bones were cremated (p. 86) has been subjected to Carbon-14 tests (p. 35), and has given a date of 3260 B.C. ± 110. The second piece of evidence comes from Megiddo. In the last of the three Late Chalcolithic stages there before the appearance of the first evidence of the next phase there were found a number of sealings impressed on jars. These are of a type assigned by most authorities to the Jemdet Nasr period in Mesopotamia, which is dated 3200 to 2800 B.C. So it seems that a central date of 3200 B.C. for this stage would agree with the evidence.[1]

Therefore, in the last centuries of the fourth millennium we have coming into Palestine a number of groups of people, of which three can now be identified, and it is very probable that further research will add to their number. Of their way of life we know very little, for most of the evidence about them has been recovered from tombs. But this fact in itself tells us something. Traces of their houses have been found at Megiddo and Tell el Far'ah, and at Jericho there is evidence, from pottery finds in the earlier excavations, that they lived on part but not the whole of the site. Everywhere their houses were slight, nowhere is there any evidence that they lived in walled towns. They were villagers, not town-dwellers. Apart from that, we know that they deposited the dead in great multiple-burial tombs, with rather strange rites, but little else.

At Megiddo there is a little additional evidence, but this is again connected with ritual rather than how they lived. This is the construction, in the second level above bed-rock, of a substantial building which is probably a shrine. It included a room, 4 metres by more than 12 metres in size, with a doorway in one of the long sides. Opposite the door was a low altar, 0·50 metre high, of mud-brick, covered with plaster, rectangular in shape, with a low step on one side. A number of flat stones set in the floor were probably too slight to carry columns supporting the roof, so they too may have had some religious significance. Subsequently the altar was

[1] Addenda p. 335.

enlarged, and its base then overlaps the line of stones in the centre of the room. We may take the appearance of this building as showing a development in community life, and also of increased architectural experience, but the inhabitants were still probably villagers.

Knowledge concerning this stage in Palestinian history has been gradually accumulating over the last twenty years or so. When G. E. Wright made his pioneer study of the early material,[1] he classified the Esdraelon ware as Chalcolithic and the decorated pottery found at 'Ai, Ophel and Gezer as Early Bronze Age Ia. Père de Vaux at Tell el Far'ah classified his material as Late Chalcolithic. It can now be shown that all the groups are at least in part contemporary. Wright would therefore now prefer to call them all Early Bronze Age, as he feels there is no break between this stage and the full Early Bronze Age, whereas de Vaux would prefer still to call A and C Chalcolithic and B Early Bronze Age, as he feels that it is from that more southerly group that the Early Bronze Age spreads over Palestine. My original view would have been to call them all Chalcolithic, for they would seem all to represent the same type of occupation, of comparatively recently arrived migrants, living in non-nucleated settlements, with little evidence of their architecture, and certainly no walled towns, such as are the characteristic of the full Early Bronze Age.

Such diversity of nomenclature would obviously be a great source of confusion. This is one reason why the term Proto-Urban has been suggested. The other reason is that it suggests the actual economic stage of development. It is from the component groups of this stage that emerges the population which developed the urban civilisation of the Early Bronze Age. The stage of development corresponds to those which preceded the Old Empire of Egypt and the Early Dynastic period of Mesopotamia. In Egypt this is designated the Protodynastic Period, and in Mesopotamia the term Proto-Literate Age has recently come into use.[2] In

---

[1] *The Pottery of Palestine*, New Haven, 1937.
[2] *Relative Chronologies in Old World Archaeology*, ed. R. W. Ehrich.

Palestine neither a dynastic nor a literate period succeeds, but one which is characterised by urban development. Like the Proto-dynastic Period and the Proto-Literate Age, and covering, like them, the last centuries of the fourth millennium, the period is a formative one for an advance in civilisation, and a comparable designation seems appropriate.

CHAPTER FIVE

★

The City States of the Early Bronze Age

THE THIRD millennium marks the first appearance of the great empires of the ancient world. It also marks the beginning of the historic period in which written records supplement archaeology. The two developments are interrelated. As communal organisation developed, the need was felt for some means of recording contributions required by the central authority, of decisions which were binding on the community and of events of importance to the community. By the beginning of the third millennium a system of writing was in use in both the Nile and the Tigris–Euphrates valleys. Allied with this was the establishment of a calendar by which events could be recorded and further events given a time-scale. This invention took place in Egypt, probably somewhere about 3000 B.C., under the stimulus of the necessity of calculating the annual beginning of the inundation of the Nile. The Egyptian calendar is the parent of our modern one, and on correlations with Egypt depend all archaeological datings.

These various developments are a measure of the progress by which the towns of the two great river valleys were outstripping those in the rest of the Fertile Crescent. It is generally agreed that two major factors were responsible for this progress, both environmental. A complex society, as distinct from one in which each family produces enough food and artifacts for its own use, depends on a proportion of the community being able to produce enough food to support those craftsmen, traders, exploiters of natural resources such as quarries or mines, who do not produce their own food. The alluvial plains of the river valleys made production of food surpluses possible, so the potential of developing a complex society was greater in those areas. But the alluvial plains could only be fully exploited if the waters of the rivers could be controlled to supply enough and not too much water. Irrigation was therefore an essential. Irrigation requires a controlling organisation. It must be planned, the channels constructed, regulations made and enforced as to the use of the water. Power over all aspects of the community life tends to become concentrated in the controlling organisation, including that of intercession with the gods to ensure that the agricultural operations are fruitful. Thus control becomes concentrated in the hands of priests or of princes with divine attributes, and the production surpluses tend to come into their hands.

The second environmental factor is that the river valleys lacked many of the other raw materials. Timber, metals, building stone, even flint for making stone tools, had to be brought from a distance, often from considerable distances, such as timber from the Lebanon and copper from the Sinai Peninsula to supply Egypt's needs. These materials had to be bought from agricultural surpluses, or food had to be provided for the traders who went to fetch them. There was thus in the river valleys an exceptional stimulus for the provision of surpluses.

Towards the end of the fourth millennium the areas that lacked this stimulus and this opportunity began to be left behind. In Palestine we have been able to trace the build-up of a sedentary, agricultural population, making parallel progress to that in Egypt and Mesopotamia. The people of the Proto-Urban stage settled themselves down successfully enough for their villages to start growing into towns somewhere about the end of the fourth millennium. The origins of many towns of importance in the historic period can be traced to this stage, on sites that first acquired a sizeable population in the Proto-Urban period. But as far as we can tell, they did not progress beyond the town stage. Until David united the Hebrews about 1000 B.C., under the short-lived United Monarchy, Palestine remained a country of city states. Presumably each of the Bronze Age towns was surrounded by its agricultural lands, with perhaps dependent villages. The agricultural surpluses were enough to provide for modest needs in the way of trade and specialists. Archaeological finds show how modest those needs were. Copper or bronze is rare in the Early Bronze Age, and not really common until the second half of the second millennium. In the third millennium any imported goods are rare, and the demand for specialist craftsmen of any sort cannot have been great. The town lands produced enough food for the population, but could never produce great surpluses to put power in the hands of the local leaders, and no leader ever became powerful enough to establish a hegemony.

Most of this is a matter of inference, based on the interpretation of the archaeological record. Just because the towns of the Mediterranean seaboard did not have the stimulus and opportunity of the river valleys, they did not develop a form of writing for another fifteen hundred years or so. We can only deduce that there was no outstanding political power in Palestine, because if there had been it would presumably have been mentioned in the Egyptian records. With the establishment of the Old Empire, Egypt became sufficiently powerful to expand its interests beyond its borders. From this time onwards, Palestine was of interest to Egypt as the route connecting the Nile Valley with the rest of the civilised world. The age-long route between Asia and Egypt passed up the Palestine coast and thence inland by the Plain of Esdraelon across the Jordan Valley. Palestinian towns, at any rate those fringing the international route, were thenceforward kept under some sort of control at all times at which Egypt was powerful, and their names, or the names of their chiefs, occur in Egyptian records. At no time, however, did Egypt really rule the whole country. Garrisons might be maintained, for instance at Beth-shan, but for the most part selected chiefs were induced to become client-rulers.

Between the different towns and their chiefs there was no doubt rivalry and even warfare. This we can deduce because the towns were protected by walls. An additional reason for this, however, may have been that the whole of the narrow strip of relatively fertile land which makes up Palestine was always to some extent a frontier zone between the Desert and the Sown. As we have seen, the immigrants of the Proto-Urban period were ex-nomads, and though their descendants built up a compact area of permanent settlement, the semi-desert to the east and north-east was populated by their relatives, still nomadic pastoralists, who at intervals cast covetous eyes on the easier and richer life of the coastlands. During the Early Bronze Age they were kept at bay; the unbroken culture of the period shows that there was at least no major incursion, and that if there were any infiltrations they were absorbed.

Jericho was particularly in danger from this raiding from the east, for until in 1958 a great new road was cut down through the eastern mountains bounding the Jordan Valley to cross the valley just north of the Dead Sea, Jericho lay on the best route from the east to the central uplands. The Israelites under Joshua were following this route when Joshua sent his spies with the instructions "go view the land, and Jericho." The recent excavations have shown what importance the inhabitants of Jericho placed on their defences.

The walls of Jericho on the north, west and south side crown the mound which the successive Pre-Pottery Neolithic towns had built up to a height of nearly 50 feet. On the west they almost exactly overlie the line of the Pre-Pottery Neolithic town walls, though separated from them by a thick layer of débris. On the north and south they recede to the brow of the mound, respectively 100 and 84 feet within the line of the earlier walls. This was no doubt to obtain the advantage of a steep exterior slope. Much of the east side of the circuit has been destroyed by the modern road which cuts into the foot of the mound. The line of the walls is, however, indicated by a large oblong tower excavated by Professor Garstang, and by a chance cutting made in connection with a military water-point. This lies just south of Square H V on the plan (Fig. 3), and runs on an oblique line which passes beneath the road just east of Square H V. It is therefore apparent that even at this stage the tell had a pronounced tilt downwards to the east, almost certainly because the buildings always sloped down towards the spring. There is no means of establishing where the spring issued from the ground at that period, whether inside or just outside the walls. A gate almost certainly must lie somewhere here, for it would be needed for access to the cultivated fields to the east.

At Jericho the town walls are built of unbaked mud-bricks, for this is the natural building material in this neighbourhood, used even today. The bricks are in fact very like those used today, and are quite different from those used in the successive Neolithic periods. The latter were hand-made, in shapes that vary for the different periods. From the Early Bronze Age onwards, they are rectangular slabs made in moulds, usually about 2 inches thick and about 14 inches by 10 inches overall. The bricks are set in mud mortar with fairly thin joints and care is as a rule taken to break the joint. The brickwork rests on a foundation of one or more courses of stone. In the earlier stages, the wall is about 3 feet 6 inches thick.

Such a wall can make a solid and impressive barrier. It does, however, need constant attention to keep it in repair. The top must be kept solid to prevent water percolating in, erosion of the face must be prevented by plastering, and no denudation allowed to undercut the foundations. In addition to the dangers of deterioration, there was at Jericho a special danger from the forces of nature. The whole of the Jordan Valley is an area of seismic disturbance, and major earthquakes happen on an average four times a century. The excavations have revealed clear evidence of collapses from an earthquake with the face of the wall fallen straight forward on to the contemporary ground level. A rather curious feature in the structure of the walls is possibly intended as an anti-earthquake device. At intervals in the course of the wall, apparently in almost all phases, were cavities about 3 feet wide, and therefore not large enough to have been towers, running almost the whole thickness of the wall. The effect certainly was to localise the collapse, for in places a section would be found to have collapsed to its foundations, while the immediately adjacent section, beyond a cavity, would be standing 10 feet or so high (Pl. 20).

Finally, the walls of Jericho undoubtedly suffered on occasion from the attacks of enemies. In all the sectors examined, the walls had at least once been subjected to a violent conflagration. It is probable that these fires were not all contemporary, for the walls so affected do not seem to come at the same point in the constructional sequences. More than one attack must have taken the form of setting fire to the walls. The clearest example of this, and the clearest evidence that the firing was the intentional act of an enemy, came from the south end of the tell. Against the outer face of the wall was a layer of ash 3 feet thick, derived from an enormous pile of brushwood (Pl. 21). The town wall at this stage was 17 feet thick, and the fire had burnt the bricks red through the whole thickness, aided by the fact that the bricks of the wall had been tied together by timbers, again possibly an anti-earthquake measure, and these had been set on fire. The purpose of the fire can hardly have been simply the destruction of the wall, for in actual effect it hardened and strengthened it by burning the bricks. The disastrous effect was undoubtedly on the town inside. Everywhere where the inner face of the wall had been cleared, houses have been found to be built up against it. The firing of the wall would therefore set these houses alight, and the fire would no doubt rapidly spread to the rest of the town, for much timber was used, and the roofs seem often to have been made of reeds.

The walls at Jericho therefore had a chequered history. On the west side of the tell seventeen successive phases of building and rebuilding could be traced. This does not of course mean that the whole circuit was rebuilt this number of times, for some collapses were undoubtedly local. It is not possible to tell how many building phases are present without cutting right through the wall. Sometimes the rebuilding took the form of a thickening wall built against the interior or exterior of the earlier wall. Sometimes the collapsed wall survived in the shape of an inverted U, and the rebuild consisted of a capping which might have foundations on the same level as the original wall, thus completely masking it. To establish the complete history would therefore require a very large number of cuts.

A number of interesting features emerged from the various clearances made. On the west side there was found to be a semicircular external tower, as substantial as many medieval towers. This is a very unexpectedly early occurrence of this type of addition to a town wall, and its purpose is not very clear, since at a period in which projectiles were not in use it would not seem to add to the strength of the defences; archery was certainly not in use then, and there is not even any evidence of sling-stones. At the north end of the tell there was also an external tower, at one stage rectangular and another semicircular. Here it is possible that it was associated with a gateway. The slope of the mound is more gentle here than on the west side, and protecting the main town wall was a claw-like projection, overlapping the tower, but with a possible entrance way between the two. The plan is like the clavicula which protects the gates of Roman forts, but the town wall of the period could not be fully excavated to see if in fact there had been an entrance here.

The most unexpected feature discovered was that at a number of places the wall had been protected by an external ditch. This was the case even on the steep western side of the mound, where four separate re-cuttings of the ditch could be traced. They belonged apparently to the later stages in the history of the wall, but it is possible that later re-cuttings removed the evidence of earlier phases.

The connection between the history of the defences and that of the town inside has not yet been fully established. It was not possible to excavate an appreciable area immediately adjacent to the walls, so the correlation of the wall phases and those of the building sequence inside is dependent on the associated pottery, which has not yet been worked out. It is likely that three points will emerge. It seems probable that there is a stage of fully developed occupation before the town was actually walled; on the south side there appear to be substantial structures stretching farther down the slope than the subsequent wall, and the same may be true at the north end, but there is always the possibility that walls on the edge of the mound have been completely removed by denudation.

The second point is that there is a very marked change in architecture in the course of the period. The earliest houses are very substantial, the rooms larger and the walls thicker than in the case of the later ones, but they are much less regularly built. The rooms themselves often have rounded ends, or in some cases are wholly circular, but there seems to be no accepted town-planning system; the buildings lie at all angles, and there are changes in axis in successive building stages. The occupation also seems to have been rather more sordid, for there are thick levels of midden deposit in several places, indicating that rubbish was allowed to accumulate in the courtyards and streets.

The later stage of occupation was probably considerably the longer. In it, in each of the areas excavated, the houses assume a much more regular plan, and are consistently orientated on a north–south axis. Though the walls are less substantial than those of the earlier period, they are nevertheless solid and well built. A feature of this later stage is the large number of brick-built silos which were associated with the houses. In them grain would have been stored from one year to the next, and they are evidence of a flourishing agricultural community. The inhabitants of this stage did not apparently allow the rubbish to accumulate around the houses, but threw it over the town walls, particularly at the north-west angle. This practice may have been more sanitary, but it cannot have been conducive to the efficiency of the defences.

There was a considerable use of timber in the buildings. The evidence of this mostly came from burnt beams lying on the floor of rooms, and the timber was therefore used in the roofs and ceilings. A number of post-holes could be traced, but there does not seem to have been a consistent use of roof supports on the central axis. The rooms on the whole were not large enough to require this.

The third point is that the buildings seem to follow the slopes of the pre-existing mound, with little attempt at levelling up. On the east side in particular, above the spring, the buildings of the later stage (the earlier one was not reached in this area), slope down very steeply from west to east, probably allowing for an approach to the spring. On the summit of the mound, however, there was also a distinct slope outwards towards the walls, with the buildings stepping down in a series of terraces.

The picture of Jericho in the Early Bronze Age is therefore of a flourishing town, closely built up of solid and substantial houses. The general plan seems to have remained consistent, at any rate in the second phase, and the town wall seems to have followed approximately the same line. There were, however, some slight alterations in size. At the north end the wall was at one stage advanced some feet down the slope, but appears to have receded to the original line at a later period. On the west side, the earlier walls were all on the same line, but the fifteenth building stage was advanced 22 feet 6 inches down the slope, and an appreciable area was thus added to the later stages of the town.

Tell el Far'ah, like Jericho, grew into a town early in the Early Bronze Age, developing out of the Proto-Urban settlement. The site is one very suitable for an important town. It lies on a hill that rises steeply on the north and south, and fairly steeply on the east; only on the west is there a gentle slope joining the hill to the main mountain range. At its foot to the north and south are excellent springs, of which the valleys curve round the foot of the hill and join to form the Wadi Far'ah. The site itself commands the Wadi Far'ah, which is the only wide pass leading from the Jordan Valley into the heart of Palestine, and which is continued by a narrower valley up to Shechem, lying on the main north–south route along the backbone of the hill country. Another road leads north from Tell el Far'ah to Beth-shan. The surrounding hill slopes and valleys provide good agricultural land. Strategically and environmentally the site is excellent.

The Early Bronze Age levels have been examined at two fairly widely separated points. The town was therefore large, though its full extent is not known. In each of these areas it was clear that

the town was fully developed before any defences were constructed.[1] The rooms were rectangular, many of them of considerable size. The surviving parts of the walls were mostly of stone,
but some at least of them were carried up in mud-brick. In the
larger rooms there was often a row of slabs which must have
carried uprights to support the roof; in other cases uprights
apparently stood on slabs against the side walls. In several cases a
low bench runs along one or more sides of the room. Five
successive building levels were found, closely linked in plan and
in the associated finds. The first two can be dated to E.B. I, the
last two to E.B. II, and the third comes about at the transition
between E.B. I and II. In the northern area excavated, the E.B. I
houses were destroyed by fire, but this does not occur in the
western site, so it may have been only a local catastrophe.

The greatest change came with the fourth period, at the
beginning of E.B. II. For the first time, the town was surrounded
by a wall. On the northern site, this consisted of a great stone
rampart, over 27 feet wide and surviving to a height of 6 feet,
with the exterior protected by a glacis of beaten earth. On the
west side, it is even more imposing. There it was built of mud-
brick, of considerable width, surviving in places to a height of
13 feet, containing a fine gateway with two towers. One can
presumably infer that at the beginning of E.B. II conditions were
becoming unsettled. This may be because of pressure from
nomadic tribes from the east, for the Wadi Far'ah route would
lay the town open to such incursions, but more probably it is due
to increased competition and rivalry between the growing number of city states.

One extremely interesting find, in the buildings of Period 3,
transitional from E.B. I to E.B. II, was a pottery kiln (Pl. 22A). This
is a type in which the fire is in a lower chamber, and the pots are
stacked on a floor through which flues penetrate from the combustion chamber beneath. The method is a great improvement on
firing pots with the fuel stacked round them, which was apparently
the method up till now. It is in fact the type of kiln which
remained in use until the Roman period.

[1] Addenda p. 335.

The town of Tell el Far'ah was completely abandoned before the beginning of E.B. III. The brick rampart on the western site collapsed at the end of the Period 5 occupation, its ruins spilling over the houses of the period. On top of the ruins, some more houses of the same type were built, but their life was apparently not long. They were abandoned, and there is then a complete gap in the occupation of the site for some seven hundred years. As far as one can judge from the history of other sites, this is not due to political causes. It may simply be that the site was subject to malaria. Until very recent health measures, the population of the villages in the vicinity was strongly infected with this disease, and it was perhaps for this reason that such a particularly important site was abandoned at a period when other towns were flourishing.

At Megiddo, as at Jericho and Tell el Far'ah, a Proto-Urban occupation was succeeded by an Early Bronze Age town. The mound at Megiddo is immense, and the air photograph (Pl. 19B) shows what a very small proportion Area BB, the only area of the city proper cleared to the lower levels, forms of the whole town. Only an indication is therefore given of the history of the site during the period. The picture is unfortunately rendered less clear than it might have been by the somewhat summary methods of excavation.[1] It would appear that there was an occupation during E.B. I and II, which was probably of fully developed urban type, but of which only rather scanty and confused remains survive.[2] There is no evidence as to whether there was a town wall at this period. In E.B. III there was a major town-planning development. Hitherto, the buildings had followed the natural slope of the rock. In E.B. III some very massive retaining walls were built, behind which flat terraces were built up, and an elaborate new town plan laid out (Fig. 15). On the lower terrace is a monumental building with large rectangular rooms. On the upper is a road flanked by buildings, of which only the fringe

[1] The description of the levels and finds is given in *Megiddo II*, with an earlier summary in *Megiddo Stages*. For a critical analysis of the evidence, see K. M. Kenyon, "Some Notes on the Early and Middle Bronze Age Strata of Megiddo," in *Eretz Israel*, V, and in *Levant* I.

[2] *Eretz Israel*, V, pp. 52-53.

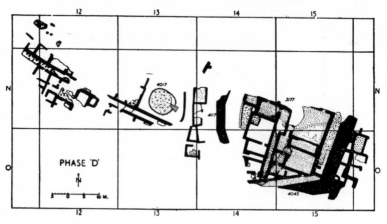

FIG. 15   Plan of Megiddo area BB in E.B. III

was excavated. Among them is a very interesting feature. It is a
conical stone structure, surviving to a height of 1·40 metres, and
8 metres wide at this height. A flight of steps leads up to the top
(Pl. 23). This is undoubtedly to be interpreted as an altar, and the
overlying débris was full of animal bones and fragments of pottery,
presumably derived from sacrificial offerings. The lower terrace
wall was interpreted by the excavators as a town wall. Though it
was certainly massive enough for this purpose (Pl. 22B), house
walls are built against its lower side, which would obviously not
be the case if it were a defensive wall. The massiveness is to be
accounted for by the fact that the terrace fill behind it was about
5 metres thick. It is highly probable that a town with such an
elaborate layout was in fact walled, but the excavators did not
locate the line; the edge of the buildings below the great terrace
wall are destroyed by erosion, and the town wall may have
disappeared in this process.

The other great city of the Plain of Esdraelon is Beth-shan, a
site represented today by a mound as imposing in size as that of
Megiddo (Pl. 24). A prolonged campaign of excavations was
carried out here by the Museum of the University of Pennsylvania, starting in 1921. The main clearance only reached the level
of the Middle Bronze Age town. Beneath this, a sounding,

24 metres by 16 metres, was sunk to virgin soil, revealing Neolithic, Chalcolithic, Proto-Urban and Early Bronze Age levels. The site therefore had as prolonged an occupation as that of Megiddo, and like Megiddo was probably a town of importance in the Early Bronze Age. The area cleared did not of course reveal much in the way of details of the successive stages, and no detailed report on the finds has ever appeared. [1] As at the other sites already described, the Early Bronze Age town developed direct from the Proto-Urban occupation, in which the excavation evidence suggests that brick-built houses had already appeared. The transition to the Early Bronze Age would appear from the pottery to come in Stratum XIV, when the scattered houses of the earlier levels were replaced by buildings with closely built rooms of rectangular plan. These, as at Jericho and Tell el Far'ah, were associated with brick-lined storage silos. The succeeding Level XIII also contained well-built houses. It is to be dated to E.B. II, and was destroyed by fire, though there is no means of telling whether this was a general catastrophe or merely a local incident. Levels XII and XI were not interesting architecturally, for the houses were small and insignificant. They are marked, however, by the sudden appearance of a particularly beautiful imported pottery, known as Khirbet Kerak ware from the site north of the Sea of Galilee where it was first found in quantity. It is discussed below (pp. 124-7); there is no doubt that it represents a foreign influence, but there is nothing at Beth-shan to suggest it was brought by invaders, for side by side with it the native wares continue, and there is no significant change in architectural features.

Level XI is the last of the E.B. levels at Beth-shan. It is difficult to judge with certainty, since only a selection of the pottery is published, but it does not seem to last to the end of the Early Bronze Age; the E.B. pottery is not, for instance, as late as that from 'Ai. Mixed with the material published from both Strata XII and XI are vessels belonging to the following Intermediate Early

[1] Interim reports were published by G. M. Fitzgerald in *P.E.Q.*, 1934, and, on the pottery, in the *Museum Journal* of Philadelphia, XXIV.

Bronze–Middle Bronze period, and even some Middle Bronze Age vessels, so there were clearly intrusions, but it would appear that the Early Bronze Age town came to an end midway through E.B. III for some unexplained reason, and, like Tell el Far'ah, Beth-shan did not become a town again until Middle Bronze II.

Another town in northern Palestine important in the Early Bronze Age is Khirbet Kerak. The site gave its name to the beautiful red and black burnished pottery that appears in Palestine in E.B. III (pp. 124-7), for many sherds were picked up on the surface by Professor Albright in 1925, before it had been encountered in excavations. The site lies just west of the place where the Jordan issues from the Sea of Galilee, and its remains appear to cover an area of some 50 acres. Only two small areas have been excavated, at the north and south ends of the site, but as thick Early Bronze Age occupation layers appear in both, it is probable that the town of this period extended over the whole site. The first settlement, founded on virgin soil, dates from the Proto-Urban period, with pottery including the grey burnished Esdraelon ware of Proto-Urban C. What other elements it includes is not clear as the material is not fully published. Occupation was in huts half sunk into the ground, as in other sites of this and the preceding period.

This Proto-Urban occupation was succeeded by houses associated with E.B. I pottery, and we would thus appear to have another example of the direct development of an E.B. town from a settlement first established in the Proto-Urban period. Above these houses were others dated by the pottery to E.B. II. Belonging to one or other of these settlements (the report is not clear on this point) was a town wall of mud-bricks about 8 metres wide. The final Early Bronze Age stage was apparently the most important of all, with deposits more than 2 metres in depth. These deposits were characterised by the presence of many vessels of Khirbet Kerak ware, and the phase therefore belongs to E.B. III. A stone-built town wall was at first ascribed to the period, but it subsequently became apparent that it probably belonged to the Middle Bronze Age. The most important building was a remarkable one, some 30 metres square, obviously a public building, but of uncertain use. Set in exceedingly massive outer walls were eight circles of an average diameter of 8 metres. Radiating from their walls like spikes of a wheel were four partition walls, which, however, did not reach the centre of the circles (as it were leaving the hubs of the wheels missing). Within this massive outer wall was an oblong hall paved with pebbles, and a court 25 metres long, to which a gateway in the outer wall gave access. Finds of ovens, figurines and burnt animal bones inclined the excavators to identify the structure as a shrine, but they put forward an alternative suggestion that it was a public granary.

With the exception of Jericho, all the sites so far discussed lie in northern Palestine. This is largely due to the chances of excavation, which has directed the attention of archaeologists in recent years to the great upstanding mounds in that area, and sites in the hill country, more difficult of excavation, have been neglected. An important site in the hill country to be excavated comparatively recently is that of 'Ai, identified in the imposing remains known as Et Tell covering a hill some 10 miles north of Jerusalem. This was excavated by Madame Marquet-Krause on behalf of Baron Edmond de Rothschild between 1933 and 1935. Unfortunately, Madame Marquet-Krause died before she could make a full publication of her results, and the volume recording the work is little more than that of an undigested field register. The site is of peculiar interest, since, according to the biblical account, 'Ai was captured by Joshua after the fall of Jericho. The excavations showed, however, that the site was abandoned at the end of the Early Bronze Age, and was not reoccupied until well on in the Iron Age. One explanation suggested is that confusion has arisen between the history of 'Ai and that of the near-by site or Bethel.

From the point of view of the history of the Early Bronze Age, the remains at 'Ai are, however, interesting on their own account, and it is very unfortunate that it is impossible, from the form of the publication, to make full use of them. The cemetery deposits, to which reference has already been made, show that the site was important in the Proto-Urban period, for there was here a mingling of the Proto-Urban A and B groups. During the Early Bronze Age, a town of considerable size grew up.[1] Three lines of stone-built ramparts can be identified round part of the site, and two elsewhere, but from the published material it is not possible to establish their date, nor whether they were contemporary. The innermost of these was probably the earliest, and at a period when the wall was moved farther out, a massive defence described as a citadel was built over it. This was certainly in use during E.B. III, for against its inner side was built a sanctuary, of which the final use can be placed in a late phase of that period; two earlier periods of use of the sanctuary were identified, but can be less accurately dated. The great interest of the sanctuary is that its component parts would seem to have the same functions as the main divisions of Solomon's Temple. The outermost enclosure was fairly large, and to this all those partaking in the ritual sacrifices would be admitted. In the far right-hand corner was a bench on which offerings would presumably be set and on this were two pottery incense burners. Beside it was the door with a step up, leading into the inner sanctuary, the *hekal*. Immediately on the right, inside the door, was another bench, on which were found thirteen saucers of a type which might have been used for liquid offerings, but are often found used as lamps. In the angle to the left of the door was the holy of holies, the *debir*, with a low plaster-covered altar, probably an incense altar, in the angle. From the outer court, the holy of holies would be invisible to the worshippers, and here the priest would have consulted the divinity. On the altar were found some fine alabaster and stone bowls, undoubtedly imported from Egypt, where they are typical of the Second and Third Dynasties. Beyond the altar were bins or *favissae* in which objects presented as offerings could be deposited. Other finds in the sanctuary included animal bones from the sacrifices, incense burners, an elaborate ivory handle of a knife and numerous platters and elegant cups with splaying sides (Fig. 23.5–8). The last also show Egyptian influence, for they are copies of stone cups particularly characteristic of the Fourth

[1] Addenda pp. 336–7.

Dynasty, c. 2613–2494. These probably indicate the date of the sanctuary, and it is probable that the fine alabaster and stone bowls were preserved from one of the earlier structures. As will be seen, in the Palestinian sequence the finds seem to come late in E.B. III. At the end of the Early Bronze Age, the early history of the site comes to an abrupt end; it was presumably destroyed by the invading nomads who will be described in the next chapter, and not occupied by them.

For many of the other great sites of central Palestine our information is meagre, for none of them has been excavated in recent years and older archaeological techniques could not disentangle the difficult and scanty evidence. At Jerusalem itself, there was certainly occupation in the Proto-Urban period, for some of the most beautiful specimens found of Proto-Urban B pottery come from a tomb discovered on the slopes of Ophel,[1] the spur to the south of the present city which was the nucleus of the pre-Israelite site. Excavations on the slopes and summit of the ridge have produced Early Bronze Age pottery, but only fragments of occupation levels. It cannot yet be said if there was an actual town. The widespread area over which finds have been made makes it quite possible. Gezer was also excavated many years ago, and the finds cannot be satisfactorily interpreted. The site, however, was certainly occupied from the Proto-Urban period on through the Early Bronze Age, on the evidence of finds in the tombs. Tell en Nasbeh and, farther north, Samaria were not occupied during the Early Bronze Age, though there had been Proto-Urban villages on both sites.

Finds made at Ras el 'Ain, in the hills south-west of Jerusalem, are an indication of the evidence which further exploration should produce. This site, a tell near the source of the River Yarkon, was not excavated archaeologically but finds were made in connection with waterworks for the supply of Jerusalem. A town wall c. 2·50 metres wide was revealed, associated with Early Bronze Age pottery. This has not been fully published, but the illustrated material[2] seems to be mainly early, probably E.B. I. From the

[1] *Jérusalem sous Terre*, H(ugues) V(incent).   [2] *Q.D.A.P.*, V.

description, it was probably not limited to this period, but nothing is mentioned which seems to be distinctly E.B. III.

It is only when we come to southern Palestine that we have satisfactory evidence again, though it is still scanty. Tell Duweir, identified as the biblical site of Lachish, is the mightiest mound in Palestine (Pl. 25), the 18 acres of its summit being equalled by Gezer and exceeded only by Hazor, which has a later origin, and its height of 40 metres probably surpasses the man-made deposits of any site. Occupation in the neighbourhood goes back to the Chalcolithic period, but the Proto-Urban groups of the north do not seem to have penetrated to this region. In the course of the Early Bronze Age, occupation began to be concentrated on the site of the city mound. Unfortunately, excavations had to be suspended before the lower levels were reached, and knowledge of the remains of the early periods only comes from caves and tombs, and from a single cutting into the side of the mound.[1] From the available evidence, it would appear that the history of Tell Duweir as a town begins fairly late in the Early Bronze Age. None of the material is characteristic of E.B. I, so it may be that the Early Bronze Age civilisation did not penetrate into southern Palestine in the first stages. In E.B. II some of the inhabitants still lived in caves, for instance Caves 1519 and 1535, but the excavation of the lowest levels of the tell was insufficient to say whether the town site also began to be occupied at this period. In the succeeding period, these caves were used for burials, which in itself is significant of a change of dwelling habits, and the lowest excavated levels on the edge of the tell show that occupation was now being concentrated in that area. In the section cut into the edge of the mound, pottery types found elsewhere at the end of E.B. II and the beginning of E.B. III occur in the lowest levels, and Khirbet Kerak ware occurs on bed-rock, so the spread of the settlement to the full extent of the later town certainly did not take place until the beginning of E.B. III. There is no evidence as to the size of the settlement, or whether it was walled. None of the tomb groups published belongs exclusively to the last stages

[1] *Lachish*, IV.

of E.B. III, but the evidence is too scanty to establish whether at Tell Duweir, like Beth-shan, occupation was interrupted before the end of the Early Bronze Age.

Tell Beit Mirsim lies, like Tell Duweir, in the fringes of the hill country, in a semi-arid area which could be fertile in years of good rain, and, like Tell Duweir, could obviously support a sedentary population, since it was the site of a settlement from the later stages of the Early Bronze Age until the end of Early Iron II. It did not, however, attract settlement until late in the Early Bronze Age, and the remains of the period are slight. The pottery published is scanty, and it is not easy to relate it to finds elsewhere, but it must certainly come late in E.B. III. No traces were found of any town wall, and the architectural remains were fragmentary.

The history of Tell Hesi, in the same general neighbourhood as Tell Duweir and Tell Beit Mirsim, is probably similar. The excavation of the site was begun as long ago as 1890 by Sir Flinders Petrie, and it was in fact at Tell Hesi that the foundation was laid in Palestine of stratigraphical excavation and of the recording of pottery in relation to the building sequence. The records therefore require much reinterpretation. But one important fact emerges in connection with the earliest occupation. A group of copper weapons is recorded from the lowest levels.[1] These include an axehead of crescentic form which can be exactly paralleled by an axehead from a fairly late E.B. III tomb at Jericho (Fig. 16.1–2).[2] This serves to place the earliest occupation of Tell Hesi in E.B. III, and is also interesting evidence of the increased use of copper weapons at this period, for hitherto they had been rare.

[1]The extension of the Early Bronze Age culture to southern Palestine does not, however, seem to have been on a large scale. At Tell Fara and Tell Ajjul, sites at which considerable excavation has taken place, no traces have appeared of a settlement at this

[1] F. J. Bliss. *Mound of Many Cities*, pp. 36–37.
[2] *Eleventh Annual Report of the Institute of Archaeology.*
[3] Addenda p. 337.

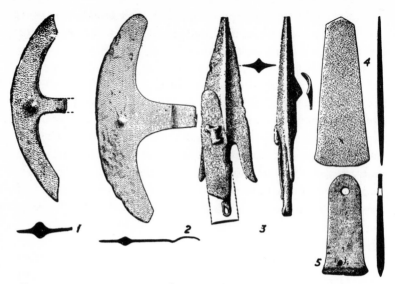

FIG. 16   Copper weapons from Jericho (1) and Tell Hesi (2–5). $\frac{1}{5}$

period, though they became important towns in the second millennium.

This outline of the history of the various sites will have suggested that much of the history of Palestine in the Early Bronze Age has still to be recorded. In all the sites which give indications of having been important towns at this period, only limited areas have been examined, or else the excavation methods have not been able to produce a clear picture. But stray finds and surface exploration have added emphasis to the widespread nature of the culture. In Transjordan in particular surface exploration has located many sites of the period, but none of them has been examined. In Palestine proper the scantiness of the evidence is in part due to the very nature of the culture. In very many cases the Early Bronze Age towns are the ancestors of the later ones, and their remains therefore lie buried deep beneath the later accumulation.

As the picture is outlined at present, the major towns, and those starting earliest and lasting longest, are in the north and centre with the towns of southern Palestine only growing up later. This is partly due to the earlier history of the areas. The preceding Proto-Urban cultures, described in the last chapter, do not occur in southern Palestine, where the Chalcolithic of the Ghassulian and allied groups may have continued later. On the pottery evidence, it is out of the Proto-Urban cultures that that of the Early Bronze Age was evolved. The Ghassulian groups seem to have lacked the necessary impetus to develop into towns, and it was from the north that the habit of town-dwelling spread to the south, perhaps not much before E.B. III. The other factor stimulating development in the north was probably contacts with the towns of coastal Syria. The seaports of the Phoenician coast early tended towards urban development, for they were dependent on trade rather than agriculture, and contacts with Egypt were established at a very early date. The first town at Byblos is dated to c. 3100 B.C., and there are many similarities in form and technique between the Byblos pottery and that of Palestine at this stage. The impulse towards urban development may have come from the same direction.

The summary of the evidence from the sites excavated will have shown that it is not possible to gain a very clear picture of the way of life of the people of Palestine at the time. In no single instance have we enough of a town plan to say if the houses were all on a similar scale, or whether some exceeded others in size sufficiently to indicate markedly different wealth and social status. On the whole, the evidence suggests reasonable prosperity but no very great wealth. The population was apparently mainly agricultural, and there is little evidence of trade. There were some contacts with Egypt, which will be referred to in connection with the pottery, but most of the objects found were probably home produced. The most striking evidence of this is the relative scarcity of metal. The period is conventionally known as the Early Bronze Age, but in fact there is no certain evidence that bronze was used, and even copper is not very common. As has already been described, copper was worked in Palestine in the Chalcolithic, and occasional implements are found from then on.

Copper beads are found in E.B. III tombs, and the weapons found at Jericho and Tell Hesi suggest that at this stage it was coming into more common use. But the population was certainly not dependent on it for everyday use, and flint remained much the most common material for tools and weapons.

Very little evidence survives as to religion. The sanctuary at 'Ai provides the only really clear evidence of a religious structure.[1] Its foreshadowing of the plan of the Jewish Temple has already been mentioned, but it would be hazardous to suggest that the elements of the Semitic religion are already present, for archaeology has not yet supplied the connecting links over the millennium and a half or so separating the two periods. It was not apparently a period during which any physical representation of deities was made, for no cult objects or figurines are found.

[2]The burial practices do not seem to indicate any complicated belief in a life after death, though the dead were considered to have some needs. The best evidence on this comes from a series of tombs at Jericho which covered almost the whole of the Early Bronze Age. Throughout the period the dead were buried in tombs with multiple interments, twenty or so in the earlier tombs, rising to fifty or a hundred in the later ones. With them were placed bowls and jugs, presumably containing, or symbolising, food and drink, and little juglets presumably for oil or scent. The only personal ornaments seem to have been beads, of carnelian, bone, shell, stone or frit. The tombs were large rock-cut chambers, but in every case the roof and most of the entrance shaft had disappeared in subsequent erosion, so little could be established about their form. The burial practices were strange. Apparently the bodies were originally placed in the tombs complete. But when the available space became full many of the bones of the earlier burials were thrown out. Most of the bones are found completely disarticulated; even if a trunk is complete it may lack some limbs, and though large numbers of skulls were found, sometimes placed together against the wall of the tomb,

---

[1] Another has recently (1959) been discovered at Tell el Far'ah, published too late for its description to be included.   [2] Addenda p. 338.

the numbers of long bones are quite insufficient to account for the rest of the body. It would seem that even before the flesh had completely decayed it was no longer felt necessary to treat the body with any reverence. The skull alone remained worthy of care, and it alone was left with any consistency in the tomb.

Much of the evidence of the distribution of the Early Bronze Age towns, and of their relative dates, comes from the pottery, which is very abundant on all sites of the period. Technically, the better-class ware is of quite high quality, and very attractive in appearance. The attractiveness is due more to the surface finish than to the forms, which are relatively simple. The especial characteristic of the period is a burnished slip, usually red, but occasionally black. The burnishing, always by hand, is sometimes continuous, and sometimes in criss-cross or other patterns, and the ware is a pleasure to handle. This practice of burnishing was coming in during the Proto-Urban period. It was hardly found in the Proto-Urban A pottery of Jericho, but almost half this pottery in the Tell el Far'ah tombs was treated in this way. It does not, however, reach its full development until the Early Bronze Age. Another type of surface treatment, found mainly on jars, is decoration in bands of red or brown. In the north the bands show veining, as if from the hairs of the brush, and is known as grain-wash; in central and southern Palestine the bands are solid, and the technique is derived from the Proto-Urban B pottery.

One reason for the improved technical quality of the pottery is due to a factor already mentioned in connection with the finds at Tell el Far'ah. This is the use of a proper kiln for the firing of the pottery, with a separate combustion chamber. Most of the pottery of the period is well and evenly fired. The second reason is the increased use of a potter's wheel. The first tentative beginnings of the use of a tournette or primitive wheel are found in the Proto-Urban period, when many of the bowls have a smooth and regular rim. The body of the vessel was apparently first made by hand, for the lower part is quite noticeably irregular, and then it is placed on some form of turntable, and the rim is smoothed. This practice was developed during the Early Bronze Age. The form of wheel was probably improved and became faster, though it was never a true fast wheel. For a long time, however, the practice continued of making part of the vessel by hand. Only in E.B. III were some of the smaller bowls made entirely on the wheel, and throughout the period the larger vessels were hand-made except for the rim. In spite of this, vessels were made of a very great size, so large that intact vessels hardly ever survive. The type of jar known as the hole-mouth jar, neckless with a simple in-curved rim, which was used for cooking and for storage, may be as much as 3 feet in height, and the storage jars, with short necks, usually collar-rims, and ledge-handle, may be equally large.

The development of the pottery is the basis for the evidence on which the history of the various sites has been outlined earlier in this chapter. The degree of definition is not yet very close, for the number of closely stratified groups is not yet great. In Figs. 17–19, 21–22 are shown selected forms from tomb groups at Jericho which seem to belong to E.B. I, E.B. II and early E.B. III and mid-E.B. III. In the first group, some of the forms, such as the bowl (Fig. 17.4) and the juglet (Fig. 17.8), are derived from Proto-Urban A, and the juglet (Fig. 17.12) from Proto-Urban B. In the next group the same forms continue, and other forms derived from Proto-Urban A, the bag-shaped juglets and jars (Fig. 18.11–14), are also found, as well as later forms such as the bowls with inverted rim, and the first appearance of the piriform juglets (Fig. 18.20–21). In the early E.B. III group, the early forms such as the round-based juglets and the bag-shaped juglets have disappeared, the piriform juglets have become very common (Fig. 19.20–28), while the early types of bowl are rare and devolved (Fig. 19.1) and the new types of jug (Fig. 19.15–19) appear. A small, round-based bowl, often used as a lamp, is common (Fig. 19.5–6), and a flat-based saucer, also used as a lamp, is just appearing (Fig. 19.10). Side by side with the native wares are vessels of Khirbet Kerak ware (Fig. 19.12), to which reference has already been made (Fig. 20). These vessels are hand-made, and have a most striking highly burnished finish, on a slip with sharply defined zones of red, black and light brown colour. The surface of the vessels is some-

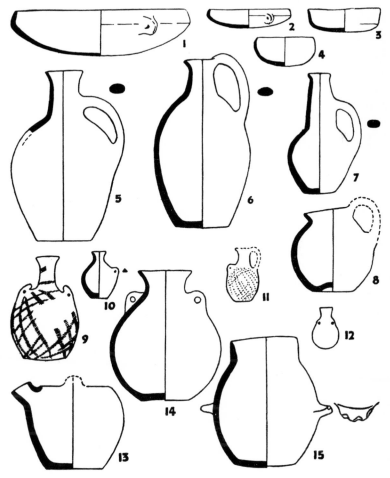

FIG. 17 Pottery from early in the Early Bronze Age from Jericho
Tomb A108. $\frac{1}{5}$

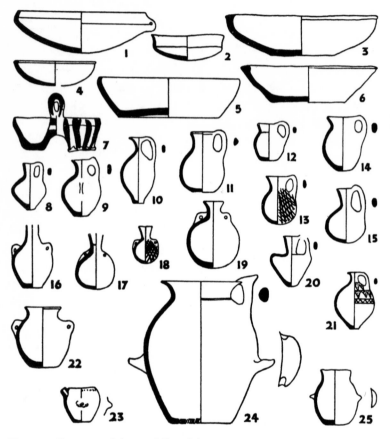

FIG. 18 Pottery of the middle of the Early Bronze Age from Jericho
Tomb A127. ⅛

times decorated with flutings. This type of pottery is also found in northern Syria, but, as in Palestine, it is intrusive there. Its home appears to be in north-eastern Anatolia.[1] In Syria its appearance is accompanied by disturbances, suggesting actual invading groups. In Palestine there is no clear evidence of disturbance, so it may be deduced that at most there was some infiltration or perhaps trade. The sites at which the greatest quantities are found, Beth-shan and Khirbet Kerak, are both on the route crossing the Jordan from Syria, and the amount becomes steadily less farther west and south, though a little is found as far south as Tell Duweir.

In the mid-E.B. III group, the earlier forms have completely disappeared. The number of round-based bowls is decreasing and that of the flat-based saucers increasing. The place of the earlier bowls seems to be taken by flat-based platters. Round-mouthed jars with side spouts, which have antecedents in earlier groups, become common. A later stage in E.B. III is represented by the pottery from the 'Ai sanctuary (Fig. 23), and by Tomb 351 from the earlier excavations at Jericho.[2] In these groups the flat-based saucers and platters have entirely superseded the earlier forms, and both the native and Khirbet Kerak types of burnished pottery have disappeared.

The sequence of Palestinian Early Bronze Age pottery can be established on internal evidence. But absolute chronology can only be established by contact with Egypt. Fairly adequate links can be shown.[3] On Fig. 19, No. 15 is a type of jug of hard, thin ware, with a fine burnished red slip, which is usually known as metallic-ware. It is found at Megiddo, Tell el Far'ah, Jericho and other sites. The Megiddo evidence as to its associations is not clear, but at Tell el Far'ah it appears in the E.B. II levels;[4] at Jericho it occurs in a group which continues into E.B. III. This type of jug is also found in Egypt, being probably imported from Syria or Palestine. In Egypt, it is found in tombs of the First Dynasty, dating from

[1] S. Hood, *Anatolian Studies*, I.
[2] *L.A.A.A.*, XXII, Pl. XXXIV.
[3] Addenda p. 338.
[4] *R.B.*, LXII, Fig. 14. 23, 29.

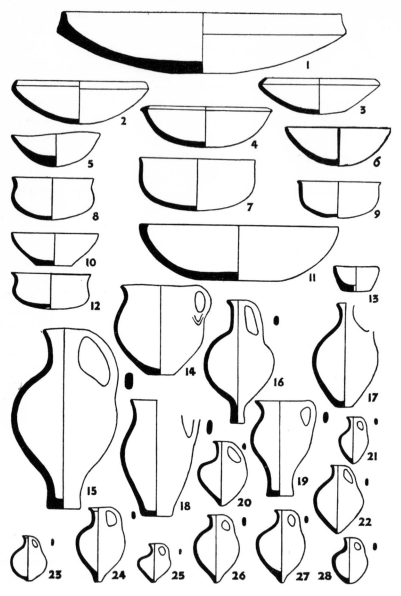

FIG. 19   Pottery of the beginning of E.B. III from Jericho Tomb F4. $\frac{1}{5}$

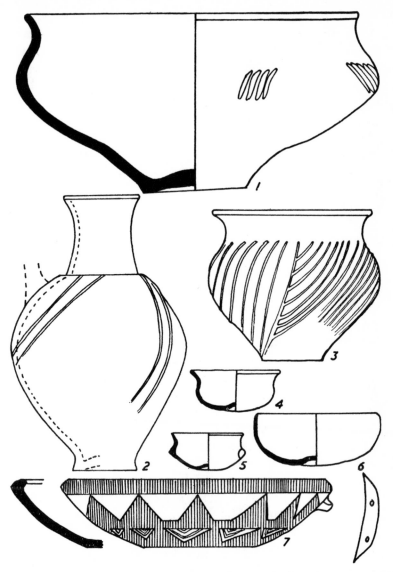

FIG. 20   Khirbet Kerak ware from Beth-shan. $\frac{1}{5}$

c. 2900 B.C.[1] It follows that E.B. II in Palestine must date from
about that same period, and it may be estimated on the basis of
this evidence and that for the preceding Proto-Urban period
(see p. 98) that E.B. I begins about 3100 B.C. The link of the 'Ai
sanctuary with the Fourth Dynasty of Egypt has already been
mentioned, and the pottery from this sanctuary, which seems to
come late in E.B. III, may therefore be dated to *c.* 2600 B.C. On
present evidence it is difficult to decide how long it continued.
It is unlikely that the next main period, the Intermediate Early
Bronze–Middle Bronze period, begins much before 2300 B.C.,
and there seems at the moment little to fill in the gap.

This may be partly due to a serious environmental change that
took place about this time. The evidence from Jericho shows that
very substantial erosion took place at the end of the Early Bronze
Age. All the Proto-Urban and Early Bronze Age tombs as found
were roofless, though the beginning of the curve of the roof, and
fallen fragments from it, in most cases make it clear that they had
originally been roofed. On the other hand, the tombs of the
succeeding Intermediate Early Bronze–Middle Bronze period
had their roofs intact. Six feet or more of the soft rock of the
hill slope in which the tombs are cut had therefore been eroded
in the interval. One tomb produced even more striking evidence.
The tomb K2 belonged to the Proto-Urban period, and had,
as always, lost its roof. Its contents were all set in a deposit of
concrete-like hardness, formed of gypsum. Gypsum is deposited
by a lowering of the water-table,[2] and a lowering of the water-
table is naturally associated with erosion. A lower bracket for the
period at which this erosion took place is provided by the fact
that into the deposit in Tomb K2 was cut a tomb of the Intermediate Early Bronze–Middle Bronze period. The deposit was
already so concrete-like that the shaft and roof of the tomb

[1] A date of *c.* 2900 B.C. for the beginning of the First Dynasty of Egypt
would best suit the Palestine evidence. However, in the chronology proposed
for the forthcoming revised edition of the *Cambridge Ancient History*, the First
Dynasty is dated 3100–2900. If this is accepted, Palestinian dates must be
revised accordingly.

[2] The interpretation is that of Professor F. E. Zeuner.

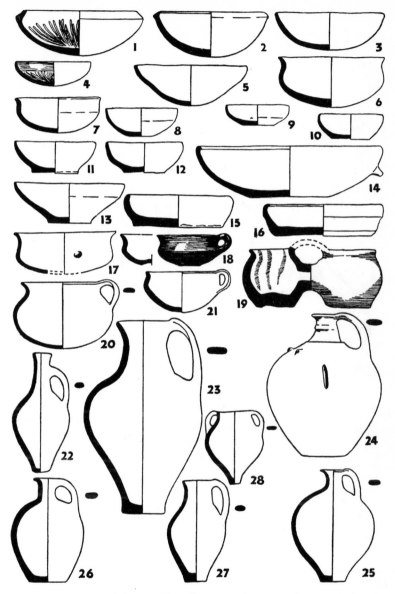

FIG. 21   Pottery of the middle of E.B. III from Jericho Tomb F2. ⅕

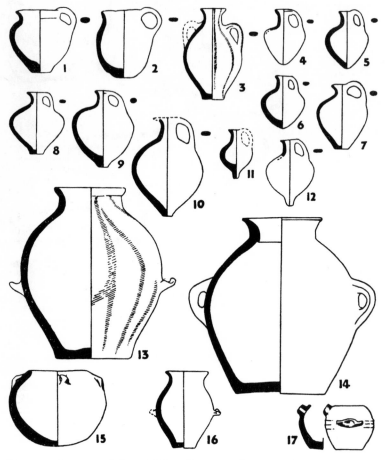

FIG. 22   Pottery of the middle of E.B. III from Jericho Tomb F2. $\frac{1}{5}$

chamber could be cut in it as if it were rock. Since all the E.B. III tombs were roofless, and all the E.B.–M.B. ones had intact roofs, the erosion must have taken place some time after 2600 B.C., and before c. 2300 B.C.

Erosion is almost always the result of deforestation. On environmental grounds, it is to be presumed that the hills of Palestine were once wooded, as are those of the Lebanon. Timber was already scarce in Palestine in the time of Solomon, since he had to obtain his supply of timber for building the Temple from Hiram, King of Tyre. The evidence suggests that very considerable deforestation had taken place during the Early Bronze Age, with resultant erosion. This seems very probable on two grounds. Both at Jericho and Tell el Far'ah there is evidence of abundant

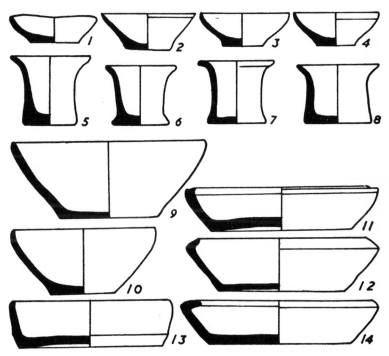

FIG. 23   Late E.B. III pottery from the Sanctuary of 'Ai. $\frac{1}{5}$

use of timber. At Jericho many instances of burnt timber fallen from the roof have been found, and in several stages of the town walls numerous horizontal lacing-timbers were employed. At Far'ah in most of the rooms there were slabs on which must have stood posts to support the roof. The second reason for deforestation would have been the clearance of fields for agriculture. With the growth of comparatively large centres of sedentary occupation, each settlement would have required a large area for crops. The two factors apparently produced an effect from which the countryside of Palestine has never recovered.

It is therefore possible that the last century or so of the Early Bronze Age marked a decline in town life as fields began to be affected by denudation, and that as a result some towns were abandoned, or the occupation was restricted and therefore the evidence of it has not been found. It may be that some of the population migrated to Transjordan, where surface exploration suggests that there was considerable occupation late in the Early Bronze Age, and where types of pottery are found that do not occur in Palestine.

The final end of the Early Bronze Age civilisation came with catastrophic completeness. The last of the Early Bronze Age walls of Jericho was built in a great hurry, using old and broken bricks, and was probably not completed when it was destroyed by fire. Little or none of the town inside the walls has survived subsequent denudation, but it was probably completely destroyed, for all the finds show that there was an absolute break, and that a new people took the place of the earlier inhabitants. Every town in Palestine that has so far been investigated shows the same break. The newcomers were nomads, not interested in town life, and they so completely drove out or absorbed the old population, perhaps already weakened and decadent, that all traces of the Early Bronze Age civilisation disappeared.

★

CHAPTER SIX

The Arrival of the Amorites

In 2294 B.C.[1] the Old Empire of Egypt fell before the attacks of Asiatic invaders, and the period known as the First Intermediate began. Such a period ranks with the Dark Age of Europe which followed the collapse of the Roman Empire in the face of the attacks of the northern barbarians in the fifth century A.D. Civilisation suffers an eclipse, history becomes misty and indefinite, literacy almost disappears. It is at such periods that archaeology becomes once more the only means of tracing the course of events, as it had been in the prehistoric period. Just as the Dark Age of Europe is gradually being illuminated by archaeology, and the events recorded in poetic sagas are being given precision, so in the Near East events during this intermission in civilisation are gradually being traced by excavation and other archaeological methods.

It is only comparatively recently that it has been recognised that there was in Palestine between the two periods of civilisation of the Early Bronze Age and the Middle Bronze Age a stage comparable with the First Intermediate of Egypt. The picture of the period has for long been blurred by the attempted assimilation of features in it into either the Early or the Middle Bronze Age. The first to recognise that there was an entity to be distinguished was Sir Flinders Petrie. At Tell Ajjul in 1931 he found a number of tombs of distinctive character, which he ascribed to the Copper Age. The ascription was reasonable, since many of the tombs were characterised by the presence of copper weapons. But more recent work has shown that these tombs belong to a phase

[1] The date ascribed to the end of the Sixth Dynasty. The new *Cambridge Ancient History* dating is 2185 B.C.

between what have long conventionally been called the Early Bronze and Middle Bronze Ages, and it is therefore confusing to give it a name suggesting an earlier technological stage. It is in fact an intermediate phase, just as is the First Intermediate of Egypt, and it is therefore more apt to call it the Intermediate Early Bronze–Middle Bronze period, and, as will be seen, it corresponds in date approximately to the First Intermediate of Egypt.

At most sites our evidence consists of the abrupt appearance of a new type of pottery. The most characteristic form is a tall, ovoid jar with flat base and flaring rim (Fig. 33.2–3). Smaller pots with lug handles at the neck and bowls either barrel-shaped or slightly waisted (Fig. 32.2–3) are also common. The typical decoration is incised, usually a combination of straight and wavy lines, or else a series of stabs. The burnished finish of the Early Bronze Age vessels and the painted decoration also typical of that period is never found. The ware is usually brittle and not well fired, but the actual making of the pots, with remarkably thin walls, is skilful. A striking characteristic is that though the bodies of the jars are made by hand, the rims are usually made on a fast wheel. This combination of a hand-made lower part and a wheel-made rim is also found in the Early Bronze Age, but the contrast and differentiation are not nearly so marked.

There is rarely any difficulty in distinguishing this pottery from that of the Early Bronze Age, and there is none in distinguishing it from that of the Middle Bronze Age, when the shapes of the pots are quite different, and they are completely made on a fast wheel. On this evidence alone, therefore, it is safe to postulate an invasion of a new group. Some broad similarity between their pottery and that of the Early Bronze Age people, such as the flat bases of the jars in contrast with the pointed bases of those of the Middle Bronze Age, and the use of ledge handles, though in quite distinct forms, may suggest some links; they are probably, however, only those of a remote common ancestry. As will be suggested at the end of the chapter, there is good reason to believe that these newcomers were the Amorites.

The differences extend over a far wider field than merely that of pottery; in way of life, in architecture, in burial customs, in weapons, in social organisation. These differences are illustrated particularly clearly at Jericho.

As has already been described, the latest of the Early Bronze Age town walls at Jericho was destroyed by fire. With this destruction, town life there came to an end for a space of several hundred years. Newcomers, who were presumably the authors of the destruction, settled in considerable numbers in the area, but they did not build for themselves a walled town. They spread all down the slopes of the mound and over a considerable part of the adjoining hillside. But on the town mound the only evidence of the earlier stages of their occupation is a considerable spread of their characteristic pottery, mingled with household débris. Similarly, on the adjacent hillside, occupation débris and pottery is found, but no structures. It was only after the ditch of the Early Bronze Age town had silted up to a depth of 2·50 metres that the first structures appear. The newcomers therefore were essentially nomads. They destroyed existing towns, but did not create their own. It is perhaps one of the clearest instances in the long history of Palestine of the temporary triumph of the Desert over the Sown.

The evidence from the tombs of these newcomers throws considerable further light upon them, and emphasises both their differentiation from their predecessors and their nomadic organisation. The tombs of the Early Bronze Age had all contained multiple burials. In the Intermediate Early Bronze–Middle Bronze period, the burial practice is essentially that of single burials, though occasionally there are two bodies. As a result there are enormous numbers of tombs of this period. All energy and constructive ability seem to have been directed towards habitations for the dead instead of for the living.

Though the practice of single burials is so characteristic, the burial customs in other respects show many variations, and these variations are probably to be explained as evidence of a tribal organisation, each group maintaining its own burial customs. The tombs can be classified in five types.

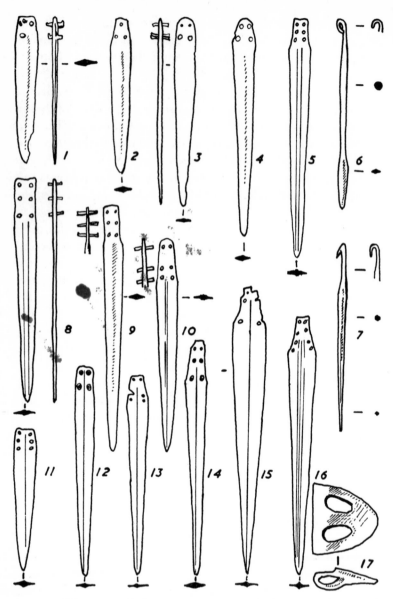

FIG. 24 Weapons of the E.B.–M.B. period from Jericho (1–10), Tell Ajjul (11–16) and Megiddo (17). $\frac{1}{5}$

The first type is the Dagger-type tomb. In this type the tomb is small and very neatly cut (Pl. 26). In the tomb chamber is found the intact skeleton, lying in a crouched position necessitated by the small size of the tomb chamber. If the burial is of a man, he has with him a dagger (Fig. 24.*1–5*), if of a woman, there is usually a pin and beads. The whole burial custom is simple and austere, and the prominence given to weapons suggests a group of warriors.

Pottery-type tombs form the second category, so called because always pottery and never daggers comprise the funerary offerings. A further difference between this group and the last lies in the form of shaft and chamber. The shaft is very wide and deep, the chamber large in area, though only about 3 to 4 feet high; both chamber and shaft are very roughly cut. The final difference is that the body was put in literally as a bag of bones, disarticulated and lying in disorder, apparently dumped in in some sort of textile or matting container (Pl. 27). The labour of excavating such enormous tombs to contain these disordered bones seems a remarkable proceeding. The reason may lie in a nomadic habit of transporting bodies of those who had died during the course of the seasonal migrations of the tribe to a tribal burying-place. The pots placed with the burials seem to have been made especially for funerary purposes, for they are not found on the habitation sites. They are ugly, clumsy little things, showing the same combination of hand-made bodies and wheel-made rims as others of this period (Fig. 25). Another characteristic find is a four-spouted lamp, usually placed in a niche cut in the wall of the chamber. The rock of the niche is often blackened by smoke, showing that the lamp was in fact intended to light the habitation of the dead.

In the third group there is to some extent a combination of features of the Dagger-type and Pottery-type tomb. Shaft and chamber are of medium size, nearer, of the two, to that of the Pottery type, but not so large as the majority, and not so roughly cut. The burials are of intact skeletons, and with them are placed both weapons and pots. A new feature is that the weapons may include a javelin, a short copper weapon with a small spear-shaped or poker-shaped head and a curled end to the tang (Fig.

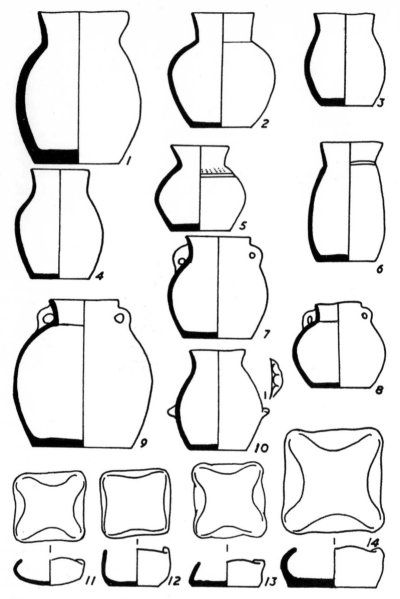

Fig. 25 Pottery of the E.B.–M.B. period from the Pottery-type tombs at Jericho. $\frac{1}{5}$

24.6–7). The most striking differentiation of the group from the others is that the tomb shaft is approximately square in plan, and for this reason they have been called the Square-Shaft-type.

Group four can only be called the Outsize-type, for everything about these works is on a grand scale. Like the Square-Shaft-type, they may contain both pots and weapons, and the skeleton is intact. But the chamber and shaft are of enormous dimensions. Particularly in the height of the chamber they contrast with the Pottery type. The largest chamber was 11 feet 3 inches in diameter and nearly 8 feet high, and the largest shaft 11 feet 9 inches in diameter and 22 feet 9 inches deep. The pottery offerings too are on the grand scale both in numbers and in the size of the vessels, which are large plump jars in place of the universal dumpy little pots of the Pottery-type (Fig. 26).

The final type is less interesting, for the offerings were so paltry. The tombs were usually not cut very deeply into the rock, and therefore have often lost their roofs in denudation. The skeleton was dismembered, as in the Pottery-type, and the sole objects placed with the bodies were some beads or a pin, or fragments of bronze studs, possibly all simply belonging to articles of apparel or adornment. As beads were the most constant find, this class was called the Bead-type.

There was almost nothing to show what was the relationship of these five tomb-types to one another. One instance did occur of a Pottery-type tomb cutting into a Dagger-type chamber, but that is not enough to show that all Pottery-type tombs are later than the others. For the rest, the Dagger-type tombs are so distinct from the Pottery-type that there can be no possibility of one having developed from the other. In view of the general character of these newcomers to Palestine, especially their lack of interest in town life, the habit of the Pottery group in burying collections of disarticulated bones, which may suggest a nomadic background, and the emphasis on weapons in the case of the Dagger group, which suggests that they were warriors, the most satisfactory explanation seems to be that the difference in burial customs is due to a tribal organisation. The newcomers would thus be

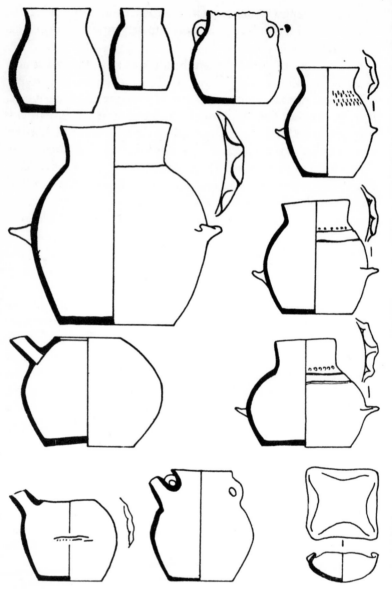

FIG. 26 Pottery of the E.B.–M.B. period from the Outsize-type tombs at Jericho. $\frac{1}{5}$

142

nomadic tribesmen, uniting as a predatory band to invade the richer lands of the coastal fringe, but still retaining individual tribal habits.

It is on the distinction between the Dagger-type and Pottery-type tombs that tribal distinctions can most confidently be argued. The Square-Shaft-type of tomb also seems to introduce new features, notably the shaft plan which has been used to designate the group, and the placing of both weapons, with a javelin as a new feature, and pottery, with the burials. The Outsize group adds entirely new pottery forms, as well as the feature of their enormous size. These differences are not, however, as great as those between the Dagger-type and the Pottery-type tombs, and it is not impossible that they are evolutionary. Another group of tombs does in fact seem to combine features from most of the other classes. It may therefore be that, after the arrival of a number of tribal groups with separate burial customs, there was some mingling of characteristics, but this has yet to be proved.

It is interesting to find that at two other sites, Tell Ajjul in the south and Megiddo in the north, there is evidence of a similar organisation. The evidence is again from burial customs. Petrie excavated at Tell Ajjul two separate cemeteries, the 100–200 Cemetery (the tombs being numbered within this series) to the east of the tell, and the 1500 Cemetery to the north of the tell. In the 1500 Cemetery the tombs have (with one doubtful exception) surface openings which are rectilinear and approximately rectangular in shape. They are thus like the Square-Shaft-type at Jericho. A notable feature is a central nucleus of three rows of three tombs of which the chamber was lined, and probably originally roofed, with stone or brick. The tombs of the 1500 Cemetery contained, with very few exceptions, single intact skeletons. In over a third of the tombs a dagger was included among the offerings, in some cases as the sole offering. The pottery vessels were very restricted in type. They consisted entirely of jars with extremely vestigial ledge handles and sometimes with a spout; a few lacked the ledge handles (Fig. 27.4–6).

In the 100–200 Cemetery most of the tombs have a rounded

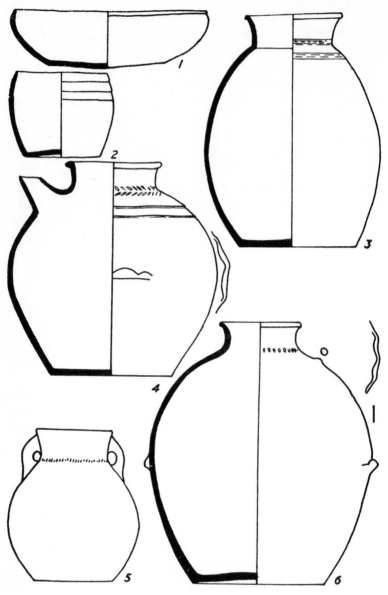

FIG. 27   Pottery of the E.B.–M.B. period from Tell Ajjul cemetery
100–200 (1–3) and cemetery 1500 (4–6). ⅕

144

shaft and contain disarticulated skeletons. There are more varieties of pottery than in the other group. The majority of the vessels are again jars, but none of them have the vestigial ledge handles; in addition there were some dishes and bowls. There were only two daggers in the whole cemetery, but on the other hand there were two javelins. A minority of the tombs were similar in plan to those of the 1500 Cemetery, and in a few cases there were intact burials.

As a general summary it may be said that Cemetery 1500 was exclusive and homogeneous in its tomb types, method of burial of body and predominance of daggers, but borrowed some of the pot types, the jars without ledge handles, from the other cemetery. Cemetery 100–200 borrowed some examples of tomb type and burial method, and the occasional dagger-offering, but has its own pottery types.

These Ajjul groups do not correspond exactly with any of those at Jericho. The single, intact, crouched burial is for instance found in tombs with the rectangular shaft. Others of these tombs with the rectangular shafts may contain intact burials with both dagger and pots, and to this extent resemble the Square-Shaft-type at Jericho, but the pots are different. The Jericho pottery which most resembles the Ajjul type comes from the Outsize group, but the repertory is not identical, and the Ajjul tombs do not approach those of Jericho in size. The tombs at Ajjul with disarticulated skeletons have not the characteristic plan and section of the Jericho ones, and the pottery is quite different.

The characteristic the tombs of the two places have in common is the practice of single burial. There is also the same emphasis on weapons, and the occurrence of the peculiar practice of disarticulated burial. Though the pots of the two sites are largely different in form, in character of manufacture and ware they are similar, and it cannot be doubted that they belong to the same general phase. How the groups at Jericho and Ajjul are related, as indeed how those at the same site are related between themselves, must remain uncertain. At Ajjul, as at Jericho, arguments for a chronological succession, from pots with ledge handles, for instance, to those without, or from rectangular-plan shafts to rounded shafts, are not really satisfactory, though such a succession remains a possibility. The merging of characteristics at Ajjul which fall into separate groups at Jericho, and the fact that at Ajjul the differences between the groups are less sharp cut, might suggest that a gradual amalgamation was going on, which would be quite in place in a site which represents a further penetration into the country of groups certainly originating in areas to the north and east. Alternatively, the Ajjul burials may be those of yet further tribal groups. It is a subject that needs further investigation.

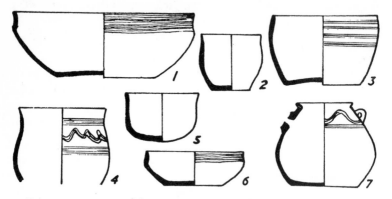

FIG. 28   Pottery of the E.B.–M.B. period from Tell Duweir. $\frac{1}{5}$

At Tell Duweir, a cemetery (the 2000 Cemetery) resembles in many respects the 100–200 Cemetery of Tell Ajjul. It lies on a hill spur some 700 metres north of the tell. About a hundred tombs were located, closely grouped on the edge of the hill. A minority of the tombs were approached by square shafts, but the great majority had either round shafts and chambers, or else no shafts at all, possibly as the result of erosion. Unfortunately no evidence was recovered as to the position or condition of the bodies, perhaps because all the skeletons were dismembered. All the tombs contained pottery vessels. The range of forms is not unlike that of the Ajjul cemetery, except that there are greater numbers

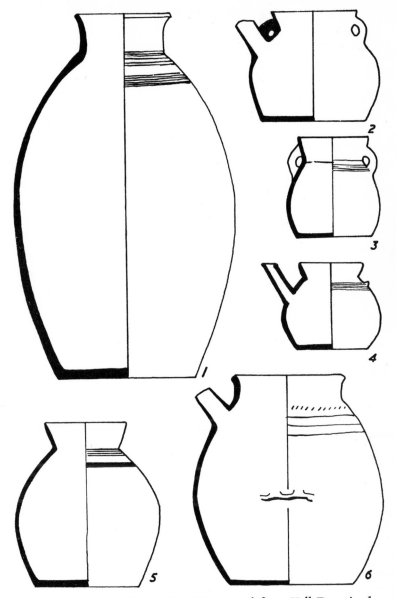

Fig. 29 Pottery of the E.B.–M.B. period from Tell Duweir. $\frac{1}{5}$

of bowls and cups, and that the jars tend to be narrower and taller. A very few, of a fatter form and with vestigial ledge handle, resemble those from the Ajjul 1500 Cemetery, and there are some spouted jars which also occur in that cemetery. Two tombs have a dagger, of which one also has a javelin, and two others have a javelin. It would appear that this group is allied to the group burying in the 100–200 Cemetery at Tell Ajjul; the differences in the material might be accounted for by a later date, with a typological development of forms and a slight mingling with features characteristic of the other Ajjul group. As always, interpretation is difficult, as one never finds different combinations of characteristics in stratigraphical relationship.[1]

Megiddo adds yet other details. A number of tombs were excavated on the rock surface sloping down from the foot of the tell on the east. Included among them were two groups which must fall in the Intermediate Early Bronze–Middle Bronze period.

The first group was in Tomb 1101–1102B Lower. This locality was part of a complex of interconnecting rock-cut chambers, cave-like in form, entered from the slope of the hill. Their final use was in the Early Iron Age (the "Upper" deposits) after there had been considerable roof falls which covered the remains of the early periods. The "Lower" deposits in themselves represented several successive uses.[2] The first falls in the Proto-Urban period, when there was domestic occupation. A second phase of domestic occupation, with stratified layers of household rubbish, was in the Early Bronze Age, probably entirely E.B. III. Lying on top of some 0·50 metres of these deposits were burials accompanied by the vessels shown on Fig. 30 and a group of copper objects (Pl.28A). The burials, representing fourteen individuals, were regarded by the excavators as disturbed, for though a few bones were in articulation, most were in no order at all. In the light of the evidence from Jericho, and the inference therefrom as regards Tell Ajjul, it is probable that once again we have to do with

[1] Addenda pp. 338–9.
[2] The picture is confused in the publication, M. Tombs, pp. 2427, by all the pottery of the "Lower" occupation being published as one, whereas the description makes it clear that there were clearly differentiated deposits.

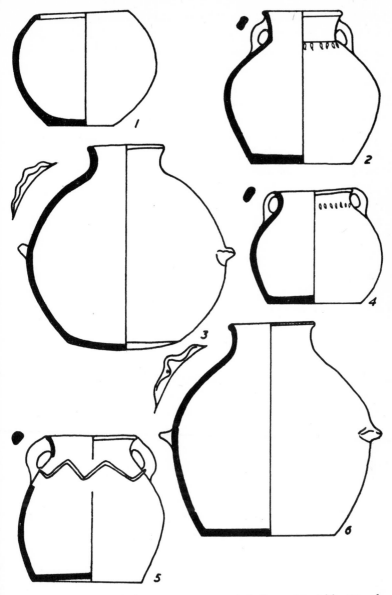

FIG. 30 Pottery of the E.B.–M.B. period from Megiddo Tomb
1101–1102B Lower. ⅛

burials after the flesh had disintegrated from exposure. Some of
the bones had been blackened by fire; this was on the upper sides
only, so the fire was clearly after they had been placed in their
present position, and must represent a funeral ceremony. This is
a feature not found so far in other burials of the period.

The pottery placed with these burials (Fig. 30) has clear connections with that of Jericho, particularly in the folded or envelope
ledge handles. The copper objects (Pl. 28A) include a dagger
resembling those of Jericho and Tell Ajjul, spearheads, and a
swollen-headed toggle-pin, a most useful object, to which reference will be made later (p. 158). But though there are these
resemblances to material from Jericho and Tell Ajjul, there is no
identity between the finds and burial customs of any of the sites.

To the second group of tombs at Megiddo the excavators gave
the title of Shaft Tombs, thus emphasising the fact that rock-cut
tomb chambers approached by entrance shafts were unusual
there. But though such tombs are the normal type at Tell Ajjul
and Jericho, this particular type at Megiddo has a most unusual
and elaborate form. The shaft is square in plan, about 2
metres deep, with foot-holes in its vertical sides. At its base a
very small doorway, closed by a blocking stone, leads into a
central chamber. From this chamber small entrances led to three
others on a slightly higher level, one on the axis of the shaft, the
others on either side of the central chamber. The cutting of the
tombs had been carried out with copper tools, 5 centimetres and
12 centimetres broad, and sometimes they were finished with a
coat of plaster or whitewash. The plan was a stereotyped one,
though some variations occurred.

Many of these tombs had been re-used at a later date. But the
excavators were puzzled to account for the disordered state of the
bones, even in the case of those which had not been disturbed in
this way. They suggest that gold or other precious objects must
have been placed close to the bodies and that the disturbance is due
to robbers, even though the blocking-stone was often found in
position. The Jericho evidence makes it quite clear that here again
at Megiddo there was the practice of burying dismembered bodies.

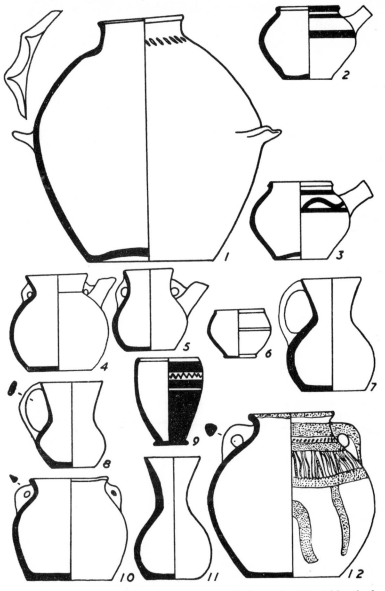

FIG. 31   Pottery of the E.B.–M.B. period from the Megiddo shaft tombs. $\frac{1}{5}$

Some of the pottery from these tombs (Fig. 31) resembles that from other E.B.–M.B. groups. It includes small jars with lug handles at the neck (Fig. 31.*10*), which are found at Jericho and Tell Ajjul, and in Megiddo Tomb 1101–1102, the jar (Fig. 31.*1*) is a common form at Jericho and Beth-shan, and is close to vessels found in the 1500 Cemetery at Tell Ajjul (though these have more vestigial ledge handles), and a bowl is close to forms found at Jericho and Tell Beit Mirsim. In addition, there are great numbers of little spouted jars which are the lug-handled jars with a spout added; these also are found at Jericho. But in addition there is a considerable number of vessels which are clearly imports, distinguished from the local vessels by being of thin hard ware and by being entirely wheel-made; they are usually dark in colour, with a decoration of straight or wavy lines in a light colour. Unique vessels in the same category are a jug and the goblet (Fig. 31.*9*). Vessels also not found at the other sites are the round-mouthed jugs with strap handles, but they are described as being hand-made and in local ware. Other finds in the tombs included mushroom-headed toggle-pins and a pin with a curled head (Pl. 28B).

These finds give a clear indication of the provenance of this group at Megiddo. The teapots are closely paralleled in shape, though not decoration, by forms found at places like Qatna in inland Syria,[1] and sherds with similar decoration have been found in Byblos. The pins point also to Syria, for an identical group has been found at Brak.[2] This group is therefore likely to have reached Palestine from the north-east.

Though, as has been indicated, a number of the forms provide links with other sites, no other group containing the remainder of the material has been found in Palestine proper. In Transjordan, however, a burial cave at El Husn has produced very similar material;[3] it includes for instance spouted jars (cf. Fig. 31.*2–3*), round-mouthed jugs with strap handles (cf. Fig. 31.*7–8*), decorated jars (cf. Fig. 31.*12*) and ledge-handled jars (cf. Fig. 31.*1*), and a pin with curled head (cf. Pl. 28B (c)). It does not, however,

[1] *Syria*, XI.   [2] *Iraq*, IX.   [3] *A.P.E.F.*, VI.

include any of the imported wares. The group perhaps reached Transjordan via Palestine, which might emphasise the probability of an entry into Palestine from the north.[1]

So far we have only dealt with the tombs of this period. In fact, by far the greater part of our evidence comes from this source. On nearly all sites the evidence within the town itself is of the slightest. At Tell Ajjul no traces of occupation were found on the tell. At Tell Beit Mirsim two strata, I and H, are assigned to this period, but the architectural remains are scanty and there is no town wall; almost all the published pottery comes from a single deposit in a cave. At Tell Duweir there was a settlement site in Area 1500, about 500 metres north-west of the tell. The traces were found in caves and pits, and there was only one poorly built house which might belong to the period. The pottery from this settlement occupation is in a different repertory of forms than that of the cemetery, a curious feature which occurs again at Jericho. At Beth-shan there are a few vessels published from Levels XII and XI which are obviously intrusive in those contexts (the stratification at this level showed clear signs of disturbances), which are an indication of some slight occupation, but again there are no structures.

The clearest evidence comes from Jericho. Immediately over the ruins of the Early Bronze town appears E.B.–M.B. pottery, and houses are found of a new type. But it is clear that there was prolonged occupation before the first houses were built. They are found mainly on the slopes of the tell, for the levels of this period on the summit have disappeared in erosion. Half-way down the slope of the tell these houses overlie the ditch of the last Early Bronze Age defences. To the bottom, this silt contained E.B.–M.B. pottery, and a depth of 2·50 metres had accumulated before the first house was built. There was thus a prolonged occupation of a camping nature. This occurs not only all over the tell, but on the surrounding hill slopes as well, for in the cemetery area patches of E.B.–M.B. domestic pottery are found, without any associated structures. When the first houses appear on the tell they are slight in character, and entirely different from the

[1] Addenda p. 340.

FIG. 32   Pottery of the E.B.–M.B. period from the tell at Jericho. $\frac{1}{5}$

preceding houses of the Early Bronze Age town. They are built
of rather soft rectangular bricks of a curious green colour. The
walls are only one course thick, the rooms small and rather
irregular in shape (Pl. 29). One structure may have been a shrine
or temple. Beneath its wall was an infant foundation burial, and
in two adjacent rooms were solid blocks of brickwork, about a
metre cube, which may be altars. The settlement, even after
houses began to be built, seems to straggle irregularly down the
slopes of the mound, and there is no town wall. The pottery
found in the settlement (Figs. 32, 33) is surprisingly different from
that in the tombs, even allowing for the fact that many domestic
forms, such as cooking-pots, are not ordinarily found in tombs.
Even the jar forms are different, many having the high, flaring
rim found in the Tell Ajjul and Tell Duweir cemeteries. Bowls
and cups are found on the tell, which are very rare in the tombs at
Jericho, and a striking feature is that it is only on the tell that
vessels are found with an incised or combed decoration in a combination of straight and wavy lines which is a feature of the
pottery of the period at Tell Beit Mirsim and Tell Ajjul. This last

FIG. 33   Pottery of the E.B.–M.B. period from the tell at Jericho. $\frac{1}{10}$

differentiation also occurs at Tell Duweir. This distinction between tell and tombs constitutes a problem that cannot as yet be answered; as with the problem of the interrelationship of different groups of which the cemeteries provide evidence, further research is required.

[1]There remains the problem of Megiddo. As the material is published, there appears to be an overlap, with pottery of the Early Bronze, E.B.–M.B., and Middle Bronze appearing side by side in Strata XVI, XV, XIV and XIII.[2] But I have shown[3] that this is due to intrusive burials and other disturbances. No such mixture occurs in the tomb groups, and it is virtually certain that

[1] Addenda p. 340.   [2] *Megiddo*, II.   [3] *Eretz Israel*, V.

on the tell the occupation of the three periods is as distinct as it is elsewhere. Owing to these disturbances it is difficult to be certain which, if any, of the structures in these levels belong to the E.B.– M.B. period. There is a strong probability that at least one building period does come here. In Area BB of the excavations

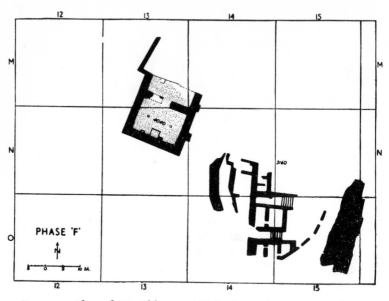

FIG. 34   Plan of Megiddo area BB in the 2nd E.B.–M.B. phase

three adjacent temples are attributed to Stratum XV. It is highly improbable these are all contemporary.[1] The second plan was probably as is shown on Fig. 34, though whether the somewhat monumental approach from the east is contemporary or not cannot be proved. This temple seems to have succeeded two similar ones to the north-west. This one was subsequently rebuilt with a much smaller cella (Fig. 35), and incorporated in the rebuild was an axehead of fenestrated type (Fig. 24.17), which can be shown to be typical of the E.B.–M.B. period.[2] In the pottery associated with all the successive builds of the temples, there is

[1] *Eretz Israel*, V, p. 35.   [2] *Eleventh Annual Report of the Institute of Archaeology.*

an appreciable proportion of E.B.–M.B. types, and though the lack of adequate stratification makes it impossible to be certain it seems quite possible that all three stages belong to the period.

This would obviously be in considerable contrast to the evidence from elsewhere. In support of such an attribution, it may be suggested that in their care for the disposition of the dead the E.B.–M.B. people do everywhere show considerable concern

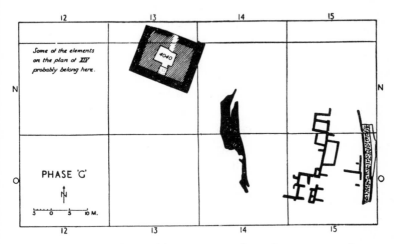

FIG. 35   Plan of Megiddo area BB in the 3rd E.B.–M.B. phase

for things spiritual, and there is also the possible shrine at Jericho, just described. It is also a fact that in the Shaft Tomb people at Megiddo we have clearly a much more sophisticated group than elsewhere, with an almost architectural approach to their tomb-digging. Moreover, they would appear to have come from a comparatively civilised area, in which there was a well-developed architectural tradition.

But in the general picture Megiddo is exceptional. Elsewhere we have a clear picture of a very numerous people, not interested in town life. They were in fact pastoralists and not agriculturists, and many of their dwellings may have been tents or shelters scattered over the hillsides, leaving little trace for the archaeologist other than the occasional potsherd. The concentrated cemeteries may represent tribal burial grounds, to which the dead were brought from a relatively wide area. Such a practice, the relic of more completely nomadic days, has already been suggested as an explanation of the custom of burying skeletalised remains. The very noticeable differences between the possessions and burial practices of all the groups described shows that though there were broad similarities there was no uniform culture in any way comparable with that of the preceding and succeeding periods, and that the groups remained separated and tribal in organisation.

Exact dates for the beginning and end of the period are difficult to fix, but the general period is clear. Professor Albright has shown[1] that the type of waisted bowl or cup, which he calls caliciform, is current in Syria in the last centuries of the third millennium, as is also a type of decoration with combined straight and wavy lines. The imported "teapots" at Megiddo point to the same date. Associated with the remains of one of the groups of people at Megiddo, that burying their dead in Tomb 1101-1102, was a type of toggle-pin with a swollen or club head. This type of pin is found at Ras Shamra in graves of the Middle Ugarit I period, associated with a cup of waisted profile decorated with straight and wavy incised lines,[2] and with fenestrated axeheads of the type mentioned above. Schaeffer has shown[3] that the type of pin is widespread, and is associated in that area with a group expert in metallurgy. At Ras Shamra the graves are in a fill underlying a temple which was of sufficient importance to receive offerings from Twelfth Dynasty Egypt in the 20th century B.C. A terminal date of c. 2000 B.C. is thus indicated in northern Syria. Two other types of pin were found at Megiddo, belonging to the Shaft Tomb people, a mushroom-headed toggle-pin and a pin with a curled head. As already mentioned, these types are

[1] *A.A.S.O.R.*, XIII, pp. 66-67.
[2] Schaeffer, *Stratigraphie Comparée*, Pl. XIII.
[3] "Les Porteurs de Torques," in *Ugaritica*, II.

exactly paralleled at Brak, and are associated in a level dated to
2200 B.C.

Palestine thus received a great invasion of nomadic groups in
the last centuries of the second millennium, which completely
blotted out the preceding urban civilisation of the Early Bronze
Age. Egypt suffered the same fate. The Sixth Dynasty of Egypt
came to an end in 2294 B.C., and Egypt was invaded by barbarians,
some at least of them Asiatics. Peaceful conditions were not
restored until Egypt was once more reunited under the Twelfth
Dynasty, c. 1990 B.C.

It seems very likely that Palestine would be affected by barbarian movements at least as early as Egypt, if not earlier, for any
Asiatics reaching Egypt would almost certainly have passed
through Palestine. For this reason it seems probable that the
Intermediate Early Bronze–Middle Bronze period in Palestine
began about 2300 B.C., and coincided roughly in period, as it did
in effect, with the First Intermediate of Egypt. As we have seen,
a late stage in E.B. III is to be dated c. 2600 B.C., and it is difficult
to stretch any period of decline even as long as three hundred
years, so this seems a minimum date for the beginning of the
ensuing period.

The centuries–old Sumerian civilisation was also overthrown
towards the end of the third millennium. In this case, the agents
of destruction are known, and this provides the clue for Palestine.[1]
It was the Semitic Amorites, coming from the semi-arid fringes
of the Fertile Crescent, who were responsible for the upheavals
in northern Syria and Mesopotamia. The Books of Numbers and
Joshua record that at the time of the entry of the Israelites into
Palestine the Amorites were in the hill country and the Canaanites
were on the coast and in the plains (Num. xiii. 29; Joshua v. 1,
x. 6). Probable evidence for their earlier presence in Palestine
comes from the Egyptian Execration Texts. These are very
probably to be dated to the Eleventh Dynasty in the 21st century
B.C., when the recovery of Egyptian power was beginning, which
led to the full Middle Empire of the Twelfth Dynasty. In them a

[1] Addenda pp. 340–41.

number of Asiatic places are classed as rebels. They can hardly have been actual rebels, since they were not breaking away from a previous sway, for any such sway had disappeared centuries before, but were more likely opposing the spread of Egyptian influence. Some places accused, such as Byblos, can be identified, but most only doubtfully so. Some places have one chief, others two or three, and there is a very slight indication[1] that the coastal towns had a single chief, and therefore a centralised organisation, and that inland places had several, and therefore still had a tribal organisation. Albright suggests that the names of these places and their chiefs are in the Amorite form of the Semitic language, and that the reason that the places cannot be identified is that they were of districts rather than of the towns which later became known to history. The deductions are based on rather scanty evidence in the texts themselves, but the archaeological evidence which has accumulated since he wrote does seem to present the same picture.

The end of the Intermediate Early Bronze–Middle Bronze period is as sharp cut as its beginning. Materially, the Amorites seem to contribute nothing to the ensuing period. The higher culture of the Middle Bronze, with its reversion to town life, seems completely to submerge and absorb that of the more primitive groups found in the land by the first wave of newcomers who bring the new culture. That the Amorites remained side by side with new groups, whom we can specifically recognise as Canaanites, is established by linguistic and literary evidence. We can deduce that they remained pastoralists from their concentration in the hill country, while the Canaanites occupied the more favourable agricultural land, but they must rapidly have given up their distinctive burial customs and pottery forms. It was a process comparable with the Romanisation of Iron Age Britain or the Normanisation of Saxon England; a minority of invaders impose their higher culture on the more backward population they find in occupation. The contacts of the newcomers with the Phoenician coastal towns can be clearly estab-

[1] Albright, *J.P.O.S.*, VIII.

lished, and at Byblos and elsewhere a Twelfth Dynasty date for the allied culture can be shown. The culture of the Middle Bronze Age was therefore introduced into Palestine not before the 20th century B.C. How early this happened it is difficult to establish, but a conventional date of *c.* 1900 B.C. is unlikely to have a margin of error of more than fifty years either way.

★

CHAPTER SEVEN

The Middle Bronze Age
and the Hyksos

As WAS the case with the beginning of the Intermediate Early
Bronze–Middle Bronze period, the beginning of the Middle
Bronze Age was ushered in by the appearance of a new group of
people. This is clearly indicated by the appearance of new pottery,
new weapons, new burial customs and a revival of town life.
Unlike their predecessors, they came from an area possessing a
developed civilisation, for it is with the Phoenician coastal towns
that close links were established. In the early stages, there were
also links with some of the settled areas of inland Syria, but these
grew less as the Middle Bronze Age culture of Palestine developed.
With Canaanite Phoenicia, the ties which were established about
1900 B.C. were permanent, and on the evidence of the pottery
we can say that the same basic culture grew up in an area stretching
from Ras Shamra in the north to the desert fringes of Palestine
in the south. Moreover, the culture now introduced into Palestine
was to have a very long life. In spite of the fact that a series of
events took place of major political importance, there is no
cultural break until at least 1200 B.C. These political events we
know of on literary evidence, for we are now in a period in
which written history can supplement (but by no means replace)
archaeology. Archaeology can show a recognisable progression
of artifacts such as pottery, and can show that towns suffered a
succession of destructions, but after these destructions the old
culture was re-established.

This period therefore marks the genesis of the Palestine that we meet in the Old Testament, the Palestine through which the Patriarchs journeyed in their wanderings, and the Palestine in which their descendants subsequently settled. The early Israelites found this Canaanite culture in the land, and much of it they absorbed. In the times of the Hebrew Kingdoms, the reformers amongst the kings and prophets were still struggling against aspects of which they disapproved.

The new pottery (Fig. 36) which appears is in very striking contrast to that of the preceding period. For the first time in Palestine it was entirely made on a fast wheel. Ever since the Proto-Urban period some vessels had been finished on a form of slow wheel. In the E.B.–M.B. period the rims were made on what must have been quite an efficient wheel, but the bodies of the vessels are still very obviously hand-made. The new vessels are as well made as at any time in Palestinian history, all on the wheel except for coarse cooking-pots. The old flat-bottomed jars and ledge handles disappear, and a completely new set of forms appears: jars with pointed bases and loop handles, bowls with sharply angular forms, dipper juglets with a single handle and pinched mouth—in fact a whole new repertory. Not a single form can be traced through from one period to the other. It has been claimed that the most domestic vessel of all, the cooking-pot, which at this period has a flat base, upright walls with an applied band, and holes pierced through below the rim, is of Early Bronze Age origin, but there is no certain evidence of this, and much evidence that it does only appear now. Another characteristic of the new pottery is that bowls, jugs and juglets are usually covered all over with a deep red slip which has been given a highly burnished finish. The vessels have often been finished on the wheel with very fine combing, even in cases of vessels which were subsequently given a red slip and burnished.

This red burnished pottery and the sharply angular forms of the bowls suggest metallic prototypes. No examples of these metal prototypes have been found in Palestine, which is not surprising, for such vessels are frail and corrode easily in the soil. Just such a bowl, in silver, has, however, been found at Byblos, where it was buried in a jar as a foundation deposit, with a quantity of clay sealings which suggest that this type of metal vessel began to be made at Byblos during the E.B.–M.B. period.[1]

This is an important pointer both for the date of the new development in Palestine and also for the direction from which the new peoples came. Byblos does in fact provide clear evidence as to date, for in the period of the renewed prosperity of Egypt during the Twelfth Dynasty, relations which had existed with this important Syrian port were resumed and the chieftains of Byblos became clients of Egypt. As a result, the royal tombs at Byblos can be closely dated by Egyptian objects. In tombs of the period of Amenemhet III and IV (second half 19th–beginning 18th centuries B.C.) there appears pottery which is very close to this new pottery in Palestine. Moreover, on a number of other sites in coastal Syria we find the same kind of pottery, and it is clear that part at least of the new population of Palestine must have come from this area.

The new groups brought with them other new developments in addition to wheel-made pottery. The most important of these was the use of bronze for weapons. The evidence for the first use of bronze is not as clear as it might be, owing to lack of analyses of metal, but at Megiddo the question was systematically investigated, and it is consistently in groups associated with this new kind of pottery that bronze first appears. The forms, moreover, of the weapons are distinctive: a short broad-shouldered dagger with short riveted hilt-plate and elaborate multiple ribs on the blade, a narrow parallel-sided axehead with shaft-hole and nick, presumably to help bind the head to the shaft, and a socketed spear. Arrowheads in metal do not yet appear, as presumably bronze was still too precious to be used on such expendable objects. This identical equipment is found on a number of sites in Palestine at this period, for instance Megiddo, Jericho, Tell Ajjul and Gezer, and here again the process can be paralleled in Syria.

The M.B. I sites which, on the evidence of the pottery, show

[1] Kenyon, *Amorites and Canaanites*, Schweich Lectures, 1963.

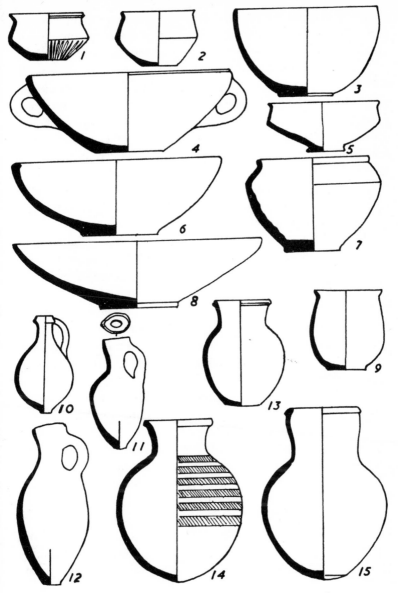

FIG. 36 Pottery of Middle Bronze I from Ras el 'Ain (2–4, 6–10, 13–15) and Tell Ajjul (1, 5, 11–12). $\frac{1}{5}$

the closest associations with coastal Syria are in southern Palestine. At Tell Ajjul closely similar pottery was found in a number of burials within the area of the subsequent town. These were called by Petrie the Courtyard Cemetery,[1] since they lay beneath the courtyard of the large building he called the Palace, but it is clear that they are in fact earlier than the courtyard. How much occupation there was at the time on the town site is not at present clear. At Tell Beit Mirsim there was, however, undoubtedly a developed town. Two strata, G and F, are ascribed to this period.[2] Only a portion of the town of this period was cleared, but though it was badly mutilated by subsequent buildings enough remained to show that it was laid out in an orderly manner and was closely built up. It was surrounded by a great wall about 10 feet thick, with solid towers at intervals, and the houses were built closely against the wall at the back. One building was sufficiently preserved to show what a typical dwelling-house of the period may have been. It seems to consist of a large hall with roof supported on a line of pillars, and with a series of smaller rooms opening off it. Within M.B. I there was apparently a considerable destruction, for the interior buildings of Stratum G were completely rebuilt in Stratum F, and the city wall strengthened and thiickened.

The same pottery occurs at Ras el 'Ain in central Palestine. As mentioned above (p. 117) this was not an archaeological excavation, and a connected story therefore does not emerge. But some of the pottery was apparently (but not certainly) found in occupation layers on the town site, while some was from graves not far off. These graves are of a form unusual for Palestine. They consist of rectangular pits lined on the long sides by stone walling, and covered by stone slabs. In the walls of three of the graves (the fourth was that of a child) were recesses in which apparently bones from earlier burials were placed. The graves were, however, essentially for single burials, unlike the multiple burials of later

[1] *Ancient Gaza*, II.
[2] Called by Albright M.B. IIa, since he calls the Intermediate Early Bronze–Middle Bronze Period M.B. I.

stages of the Middle Bronze Age, and the bodies were placed in them in a slightly flexed position with the head to the east. With each of the adults was a bronze weapon, either a spear or a dagger. Most of the graves were liberally provided with pottery vessels. Many among them closely resemble the M.B. I vessels from Tell Beit Mirsim and Tell Ajjul. But others are of a type not found there, especially a class of globular, round-mouthed, handleless jar, sometimes plain and sometimes with decoration in encircling bands of red or brown. This type of vessel is characteristic of inland rather than coastal Syria, so some at least of the newcomers probably came from that direction.

Similar types of jar are also found at Megiddo. Here they are associated with the same types of angular, carinated bowls and plump dipper juglets, both with well-burnished red slip, as at the sites already mentioned, but there is a much more elaborate repertory of forms (Fig. 37). Particularly characteristic are wide bowls with thickened rims, on which is a band of red wash, jugs with narrow splaying necks and elaborate multiple-strand handles, and plump dipper juglets with decoration in bands of red or red and black. These vessels have been found nowhere else in Palestine, and their ancestry is not as yet apparent.

The great majority of these vessels at Megiddo come from burials. In two cases, these were in re-used E.B.–M.B. shaft tombs, but most of the burials were in simple graves on the tell. The pottery unfortunately is published mixed with that of the level on the tell to which the base of the grave happened to penetrate, but by a sorting out of provenance it is possible to establish that there were some fifty burials of the period in Area BB. It is more difficult to establish whether any of the buildings of which the plans are published belong to this period. The burials seem to spread almost all over the area, but, as will be seen, there does seem, in later stages of the Middle Bronze Age at Megiddo, to have been strange juxtapositions of burials and houses; it is therefore possible that some part of the fragmentary walls shown on the plan of Stratum XIII do belong to this phase.

At Jericho, the town certainly only developed slowly at the

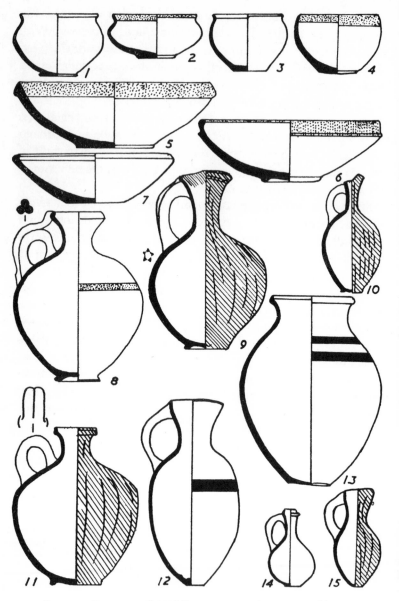

FIG. 37 Pottery of Middle Bronze I from Megiddo. $\frac{1}{5}$

beginning of the Middle Bronze Age. In the main cemeteries, no tombs of the period have been found, and the only certain evidence on the tell is a brick-built tomb and a grave, close together on the east side of the mound. The tomb had walls of mud-brick with probably a corbelled roof, but little of that or of the entrance shaft survives. In it were the remains of about a dozen individuals, the earlier bodies being disarranged to make room for the later ones. The grave contained the bodies of two individuals, lying on their left sides in a flexed position. The accompanying pottery resembles that of the southern sites, and not that of Megiddo. Again at Jericho it is difficult to establish the extent of the occupation. Only a relatively small area of the Middle Bronze Age town survived subsequent denudation, and of this area only a small portion has been excavated to the M.B. I levels. Again we cannot say if there were buildings on one part of the town site and burials in another.

The general picture that does emerge does, however, suggest that the occupation was on a small scale in the first stages. If any towns on the scale of the M.B. II ones had existed, they would certainly have been found. It would seem that the newcomers settled on some of the old town sites and started to build houses, but that they did not need the whole area for this purpose; on part of the site they seem, in most cases, to have buried their dead, perhaps wishing to keep the graves close to the settlement to avoid the risk of desecration in an alien land.

The comparatively meagre amount of finds of the period suggests also that it was not of long duration. As was mentioned in the last chapter, it is difficult to give a precise date to the beginning of the Middle Bronze Age. It may begin anywhere between 1950 and 1850 B.C., and the suggested date of 1900 B.C. is only given as a mean between the two. The occurrence of similar pottery at Byblos in tombs and deposits of the period of the Twelfth Egyptian Dynasty gives a general indication of the date. At Byblos, it would seem that this pottery continued in use down to the end of the dynasty and as late as the beginning of the Thirteenth Dynasty, that is to say to the beginning of the 18th century. In Palestine it is unlikely to have been so late as that before the individual Palestinian version of the culture in Middle Bronze II, and particularly of the pottery with its remarkably homogeneous character, developed, for to put the transition as late as 1800 B.C. would compress too much the abundant M.B. II material, in which a whole series of stages can be shown, and would stretch too much the relatively scanty material of M.B. I.

A tentative date of 1850 B.C. is therefore suggested for the beginning of M.B. II. As will be seen, its end may be taken to coincide with the revival of the Egyptian Empire under the Eighteenth Dynasty early in the 16th century B.C. For the intervening period, there is at present no safe means of establishing exact dates. The pottery and other finds can be shown to exhibit characteristic forms at different stages, but to give a term in years to these stages is only hypothetical. In the Jericho tombs five successive characteristic assemblages of pottery and other finds can be recognised,[1] and the finds in the tombs at places like Megiddo, Tell Fara and Tell Duweir fall into the same categories. Figs. 38–42 show the salient and diagnostic forms in what we will refer to here as phases i, iii and v of M.B. II. The characteristics of the successive phases can be briefly summarised.

The pottery of phase i (Fig. 38) is close to that of M.B. I, and has developed directly from it. At Megiddo a set of tombs showing transitional characteristics can be identified. The chief difference is that the use of a burnished red slip is dying out. The carinated bowls have a less sharply inclined-in wall, the dipper juglets become less plump, and have a pointed and not a small flat base. A characteristic small bowl has a globular body and short outcurving neck (Fig. 38.9–10); it is often finely burnished on a cream slip. Larger bowls with upright necks are also common (Fig. 38.8). The characteristic oil flask is the piriform juglet (Fig. 38.13–16); in the earlier groups it has a small ring base, but the button base was already found in the phase i groups at Jericho. Allied to this form is the cylindrical juglet (Fig. 40.2–5), which is a form which is occasionally found in M.B. I, but it is not really

[1] *Jericho*, I. II.

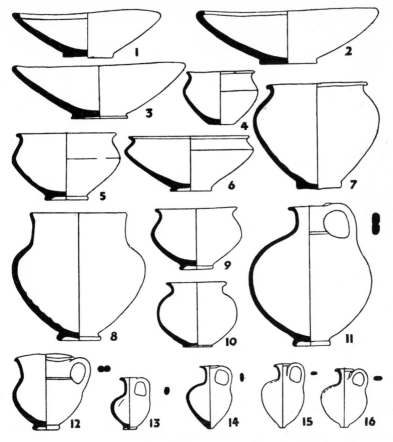

FIG. 38   Pottery of Middle Bronze II phase i at Jericho. $\frac{1}{5}$

adopted in Palestine till phase iii; an occasional isolated example occurs in i and ii, but it is not characteristic. Neither pedestal vases (Fig. 39.*18–20*) nor flaring carinated bowls (Fig. 39.*9–11*) are found. No specially constructed lamps are found in this phase at Jericho, and broken bases of other vessels seem to have been used for the purpose.

In phase ii most of the characteristic forms of phase i continue. To them are added flaring carinated bowls and pedestal vases;

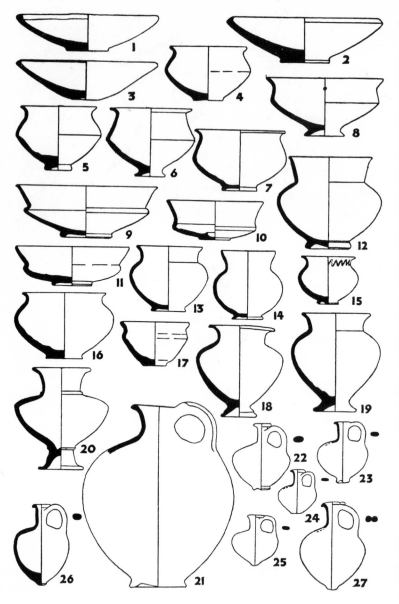

FIG. 39 Pottery of Middle Bronze II phase iii at Jericho. $\frac{1}{5}$

at this stage the latter form does not have a cordon round the neck or base. True lamps, round saucers with a slightly pinched nozzle, appear, the ancestor of the lamps which continue into the second half of the first millennium B.C., when the closed Hellenistic type is introduced.

Most of the early forms also continue into phase iii (Figs. 39–40). At this point, cylindrical juglets begin to appear in numbers, though piriform juglets are still in the majority. Pedestal vases are found both with and without cordons. Up to this stage, all the toggle-pins found have plain heads above the eyelet, but the type with a decorated head begins to appear.

By phase iv most of the early forms have died out. The small globular bowls and the larger necked bowls are no longer found. A few piriform juglets still appear, all with developed button bases, but cylindrical juglets are in the majority. At this stage, faience bottles and flasks first appear.

In phase v (Figs. 41–42) the later elements alone are found. Piriform juglets have completely disappeared, and there is a tendency for the flaring carinated bowls and pedestal vases to become larger. A deep hemispherical bowl is relatively common. The majority of the toggle-pins have decorated heads.

Many of these features have for long been recognised as of chronological significance, but the evidence of the Jericho tombs has enabled more precision to be given to some of the characteristics. Further work will no doubt add a greater precision.

During M.B. II the towns of Palestine show great development and all the evidence of an eventful history. Each town excavated was rebuilt several times within the period and each suffered several destructions. Most of the excavation was, however, carried out before a precise knowledge of the pottery sequence had been acquired, and therefore the sequence of events can only be established in outline.

In the case of the history of the town of Jericho, the material has not yet been fully worked out, but a broad outline can be given of the sequence in the limited area excavated. The Middle Bronze Age town only survives on the east side of the mound,

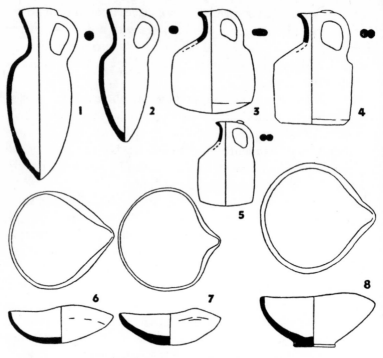

FIG. 40   Pottery of Middle Bronze II phase iii at Jericho. $\frac{1}{5}$

where throughout its history there was a slope down to the source of the spring. In this area a small section only has been excavated to the base of the M.B. levels. This section showed that the town was enclosed with a brick wall about 2 metres thick, running along the extreme edge of the present mound, and partly cut into by the modern road. The wall was of the same character as the Early Bronze Age town walls, and the newcomers must have reintroduced this style of defence from the north. Almost certainly the gate lies on the extreme southern edge of the excavated area, for the back of a massive structure, probably a tower guarding an entrance passage, just came within the area cleared. Inside, the buildings climbed the mound in a series of terraces, those immediately within the wall being probably yards

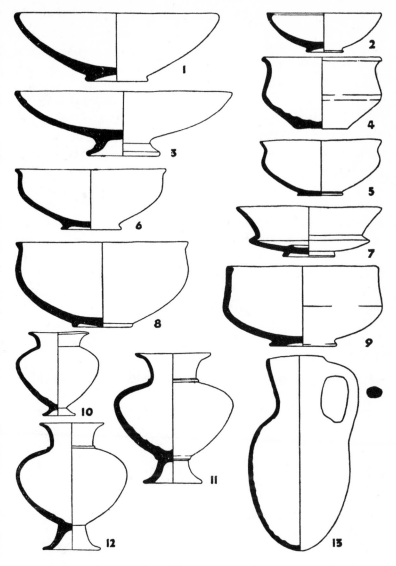

FIG. 41   Pottery of Middle Bronze II phase v at Jericho. $\frac{1}{5}$

or storage enclosures. The town wall has some three building stages, and there was also a complicated series of reconstructions of the internal buildings. The pottery has not yet been correlated in detail with that of the tombs, but it is possible that for this stage in the history of the town it roughly covers phases i to iii.

At Tell Beit Mirsim it is probable that Stratum E belongs to the same period. The surviving remains were fragmentary but seem to indicate a spacious layout. The plan of only two houses could be identified. Both were substantial, with a main hall in which the roof was supported by a central line of posts (the old style found already in the Early Bronze Age) with smaller adjoining rooms. The pottery of the period is exceptionally fine, all the better-class vessels being finished with a highly burnished cream slip. Within the life of Stratum E, but overlying pottery of an E type, a town wall was built, but since it is in the style described below, of the next epoch in the history of Palestine, it may be that Stratum E lasted into that epoch.

At Megiddo there is a complicated succession of building periods, which it is very difficult to disentangle owing to uncertainties in the stratification.[1] Early in the sequence comes a very fine town wall, associated in Area AA with a gateway with a sloping ramp leading up parallel to the line of the wall to a gateway in a court, in which there is a right-angled turn to an inner gate.[2] The wall is characterised by a series of shallow recesses, and is a most impressive example of the town walls of the period. In Area AA the evidence suggests that this may even belong to the end of M.B. I, though in Area BB it suggests that it is somewhat later, about phase ii of M.B. II. The house plans in both areas are fragmentary for this stage in M.B., but show that there was a succession of substantial buildings.

This phase can be taken as representative of the fully developed culture of Canaanite Palestine, a culture of prosperous city states. On it supervenes another influence. It is represented by an entirely different method of defence, a defence in depth in contrast to

---

[1] Levant I, pp. 25–60. [2] *Megiddo*, II, Fig. 378.

the single-wall type of the earlier stages of the Middle Bronze Age and also of the preceding Early Bronze Age.

The evidence for this is especially clear at Jericho. We have seen how on the west side of the tell there had been, during the Early Bronze Age, a succession of town walls crowning the crest of the mound. As the successive walls were built, the layers of débris from their collapse gradually raised the level, but the angle of the slope remained approximately the same, being the angle of rest of the débris, in a slope of approximately 25 degrees from the horizontal; in the later stages, the foot of this slope was somewhat steepened by a ditch. Above the débris of the final collapse were the remains of the E.B.–M.B. houses. In the main area of excavation, the summit of the slope has disappeared in erosion, and therefore there is no trace of the early M.B. wall which has been found on the east side; at the north-west angle, however, some slight clearance in the area where a trench was

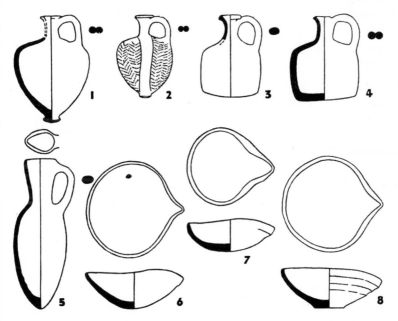

FIG. 42   Pottery of Middle Bronze II phase v at Jericho. $\frac{1}{6}$

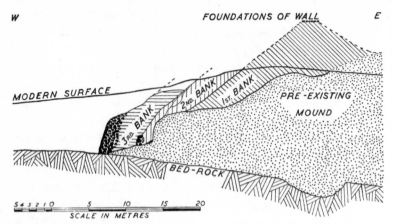

FIG. 43   Reconstructed section of Middle Bronze II rampart at
Jericho

cut in earlier excavations has located what are probably the
remains of this wall. This wall at the north-west angle, and all
the remains in the main area of excavation, were enveloped in a
great rampart, consisting of an enormous fill of imported material,
faced by a thick layer of plaster, which was keyed by a series of
tongues into the fill behind (Pl. 30). The foot of the rampart was
revetted by a stone wall; from this the stones of the original line
have been removed for subsequent rebuildings, but its character
can be deduced from the similar revetment in the final stage
(Pl. 31). In the north-west angle the plaster facing can be traced
up to the highest surviving point on the tell, where the foundations survive of the town wall which crowned the whole defensive
system. Inside the town the great artificial bank sloped down
probably some 13 feet; evidence of this survives in the south-
western area. The new defences were therefore 66 feet wide from
the foot of the revetting wall to the line of the town wall, and the
latter was 46 feet higher than the ground level at the foot of the
defences (Fig. 43).

On the west side of the town, three successive stages of this
rampart could be traced, a second plaster-faced bank, with a steeper

slope but a less solid plaster facing, and a third bank, of which the plaster facing does not survive, but which provides the best evidence of the revetting wall at the foot of the bank (Pl. 31). This wall was based on bed-rock, and the rock outside had been stripped of all earlier deposits, but there was no trace of the ditch which had been presumed to exist. This final revetting wall is the most impressive surviving fragment of the defences of Jericho at any period, but one must remember that it formed a comparatively minor element in the whole defensive system. It is, however, the element in the system which has been traced over the widest area. The plaster facing of the original bank has been traced on the north, west and south sides of the tell, but the final revetting wall was traced, by the Austro-German expedition of 1907-09, curving round at the north end to the east of the present road, and at the south end extending as far as the line of this road. From this it would appear that there was an appreciable extension of the town to the east in the second stage of the Middle Bronze Age, and there is confirmation that this was so in the excavations of Area H (plan, Fig. 3). The earlier M.B. town wall had run along the extreme eastern edge of the excavated area. After the abolition of the latest stage of this wall, there are a series of subsequent building levels that cross its top and are truncated by the modern road to the east; they must therefore have run up to a town wall appreciably farther out. This eastern side of the rampart was therefore clear of the town mound, and did not, as elsewhere in its circuit, crown a pre-existing slope. It must therefore have formed a free-standing bank on flat ground, a point which is of importance in relation to similar defences elsewhere. This extension of the defences to the east was presumably intended to enclose the source of the spring, though how the water would be conducted through the ramparts without its channel providing a point very vulnerable to attack is a problem on which we have no evidence.

Most of the material in the bank is derived from earlier deposits, together with a not very enlightening collection of M.B. sherds. The material from the successive levels in Site H, with the sharp differentiation between those contemporary with the earlier lines of the wall and those passing over their top and running out to the vanished line to the east, will, however, provide strong evidence for the period at which the new type of defence was built, when it has been worked over in detail. A first impression would suggest that the new developments came somewhere about the end of phase iii, but this is not a final verdict.

This type of defence is widespread in Palestine in the Middle Bronze Age. The best parallel to Jericho comes from Tell Duweir. Here there was a very similar rampart containing material derived from earlier levels, faced by a smooth hard plaster slope (Pl. 32) and probably[1] revetted at its foot by a massive wall. Outside was what is known as the Fosse, but it is not an effective ditch forming part of the defences, for it is flat-bottomed, with the outer edge only a metre high; rather was it a cutting into the slope of the rock in order to give a steeper slope to the inner side. The Duweir evidence points to approximately the same date as Jericho. Sealed beneath the plaster surface were rock-cut tombs belonging to phase iii, which provide a *terminus post* for the construction of the bank, and débris containing 16th-century pottery that accumulated in the Fosse indicates that the defences had ceased to be kept in repair by that date.

A very similar plastered bank has been found at Tell Jeriseh, where the constructional methods are similar to those of Jericho.[2] A similar type of defence is found at Tell Ajjul,[3] where it makes an impressive sweep round the great mound, and at Tell Fara,[4]

---

[1] It is probable that the whole of the fill in *Lachish*, IV, Pl. 96, from 6 feet in fact represents the M.B. bank, for in *ibid.*, Fig. 4, it is clear that from that level upwards there is an appreciable quantity of M.B. material, mixed with earlier sherds from derived deposits. From the section it also appears very probable that the great revetment is the equivalent of the revetment at Jericho, for though the line was used in the Iron Age it is clear from the account in *Lachish*, III, p. 89, that there must have been patching of an earlier line. The pocket behind this wall in the section may represent an earlier stage, as at Jericho.

[2] *Q.D.A.P.*, X.   [3] *Ancient Gaza*, I, p. 11.   [4] *Beth-pelet*, I, p. 16.

though in both cases a ditch seems to form part of the system. Both at Tell Beit Mirsim at a late stage in Stratum E,[1] and at Megiddo in Stratum X, there were ramparts of *terre pisée* at the base of the town wall, though their surviving remains were perhaps not so impressive as those already described.

The most impressive site of all to be surrounded by this type of defence is the one most recently excavated, Hazor. Here a great rectangular area of *c.* 183 acres was enclosed by a bank, and, where the external slopes did not render it unnecessary, a ditch[2] (Pl. 33). It would appear that this great site was first occupied in M.B. II, though it is possible that there may be an earlier nucleus beneath the restricted area, the tell, in the south-west corner, to which Iron Age occupation was confined.[3] The full evidence is not yet published, but it would seem probable that a major settlement was only established at Hazor at the time at which this new type of defence was introduced. The material so far published would agree with a dating of about phase iii.

Such an entirely new system of defence must certainly have been introduced from outside. It must also reflect new conditions of warfare, for it is axiomatic in military history that new systems of defence are the sequel to the appearance of new methods of attack. It does not seem possible to identify these new methods of attack either as chariot warfare, for there is no satisfactory evidence of the use of chariots in this area until the time of the Eighteenth Dynasty, or of the use of archery, for bronze arrowheads are not found in Palestine until the Late Bronze Age. The most probable explanation is that the bank was intended to impede the use of battering rams, which it would be almost impossible to drag up the steep and slippery slope to reach the town wall, or to operate them when standing on such a slope.

It must, however, be strongly emphasised that though the system of defences was new, the life in the towns within them continued unbroken. As will be seen, there was no break in culture. The type of defensive system was something which was superimposed on the other elements of town life.

[1] *A.S.O.R.*, XVII, pp. 27 ff.   [2] *Hazor*, I, p. 75.
[3] At an early stage in MB II, occupation was confined to the tell, with only tombs in the area to the north.

The clue to the problem lies in the fact that this type of defence is not confined to Palestine. To the south, at Tell el Yahudiyeh, a little south of Cairo, a great plaster-faced sand bank, still 41 feet high, surrounds an area of more than 23 acres, the bank here standing up from the level of the surrounding country like the walls of a Romano-British town. To the north, the ancient tell of Qatna, east of Homs, was surrounded, at a distance of *c.* 400 metres on three sides and 600 metres on the fourth from the foot of the tell, by a similar great free-standing, plaster-faced bank, here associated with a fine inturned entrance with the passage divided by three piers. At each of these places the defences are associated with pottery native to the area. The same types of defence can be traced even farther north, at places like Carchemish. It would seem that the method of defence came south to Palestine and Egypt, and we may with some certainty ascribe its intro-duction to the Hyksos, who secured control over northern Egypt *c.* 1730 B.C.[1]

The best explanation of the Egyptian word Hyksos is "rulers of foreign lands," and therefore it is of no help to identify them, though other Egyptian references make it clear that they were Asiatics. The majority of the names identifiable on Hyksos scarabs are Semitic, but there are a number which are not, and the Hyksos must therefore include other ethnic elements as well. Now in Asia in the first half of the second millennium B.C. we have literary and linguistic evidence of a number of groups of people on the move. In the first place there are the Hurri, who seem to have established themselves on the middle Euphrates at the beginning of the millennium, and groups of whom certainly reached the Syrian coast and Palestine in the following centuries. At the period of the Amarna letters, the first half of the 14th century B.C., a number of the chiefs in Palestine bore Hurrian names, and such names are even found in Egypt during the period of the Eighteenth Dynasty. It is therefore now clear that an important new group of people, probably of Indo-European origin, gained control of a key area in the Fertile Crescent at the beginning of the millennium, no doubt thereby causing a

---

[1] For full description, see *Amorites and Canaanites*, pp. 65–72.

considerable upheaval and setting other groups in motion, while bands of this people penetrated farther afield and probably established an alien military aristocracy in a number of towns on the Syrian and Palestinian coast.

At the same time we find mention of other alien groups designated as the Ḥabiru. Unlike the Ḥurri, the Ḥabiru, in the opinion of most scholars, cannot be recognised as an ethnic group, since no characteristic names can be associated with them. Nor can they be recognised as following some definite occupation, for sometimes they are apparently professional soldiers, sometimes they are labourers, and sometimes slaves. The only common characteristic is that they are foreigners, and the best explanation would appear to be that they were bands of adventurers and soldiers of fortune, who in times or areas of unrest would appear as raiders of defenceless towns, in times of warfare between strong states would enlist as mercenaries, and in times of peace and strong government might have to sell their services as labourers or slaves. Such groups might be recruited from various sources: from among displaced persons, such as must have been put on the move by the establishment of the Ḥurrian kingdom; from bands of adventurers seeking to conquer new territories, such as the Ḥurrians themselves; from outlaws evicted from their native cities; and above all from that reservoir of groups seeking a richer country, the Semitic Beduin of the Arabian Desert. Such groups would therefore be of mixed origin, though in any one band there might well be a predominance of one ethnic group, or even homogeneity. Such an explanation accords well with what we know of the Ḥabiru. The majority seem to bear Semitic names, for the Arabian Desert would certainly be the best recruiting ground, but a percentage of the names is non-Semitic, including even Egyptian. The wanderings and settlings of the Ḥabiru were principally in Semitic countries, and therefore they adopted a predominantly Semitic culture. Such an explanation again fits the description of Abraham as a Hebrew (to the equation of Hebrew and Ḥabiru and the Egyptian 'Apiru there is no philological objection) for he is clearly a soldier of fortune and a

wanderer, and the general story of the Patriarchs and the area
covered by their wanderings is similar to what we know of the
Ḥabiru.[1]

Therefore at the period at which the Hyksos appear in Palestine
and Egypt, we have on the move groups of Ḥurrians and Ḥabiru,
and the most probable explanation of the Hyksos is that they were
recruited from such bands, and formed a group welded into
sufficient cohesion to establish themselves as overlords in these
countries.

As regards Palestine, the effect is clear. Strong rule and efficient
means of warfare, together with the control of the riches of
Egypt, brought prosperity. New ethnic elements were established,
as shown by the Ḥurrian names of some rulers in the succeeding period, in a previously almost pure Semitic area. But the
basic culture of the country remained that established in the
preceding period, as is so often the case with the superimposition
of a ruling aristocracy rather than a complete emigration of
peoples.

In addition to the groups reaching Palestine with the initial
invasions, other alien groups no doubt settled there on the
expulsion of the Hyksos from Egypt, for the Egyptians drove
them back across Sinai, but did not systematically pursue them
beyond southern Palestine, and the expelled groups must have
been left to secure for themselves homes among the allied groups
who had settled there earlier and among the pre-existing population. If this interpretation is correct, we thus have by the 16th
century B.C. a population in Palestine which is basically Semitic,
and of which the Semitic characteristics show a great power of
survival and of absorption of other elements, with superimposed
on it a number of other groups, some Semitic, some Ḥurrian and
some as yet unidentified, while some of the newcomers had

[1] Proponents of another school of thought claim that the Ḥabiru did constitute a true ethnic group, and that the reason that non-Semitic names are
found among them is that some Ḥabiru adopted the names of the peoples among
whom they settled. Moreover, other schools are not satisfied that Ḥabiru and
Hebrew are equivalent. There are in fact many uncertainties, but the foregoing
explanation appears to be the most satisfactory.

settled direct in Palestine, and others had been in Egypt for a period, and no doubt had acquired elements of Egyptian culture and habits. But some of the Ḥabiru undoubtedly remained in Egypt, where they are recorded as late as the Twentieth Dynasty. On the other hand, others, still nomadic, continued to arrive from the north to a later period, for the Ḥabiru who constitute the menace of the Amarna age represent later groups of similar characteristics and possibly similar mixed origins.

As has already been mentioned, the culture of Palestine remained basically the same. Of this, the pottery provides undoubted evidence. There are no intrusive elements, and the descendants of the types introduced at the beginning of M.B. I continue throughout. The finish of some types is less good, and there is a tendency for well-burnished vessels to disappear, but this is the usual course of typological development. Domestic architecture and building methods remain much the same. At Tell Beit Mirsim in Stratum D (Fig. 44), the final M.B. level, there is a suggestion of rather less prosperity and increasing congestion, for the layout of the town is more cramped and the majority of the houses smaller. There appears, however, to be one house on a very much larger scale than the rest. This suggests that some families were enriching themselves at the expense of the general population. This house, in the upper right centre of the plan, consisted of a large courtyard, into which a wide doorway opened, with, in the centre of it, a basin. Obviously livestock was brought into the courtyard. Along one side was a row of rooms. There is clear evidence that these had an upper storey, which provided the living-rooms, while the lower ones served as store-rooms and possibly stables. In one were in fact found large numbers of the storage jars typical of the period. In the débris above these rooms were found a number of objects fallen from the upper storey. The most interesting is the lower portion of a stela of a serpent-goddess (Pl. 34B). The stela had a rounded back, and must have stood in a niche in an upper room. Light is also thrown on the life of the period by the find of the inlay from a gaming board and a set of playing pieces (Pl. 34A). The game, which was

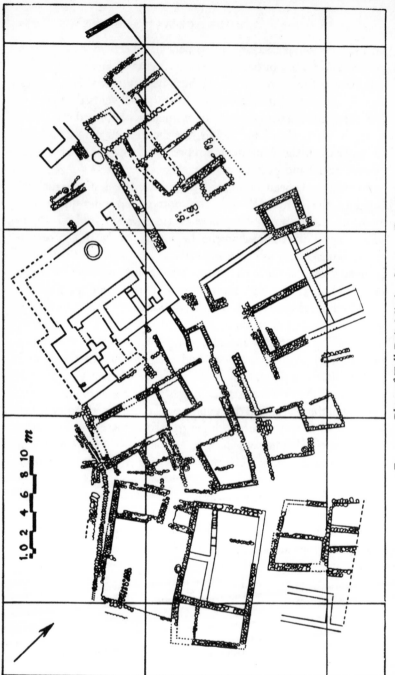

FIG. 44 Plan of Tell Beit Mirsim Stratum D

apparently Mesopotamian in origin, but was widespread in the
Orient, was played on a board of three rows, of which the top
and bottom were of four squares and the centre of twelve squares.
One side played with conical and the other with pyramidal pieces
of blue faience. The teetotum or die is numbered from one to
four.

At Jericho a considerable portion of the plan of the final Middle
Bronze Age town has been recovered (Fig. 45). This plan represents the last of several building stages which followed the
construction of the new-style defences farther to the east. Two
streets running up the steep slope of the mound have been traced.
They are about 6 feet 6 inches wide, and climb the mound in a
succession of wide cobbled steps (Pl. 35). Beneath them are well-
built drains (Pl. 36A). On to the streets open a series of closely
packed houses with small rooms.[1] Many of the features of streets
and houses recall those of eastern towns today. The ground-floor
rooms seem mainly to have been shops and stores. The shops are
single-room booths, not connecting with the rest of the building.
In many of the stores, belonging either to private houses or to
the shops, were found rows of jars full of grain, carbonised in the
fire that destroyed the town. This fire caused the collapse into the
ground-floor rooms of the upper-storey rooms and their contents.
These rooms no doubt, as today, provided the living accommoda-
tion. But they seemed to have served for industrial purposes too.
Great quantities of clay loom-weights were found, suggesting
that weaving had been carried out. In one area, fifty-two saddle-
querns and many rubbing stones were found, a number in excess
of the requirements of a private house, indicating that a corn-
milling business may have been carried on there; to this business
perhaps belonged the supply of grain in the ground-floor room
(Pl. 36B).

Buildings destroyed by fire, such as these, offer particularly

---

[1] Those on the left-hand side of the plan (Fig. 45) were excavated during
the 1930–36 excavations, and were called the Palace Store-rooms. Further
investigation has shown that they were not associated with the so-called
Palace, and were ordinary private houses.

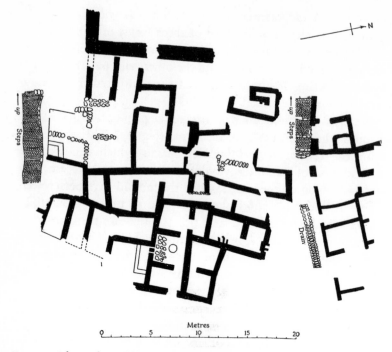

FIG. 45 Plan of Middle Bronze II houses on east slope of tell at
Jericho

favourable opportunities to archaeologists, as usually all the
contents of the houses are left in the débris. But many of the
details of the equipment of the houses are missing owing to the
limitation of archaeology, which can only concern itself with
those material remains which have survived. All evidence of
everything made of organic matter has disappeared. Thus from
the excavation of this town site we can recover no evidence of
the wooden furniture, the bedding, clothing and food. There is
fortunately at Jericho another source of information in the finds
in the tombs.

There seems to have been some considerable diversity of burial
practice, for at Tell Ajjul and Megiddo many burials were
certainly in graves containing a single body, dug on the tell. At

Megiddo, at least, it does not seem possible that unoccupied parts of the town area were used for burials. The pottery sequence seems to run right through the Middle Bronze, and during that period there are at least five building periods. The graves must therefore have been adjacent to or even underneath the houses. A few of the burials on the tell at Megiddo are in built tombs instead of single graves. These built tombs were obviously to enable successive burials to be made, the tomb being reopened each time; it is probably not the case that these tombs are structurally part of the houses, for in most cases they are not built in connection with the house within which they are situated but break through it.

The practice of communal burial is the one more generally found, for instance at Tell Fara, Tell Duweir, Tell el Far‘ah and Jericho. The tombs at Jericho are particularly well preserved, both structurally and in the contents, and may be taken as examples of the procedure. The tombs are cut into the soft rock of the lower slopes of the hills which curve round the west and north sides of the tell. They consist of a vertical shaft with the tomb chamber opening off its base. Many of these used in the Middle Bronze Age in the northern cemetery were originally cut in the E.M.–M.B. period, and were re-used at this stage; it is not clear whether this was the case in the western cemetery, which was excavated by the earlier expedition. With a single exception, the tombs contained multiple burials, but not on the scale of the Proto-Urban Period or Early Bronze Age. Exceptionally they may contain about forty burials, but the average is about twenty. Apparently the tomb shaft was filled after each burial and re-excavated for the next one. Each dead person was put in the tomb with food and equipment for the after-life, as will be described below. The body was placed on its back with limbs untidily disposed, and often with the knees raised. When the next burial was made, the body and offerings belonging to the earlier ones were pushed roughly towards the back and sides of the tomb chamber. As a result, a jumble of bones and offerings became piled up in the rear of the tomb, while the front was kept comparatively clear, and when excavated would be found occupied by the final burial (Pl. 37). From this description, it will be realised that it is impossible to deduce the relative age of objects from their height within the latest deposit in the tomb, as has been done in the past when the objects have been recorded by their height above the floor of the chamber, for the latest deposits are usually the lowest, and the objects in the pile may have slid into any position. Any deductions as to sequence can only be made from a careful study of an accurately made plan of the deposits.

Such tombs can therefore only give an overall impression of the period within which the tomb was used. It is reasonable to deduce that they were family vaults, and therefore that twenty or so deaths would cover a fairly long time, but probably under a century. The dating evidence is therefore valuable, but not very close.

In the mounding process, too, many of the objects were broken, and further damage was caused by roof fall. But at an early stage in the excavations it became clear that the contents were exceptionally interesting, since some preservative property had prevented the complete decay of organic substances, such as wood, textiles and flesh. The cause of this is not yet certain, but apparently some gases had accumulated in the tomb chambers which had killed the organisms of decay before they had completed their work. Decay had begun, and the objects had been rendered very fragile, but their form was preserved. But from this fragility the wooden objects had suffered severely in the mounding process, and in the earlier tombs to be excavated only small objects and tantalising fragments of larger furniture could be recovered.

The full possibilities from the evidence of these tombs did not become apparent until a group of tombs was discovered in which a number of burials had been made simultaneously and not subsequently disturbed. There is little doubt that each represents a family group, with adults, adolescents and children. The bodies were found laid out side by side, with all the supply of food and the general and individual equipment readily identifiable (Pl. 39). From this we can deduce what was considered to be the necessary equipment for a person of Middle Bronze Age Jericho in the after-life, and it is reasonable to suppose that this had been their equipment during life. In these mass burials, the supply of food is communal, with jars of liquid, drinking vessels and platters ranged round the edge of the tomb, and a liberal supply of meat, usually in the form of roasted sheep, either jointed or entire. In the tombs in which only single burials had been made at a time each burial had probably been accompanied by food. With the family groups was placed the family furniture, of which the important item was a long, narrow table, made with two legs at one end and one at the other, in order to stand better on uneven ground. This in fact seems to have been the only universal piece of actual furniture. Most of the dead lay on rush mats, on which they probably slept and sat during life. Only one individual lay on a bed (Pl. 38), probably a man of importance, for he occupied the centre of the tomb, and the members of his family were disposed round the edge. In another tomb were found two stools, again the only examples, and in this tomb too was a burial of someone obviously more important than the rest, placed on a low dais of mud-bricks in the centre of the chamber. It would appear that beds and stools were only found in the houses of richer members of the community.[1] The individual personal adornments were simple. With most of the bodies was a toggle-pin, usually on the left shoulder, showing that the garment was secured there, and most had a scarab, either on a bronze finger ring or suspended round the neck or from the toggle-pin; bead necklaces were rare. In a number of cases there were carved wooden combs by the heads, and in some cases in positions which suggested they had been in plaits; fragments of plaits were actually found. In most tombs a supply of toilet equipment was placed with each adult, consisting of a cylindrical juglet which probably contained oil, and often a basket holding little wooden boxes decorated with bone carvings, an extra supply of combs,

[1] Addenda p. 341.

an alabaster juglet for oil or scent, and in some cases a wig. In only a few exceptionally poor tombs was this provision omitted.

The equipment was therefore simple, and we can presume that the equipment of most of the houses of Jericho at this time was simple. The furniture was skilfully made by good carpenters, but with little adornment. All the details are sufficiently well preserved for the reconstruction of a room in Jericho at this period shown on Pl. 40 to be completely factual, the only exception being the clothes, for only fragments of textile were preserved. The date of the group of tombs which gives this evidence comes at the very end of M.B. II, in phase v, and the finds in them would therefore represent the furniture of the houses of which the destruction marks the end of Middle Bronze Age Jericho. It may be surmised that there was a serious epidemic which swept off whole families at a date so late in the life of the town that the tombs were never reopened for subsequent burials.

It is probable that the picture of Jericho at about 1600 B.C. is reasonably representative of that of many of the towns of Palestine, though the greater ones may have shown more signs of wealth. Jericho certainly was not wealthy. In all the tombs excavated, only one contained any gold, five scarabs being mounted in this material, with, in addition, a simple gold bracelet. At Tell Ajjul there was much greater wealth, with quite a number of gold bracelets, torcs, pendants and toggle-pins coming from this period and the beginning of the following one.

The culture of Middle Bronze Age Palestine was largely individually Palestinian. As we have seen, the people who brought it came from Syria and were mainly Canaanites from the Phoenician coast. By the beginning of M.B. II a distinctively Palestinian version of the culture had grown up, as can be judged from a comparison of the finds with those of Syrian coastal towns such as Ras Shamra; the pottery for instance is related but not identical. With inland Syria the links thereafter were much slighter. There is no doubt an appreciable amount of Egyptian influence. Under the Twelfth Dynasty, Egypt re-established some sort of control over the Syrian coast, as is shown by finds at

Byblos and Ras Shamra. Evidence of this in Palestine is slight, a Twelfth Dynasty funerary statuette at Gezer and a few Twelfth Dynasty scarabs, but it is to be presumed that tribute was demanded from the rulers of at least the more important towns. During the Hyksos rule in Egypt, contacts between the Asiatics there and those who had set up a comparable ruling aristocracy in Palestine were probably fairly numerous. Trade and economic contacts no doubt existed, for we learn of this both from Egyptian documents, including the famous Beni Hassan paintings showing Asiatics coming to Egypt, and also from Egyptian influence on local artifacts. The scarab is in origin Egyptian, and a few of Egyptian origin are found in Palestine, but the great majority are of local manufacture, with either simple pattern decoration or else blundered and uncomprehended versions of Egyptian hieroglyphs. The alabaster vessels resemble the Egyptian in form, but they are made out of a local stone. The wooden furniture at Jericho copies Egyptian types, but in a much simplified style. But in all this Palestine was undoubtedly the poor relation. To the mixture the coming of the Hyksos chieftains added little. From the material remains one would never deduce the setting up of a new ruling class, with its alien Hurrian elements, if it were not for the appearance of the new type of fortification.

The picture of Palestine at this time is of especial interest in that it provides the background for the beginning of the biblical story. It is highly probable that the period of the Patriarchs is to be placed in the Middle Bronze Age, and that the Israelites were the descendants of Habiru groups that entered Palestine from northern Syria at this time. The traditional character of the Book of Genesis, built up of long-transmitted oral legend, makes any exact chronology impossible. It has long been suggested that the Amraphel of Genesis is to be identified as Hammurabi of Babylon, whose reign is now dated c. 1792–1750 B.C.,[1] but too much reliance cannot be placed on this. From the evidence of their customs and laws, it is clear that the groups in question had been

---

[1] S. Smith, *Alalakh and Chronology*. Other scholars hold divergent views as to the exact dates, but nearly all agree as to the general period.

in contact with the Ḥurrians, for similar customs appear in the Mari documents of about 1700 B.C. It is certain that one cannot build up a chronology on the spans of years attributed to the Patriarchs, nor regard it as factual that Abraham was seventy-five years old when he left Harran and a hundred when Isaac was born, or that Isaac was sixty when Jacob was born and that Jacob was a hundred and thirty when he went into Egypt, for the evidence from the skeletons in the Jericho tombs shows that the expectation of life at this period was short. Many individuals seem to have died before they were thirty-five, and few seem to have reached the age of fifty. The biblical figures only reflect the veneration felt for the tribal ancestors, to whom tradition came to ascribe great years and wisdom.

But though an exact chronology is impossible, the setting of the period reflects that recorded in the biblical story. The Patriarchs were semi-nomadic pastoralists, moving into the more fertile coastlands, and living in their tents among, but separate from, the Canaanites living in the towns of the type which archaeology reveals. Pastoralists in their tents leave no evidence which archaeology can recover, but we now know something of their surroundings.

A convenient date for the end of the Middle Bronze Age is the rise of the Eighteenth Dynasty in Egypt in 1580 B.C.,[1] when Egypt drove back the Asiatics and began to recover her control over Syria. Punitive campaigns driving back the Hyksos into Palestine are recorded in Egyptian documents. Both Tell Beit Mirsim and Jericho were violently destroyed at about this time, probably by such campaigns, and were not reoccupied for many years. Other towns, such as Megiddo, were destroyed, but occupation is immediately resumed. This revived occupation exhibits the same character as the preceding. New foreign elements may have arrived with the mixed Asiatics driven out of Egypt, but there is little material evidence of this. Canaanite culture continues into Late Bronze Age Palestine.

[1] In the chronology compiled in the revised edition of the Barnbridge Ancient History, the date is 1567 B.C.

★

CHAPTER EIGHT

The Late Bronze Age and the Coming of the Israelites

IN ABOUT 1580 B.C. the one hundred and fifty years of domination of Egypt by the Asiatic Hyksos came to an end with their expulsion by the first kings of the Eighteenth Dynasty. This event had a twofold repercussion on Palestine. In the first place, the expelled groups were thrown back on Palestine. Some, or even the majority, must have settled there. In so doing they would add to the mixed racial elements which probably settled there in the preceding period. One would have expected them to have brought a considerable amount of Egyptian culture, for just as in Palestine the invaders, as we have seen, adopted the native Semitic culture, so in Egypt they became to a large extent Egyptianised; but of this there is no great archaeological evidence. Secondly, the Egyptian rulers proceeded to reassert their empire over Palestine and Syria. This probably did not amount to more than punitive campaigns, and did not, any more than under the Twelfth Dynasty, imply a close political control. Archaeology does, however, provide two types of evidence for the new state of affairs, that of the destruction of cities which may reasonably be ascribed to Egyptian campaigns, and the evidence of trade contacts showing the increased connections between Palestine and the rest of the eastern Mediterranean.

There is no direct evidence to show how quickly Egyptian authority in Palestine was reasserted. There may have been a series of campaigns over a period of twenty years or so. A number of Palestinian sites show a break which must, from the pottery

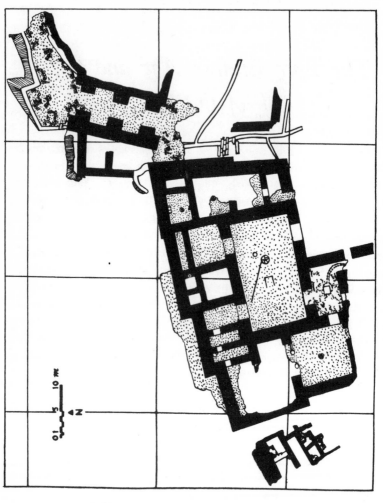

FIG. 46 Plan of Megiddo Area AA Stratum VIII

196

chronology, fall within the period 1600–1550 B.C., and which may reasonably be ascribed to conquest by an Egyptian army. At Megiddo Stratum X is succeeded by Stratum IX within this period. Here there is no interruption in the life of the city, and no catastrophic destruction. In the comparatively small parts of the tell excavated to this level, the majority of the houses were rebuilt, but as modifications of those of Stratum X and not on completely new lines. Interesting evidence of the continuity of culture is provided by the city gate (Fig. 46).[1] This consisted of a long passage divided by three pairs of buttresses, between which were presumably gates. This plan was probably a rebuilding of that of Stratum X, though the latter was too badly destroyed for certainty, and is one found on other Palestinian sites in the Middle Bronze Age, for instance Tell Beit Mirsim, Shechem and Tell Fara, and also at Qatna in Syria. The building near the gateway is a stage in the development of the three houses, which existed here from early in the Middle Bronze Age, into something in the nature of a palace, belonging to Stratum VIII.

The fate of two other sites, Tell Beit Mirsim and Jericho, was different. Both were destroyed, and neither was reoccupied for an appreciable period. At the former site the remains of Stratum D were found to be covered by a layer of ashes, and the succeeding town C was laid out on new lines and a changed orientation. The new town can be dated to about the middle of the 15th century B.C., that is to say, there was a break in occupation of about a hundred years.

At Jericho, the evidence for the destruction is even more dramatic. All the Middle Bronze Age buildings were violently destroyed by fire. The stumps of the walls are buried in the débris collapsed from the upper storeys, and the faces of these stumps and the floors of the rooms are strongly scorched by fire. This destruction covers the whole area, about 52 metres by 22 metres, in which the buildings of this period surviving subsequent denudation have been excavated. That the destruction extended right up the slopes of the mound is shown by the fact that the tops of the wall-stumps are covered by a layer about a metre

[1] Addenda p. 341.

thick of washed débris, coloured brown, black and red by the burnt material it contains; this material is clearly derived from burnt buildings farther up the mound. Such a layer represents a long period of erosion, and is typical of the fate of the mound when it was not occupied; material from the ruins on the surface is gradually carried down to the foot of the mound by violent winter rain-storms, after it has been made dry and crumbly by the heat of summer.

The stratigraphical evidence suggests in itself that there was a gap in occupation at Jericho. This is confirmed by a gap in the use of the tombs. Burials cease in all the tombs in the northern cemetery at the end of the Middle Bronze Age. There is a similar break in those in the western cemetery. But in the latter area, five were found to contain deposits belonging to the Late Bronze Age. At the time of their excavation, the pottery of the 16th and 15th centuries B.C. in Palestine was not well known, and it was not realised that this was missing both in the tombs and on the tell.[1] Moreover, the stratification of the tombs was not understood. The process by which earlier deposits were mounded up round the edge, described above, resulted in Middle Bronze Age objects being on the same absolute level as those of the Late Bronze Age inserted in front. Therefore the layers seemed to show an actual intermingling of and transition between the characteristic pottery forms of the two periods. When the material is analysed in the light of our present knowledge, it becomes clear that there is a complete gap both on the tell and in the tombs between c. 1580 B.C. and c. 1400 B.C.[1] [2]

There was thus considerable dislocation of life in Palestine in the period following the end of Hyksos domination. Conditions are likely to have remained disturbed until the period of more intensive Egyptian control under Thotmes III after his campaign in 1479 B.C. Owing to the fact that some of the more thoroughly excavated sites have a gap at this period, our information is somewhat scanty. The chronology of the pottery depends almost entirely on Megiddo, since there alone is an uninterrupted

[1] *P.E.Q.*, 1951.   [2] Addenda p. 341.

FIG. 47 Pottery of the sixteenth century B.C. from Megiddo. ⅕

sequence, but with the framework provided by that site as a guide, evidence from other sites can be fitted in. It may be taken as typical of the half-century 1550–1500 B.C. in which there was a transition from Middle to Late Bronze Age pottery.

The pottery does in fact provide very useful evidence about culture. The first interesting point is the wealth of a particular class of painted pottery (Fig. 47). The decoration is bichrome, nearly always red and black, and the most typical vessels have a combination of metopes enclosing a bird or a fish with geometric decoration such as a "Union Jack" pattern or a Catherine wheel. At Megiddo the first bichrome pottery is attributed to Stratum X, but all the published material comes from tombs intrusive into that level. It is in fact characteristic of Stratum IX. Similar pottery is found in great profusion in southern Palestine, and has even been ascribed to an individual potter working at Tell Ajjul. It may be too much to suggest that an individual potter was responsible for all the vessels found, but they may at least be ascribed to a well-pronounced school of potting. Very similar vessels are also found on the east coast of Cyprus and on coastal Syrian sites as far north as Ras Shamra.

The particular style referred to may be the product of a Palestinian school, but it is part of a larger complex of painted pottery, which started to reach Palestine in the 16th century B.C. It has certain affinities in style to Ḥurrian decorated pottery, and may be taken as evidence for renewed northern contacts, and probably the continuance of the infiltration of new groups from that direction.[1]

The second point of interest suggested by the pottery is the evidence for the opening up of the Syrian coast to trade with the eastern Mediterranean. At first this trade was almost entirely with Cyprus. Cypriot imports during the Middle Bronze Age are rare, though they begin to appear towards the end of the period. But in the transitional period covered by Megiddo IX, they become much more numerous, until during the Late Bronze Age almost as much pottery of Cypriot connections is found as that in the native tradition. As described above, there was also

---

[1] A recent study of this pottery has been made by C. Epstein in *Palestinian Bichrome Ware*.

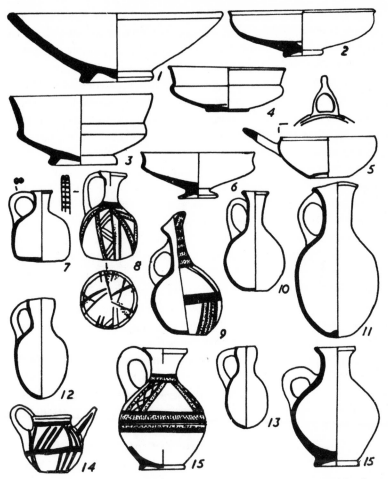

FIG. 48 Pottery of the sixteenth century B.C. from Megiddo. $\frac{1}{5}$

traffic in the reverse direction. It is clear that during the period of the strong rule of the Eighteenth Dynasty in Egypt conditions favoured maritime trade.

The third point of general interest shown by the pottery is that though there were the new elements which have just been described, the basic wares and forms continue throughout with only normal development. There is no break in culture, only the addition of new elements. This is probably a true indication of the racial position. From the period in the 20th century B.C. when the big changes in equipment appear that mark the beginning of the Middle Bronze Age, the basic Semitic Canaanite population, like its pottery, remains the same. New groups are absorbed, new rulers with alien names may establish themselves in the various towns, but the culture remains Canaanite though the race is no longer pure.

The evidence at Megiddo shows that this transition period, represented by Stratum IX, merges without cultural break into full Late Bronze Age I, represented by Stratum VIII, by about 1500 B.C. Politically, the break would come in 1479 B.C., when Thotmes III established effective control in Palestine and set up local governors or client dynasts in the principal towns. Egyptian control lasted until the troubles of the Amarna age a century later, when we find some of these local princes faithful to Egypt and some rebellious. It is probable that Egyptian control was not very close over most of the country. Egypt was interested in Palestine mainly in order to control the route to northern Syria and Mesopotamia. It was therefore important that the greater cities of the coastal plain and the Plain of Esdraelon should be in safe hands, but the smaller towns and those of the upland area were probably allowed to go their own way, with perhaps the payment of some tribute.

Egyptian monuments record the fact that Thotmes III sacked Megiddo about 1479 B.C. (the exact date depending on which system on Egyptian chronology is accepted). This event must be represented by the break between Strata IX and VIII at Megiddo. The succeeding Stratum VIII had two interesting buildings. The first was a building (Fig. 46) on a scale suggesting that it may have been the palace of the local client ruler. It is planned round a series of courtyards, and the thickness of the walls shows that there was more than one storey. Buried beneath the floor of one of the rooms was found a most magnificent treasure hoard of gold, ivory, lapis lazuli and other precious materials. This is a good indication of the wealth of the period, while the art reflects connections both with Egypt and northern Mesopotamia.

The other building of importance excavated was a temple. The preceding periods have produced surprisingly scanty evidence of the religion of the country. But for the period during which the Israelites were settling among the Canaanites, the material evidence for the religion of the latter is accumulating. The Megiddo temple is one of the earliest Late Bronze Age temples known.[1] In plan, it is extremely simple, and in structure very massive. It consisted of one main hall, in the back wall of which was a shallow niche that presumably held the cult object. On either side of the entrance was a small room, which may have served as priests' rooms or store-rooms; on the analogy of later reconstructions of the building the space between may have been a porch with a roof supported on columns. The size of the main hall is such that it is probable that the worshippers were admitted to the presence of the deity, and there is no trace of a Holy of Holies.[2]

The other site which has provided evidence of this early phase of the Late Bronze Age is Tell Duweir. Here the main clearance of the tell has not yet reached the levels of the period, but deposits and buildings belonging to it have been discovered in the Fosse at the base of the great Hyksos rampart. It would appear that after the end of the Middle Bronze Age, the ramparts ceased to be maintained in repair and the Fosse was allowed to fill with débris. This can be interpreted alternatively as a change of fashion in fortification, as a period of peace in which fortifications were not required, or a period of weakness within the city in which it was

[1] It is indeed possible that it takes its origin early in the Middle Bronze Age. It occupies exactly the place of the E.B.–M.B. temple (Fig. 35), which would be a very unlikely coincidence if the earlier sacred area had been left vacant for a matter of some four centuries. In the succeeding plans of Strata XIII to IX this space is empty of buildings, but it should be noted that the houses to the west are on a new alignment, that of the Stratum VII temple. The explanation probably is that there was a mound over the remains of the earlier temple, and that the high level on which the new temple was built caused it to be wrongly assigned to a later level, into which it may have continued to exist.

[2] Addenda p. 341.

not possible to maintain them; only further excavation can show which explanation is likely to be correct. What is clear, however, is that the site was not abandoned, for the débris contained pottery which is close to the transitional M.B.–L.B. Level IX at Megiddo, including some of the characteristic painted pottery.

This period of silting up of the Fosse, which may not necessarily have been a long one, was followed by the erection in it of a most interesting structure, a small temple, the first of three super-imposed buildings on the same general plan. The exact foundation date is difficult to fix. The archaeological evidence points to approximately 1500 B.C., and it is possible that it should be placed after 1479 B.C., when the restoration of Egyptian control under Thotmes III would provide the peaceful conditions that an extra-mural building like this would seem to require. This is certainly the latest date which the archaeological evidence would allow, and a rather earlier date would be preferable. The temple continued in use down to about 1400 B.C., since a plaque of Amenhotep III was found in the filling between it and the immediately succeeding Temple II.

The temple was simple in plan (Fig. 49), consisting of an oblong sanctuary with two attached rooms, only one of which was entered from the sanctuary. It is notable that there was no inner room, or Holy of Holies, such as was required by the Hebrew religion, and has been found in much earlier Semitic sanctuaries. The roof had been supported on columns, probably of wood, of which the bases were found in position on the central axis. The entrance was screened by a wall which prevented a view into the sanctuary from the outside. The shrine consisted of a low bench, 1 foot high, from the front of which three rectangular blocks projected (Pl. 41). It is suggested that the cult objects stood on the bench, and that the projecting blocks served as altars. The existence of three projections suggests that a trinity of deities was worshipped. On the central axis in front of the shrine were two jars sunk in the floor, which may have been receptacles into which libations were poured, while against one end of the bench was found a great pile of vessels, abandoned when the temple was

UPPER TEMPLE   MIDDLE TEMPLE   LOWEST TEMPLE

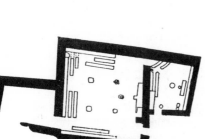

1325 - 1260 B.C.   1420 - 1335 B.C   1480 - 1420 B.C.

SCALE

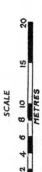

0 2 4 6 8 10   15   20
METRES

FIG. 49 Plans of the three successive temples in the Fosse at Tell Duweir

205

rebuilt, which had presumably served as containers of liquid and solid offerings. Outside the temple was found a number of pits used for the disposal of vessels which had served a similar purpose. There was also a low bench along one wall, which, on the analogy of the more numerous benches found in the later structures, may also have served for the deposit of offerings.

Unfortunately, little evidence was recovered to indicate the deity or deities worshipped in this temple or its successors. A statuette of Reshef, the Syrian god of war and storm, may suggest that he was among those worshipped, while one suggestion for the translation of the inscription on the Duweir Ewer found in Temple III (see below, p. 214) includes the name of the goddess Elath, apparently as part of a triad.

The evidence concerning this phase in the history of Palestine is thus somewhat scanty. The overall picture is one of the continuation of Canaanite culture based on that of the Middle Bronze Age in a number of largely independent towns, probably exhibiting considerable diversity of culture and organisation. Such diversity is suggested, for instance, by the differences between the temple at Megiddo and that at Tell Duweir.

During the 14th century B.C. the second phase of the Late Bronze Age begins. For this we have a considerable amount of both historical and archaeological evidence, but difficulties arise in the reconciliation of the two types of evidence.

Historically there are two important groups of events that fall within this period, the disturbances caused by the Ḥabiru recorded in the Amarna Letters, and the settlement in Palestine of the Israelite tribes recorded in the Old Testament. The period covered by the Amarna Letters is between c. 1390 and 1365 B.C. That of the Israelite settlement is a source of wide disagreement between authorities, but all except a very small minority would agree that it falls between 1400 and 1200 B.C.

The Amarna Letters are a series of documents discovered at the site of Tell-el-Amarna, in the Nile Delta, in the palace of the Pharaoh Akhenaten. They provide contemporary evidence for the break-up of the Asiatic empire re-established by Thotmes III.

The Amorite cities of northern Syria were in revolt, largely instigated by the Hittites, and their example was followed by the Canaanite cities of the south. Either as cause or effect, among the revolting cities appear bands of Ḫabiru, a name which, as suggested above (pp. 182 ff.), probably in its broadest sense covers bands of wandering warriors of somewhat mixed origin, who might be expected to take advantage of times of trouble, and who would also stimulate such trouble. The letters are written by the rulers of those towns which remained faithful to Egypt, notably Jerusalem in the case of Palestine, asking for help against the rebels and invaders. As has already been mentioned, it is an interesting reflection of the racial elements which had settled in Palestine in the preceding centuries that some of these rulers have Ḫurrian names. The help was not forthcoming, and Egyptian control of Palestine was not re-established until early in the reign of Seti I (1320–1301 B.C.), though the Hittites, who took advantage of this weakness in the north, did not advance south of Galilee.

The well-known biblical account describes the arrival of the Israelites in Palestine after a period of sojourn in Egypt, and as effecting an entry from the east, with an expansion from the Jordan Valley into the hill country. In both accounts Jerusalem is described as resisting the invaders.

The events recorded under the two headings have much in common, representing as they do the invasion of nomadic or semi-nomadic tribes amongst the settled Canaanite population. Opinions differ as to the extent to which the two accounts may be held to be of the same events from different points of view, that of the invaders and that of the invaded. Not all linguistic scholars are prepared to accept the equivalence of the words Hebrew and Ḫabiru, though the majority do. In any case, neither the Amarna Letters nor other Egyptian sources give any hint of the events recorded in Exodus. The event of the Exodus was of such primary importance in Hebrew history, and the divine assistance of which it was held to be evidence was such a basic concept in the development of Yahwehism, that its historical basis must be accepted, particularly in view of recent evidence as to the possibility of written records at a much earlier date than used to be supposed.

It is, however, generally accepted by scholars that the Old Testament account is a conflation of different ancient sources. A theory that has gained acceptance from a number of scholars is that there is evidence in the biblical account that not all the tribes which made up the subsequent Israelite nation took part in the Exodus. This school of thought holds that the religious significance of the Exodus was such that in course of time all the tribes came to believe that their ancestors took part in it. Such a theory has many attractions, particularly since it goes far to reconciling the biblical account with the other historical records and with the archaeological evidence.

This book is not, however, the place to discuss in detail this or any other theory, nor the chronological framework which can be evolved to fit any of them, since it is concerned primarily with the evidence produced by archaeology. It may, nevertheless, be remarked that to the writer it seems to be a waste of time to attempt to produce a chronology covering a period of several hundred years by adding up the different spans of forty or thirty years mentioned in the Bible. This is only too well shown by the fact that by different combinations of overlaps, omissions and reduplications it is possible to arrive at varying results which fit the very varying theories of different writers. It must surely be obvious on the one hand that such spans are largely conventional expressions for the passage of an appreciable period of time, and on the other that the length of folk memory, though it may be reasonably accurate as to the occurrence of important events, is short as regards chronological exactitude. In the absence of a fixed calendar (and there is no evidence that the Israelites made use of the Egyptian calendar) a man would remember that an event took place in the lifetime of his father, or even his grandfather, but it is very unlikely that he would be sure that it took place in that of his great-grandfather or alternatively of his great-great-grandfather.

The purpose here, therefore, is to describe the archaeological evidence. It must, however, be recognised that it is only on certain aspects that this evidence is likely to be informative. The chief aspect is that it is to be presumed that the Israelite capture of a town is likely to be marked by a destruction. But it is not clear that such a destruction would be followed by a change in culture. Migratory bands, whether of the Ḥabiru of the Amarna Letters or of the Israelites of the Old Testament story, would be most unlikely to have a large equipment of durable material objects. Their containers may well have been mainly of skin, they would lack house furnishings or ornaments, their places of worship would have been temporary and with little in the way of fitments. History and archaeology show again and again how such bands, coming amongst a settled population, tend to adopt the material culture (which alone is reflected archaeologically) of that population. This must be the case wherever within the period 1400 to 1200 B.C. one puts the arrival of the Israelites, for there is no complete break within the period. It is in fact at the beginning that the biggest change occurs, with the transition from L.B. I to II, when the culture does seem to show a marked deterioration. In the pottery, for instance, there is the introduction of a class of saucer bowls of a very plain and undeveloped form, which form one of the least attractive series in the whole of Palestinian pottery. The archaeological remains are undistinguished and the objects found suggest a low level of artistic ability. Such a situation would well reflect the state of affairs during the acclimatisation to settled life of wanderers such as the Ḥabiru bands of the Amarna Letters and the Israelites of the Old Testament. It is not, however, possible to deduce on the existing evidence any spread of conquest or, on grounds of material remains, to say that at any one time a certain district fell under the control of invaders.

Evidence for destruction does exist, but it does not yet tell a coherent story. Of all the captures of towns by the Israelites, that of Jericho is the most dramatic. It is difficult to avoid the impression that it is the record, committed to writing perhaps after very many years, of a folk memory of an important event. The capture of Jericho might certainly be expected to come early in any penetration into Palestine from the east, owing to its strategic position, to which reference has already been made (p. 104). Archaeological evidence as to the date of the fall of Bronze Age Jericho would therefore be very valuable in establishing the chronology of the Israelite entry into Palestine.

Unfortunately, the archaeological evidence is most inadequate. Above the denudation level covering the Middle Bronze Age only fragments of buildings survive. The "Middle Building" excavated by Professor Garstang,[1] and a very small portion of a house excavated in Square H III in 1954, are the only ones that can be ascribed to this period. From the Middle Building itself no actual dating evidence is published, but some Late Bronze Age pottery, probably of mid-14th century date,[2] came from beneath it The fragment of building in Square H III consisted only of the foundations of a single wall with about a square metre of intact floor beside it; on the floor was a small clay oven with a juglet lying beside it (Pl. 42). Over the rest of the area of Square H III, the modern surface was usually lower than the level of this floor. This seemed to be the case everywhere in the neighbourhood. A further area was cleared to the north in the hopes of finding more buildings, but here great rain-water gulleys were found cutting right down into the Middle Bronze levels, filled by débris of the Early Iron II occupation.

It had been believed in the earlier excavations that the defensive walls of the Late Bronze Age town had been discovered, and that they had been destroyed by earthquake and fire.[3] It became clear in the course of the recent excavations that these walls had been mistakenly identified. They actually belonged to the Early Bronze Age, and had without any doubt been buried beneath the Middle Bronze bank, which had not been recognised. In point of fact, only at one point docs the full height of the Middle Bronze Age defences survive, on the surface of the highest existing point of the tell in the north-west corner. Elsewhere erosion has gone far below the Middle Bronze Age level except on the lower slopes of the eastern side of the tell; here only these

[1] L.A.A.A., XXI, pp. 105 ff. and Pl. XIV.
[2] P.E.Q., 1951.   [3] P.E.Q., 1931.

miserable fragments of the Late Bronze Age houses described above survive.

They do at least show that a town of that period had existed. The dating evidence from the recent excavations is negligible. All one can say is that the single juglet is probably 14th century in date. The earlier excavations did produce a certain amount of pottery, and an analysis of this and of the finds in the tombs which were re-used in this period suggests that the town was reoccupied in about 1400 B.C., and abandoned again about 1325 B.C.[1] Subsequently erosion removed nearly all trace of it. Such erosion during a period of abandonment was proved for the period after the destruction of the Middle Bronze town, and the biblical account says that Jericho was cursed and abandoned for a period of some four hundred years. The filling up of the rain-water gulleys in the Early Iron Age shows that the erosion had taken place before that date. The find of the little oven still *in situ* suggests an abandonment, for such a structure would ordinarily have been levelled over in any rebuilding. The evidence thus accords with a destruction of the site and subsequent abandonment, and suggests a date in the second half of the 14th century.

Jericho thus provides possible evidence of one episode in the establishment of the Hebrew population in Palestine, the elements of which were eventually combined into the Israelite kingdom. But it has already been suggested that both the component parts of this population and the accounts combined in the Old Testament may have had different origins. It is not therefore necessary to try to reconcile the course of events described in that source with the archaeological evidence, and it is in fact very difficult to do so. When one realises that a strong kingdom was not established until about 1000 B.C., some four hundred years after the date proposed by those who believe in an early date for the Exodus and two hundred and fifty years after even the later date proposed by others, it is clear that the process of spread and of organisation into a nation was a very slow one. The biblical account may record events spread over a comparatively long

[1] *P.E.Q.*, 1951.

period, combined and adjusted by editors into a chronological sequence of which the authenticity is difficult to test, in view of the limitation of archaeological evidence pointed out above. One can thus at present only describe the course of events at different sites as revealed by archaeology, while for the present the part played in them by the Hebrews must often remain uncertain.

One of the other sites which, according to the Book of Joshua (Joshua xi. 10), fell to Joshua at an early stage in the campaign was Hazor, the mightiest of the Canaanite towns. The excavations at that site are still (1959) in progress, and only preliminary reports have appeared. The finds show that it was indeed a mighty city, protected by the great rampart erected in M.B. II (p. 33). Occupation there seems to have been continuous on into the Late Bronze Age, and to have lasted at least into the beginning of the 13th century. As far as the evidence so far available shows, the pottery certainly seems to include somewhat later material than that of Jericho. This would agree with a more gradual spread of Israelite power, as is indeed suggested by the other account of the early stages of the entry given in the Book of Judges (Judges iv. 2).[1]

One of the sites referred to in the biblical account of the early stages of the conquest is Bethel. Excavations here have shown that there was a flourishing Late Bronze Age city, with exceptionally well-built houses, which could be divided into two phases separated by a layer of débris. The earlier phase is dated to the 15th–14th centuries, and the later to the 14th–early 13th. Between the two comes a destruction which is evidence of the disturbed condition of the country, but there is no drastic break in culture. The second phase, however, was brought to an end by a terrific conflagration, leaving a deposit of as much as a metre and a half of débris, which is followed apparently after a chronological break by an occupation of a much poorer sort. Professor Albright ascribes this destruction to the work of the Israelites.

Tell Beit Mirsim, in southern Palestine, of which the abandonment at the end of the Middle Bronze Age is described above, was apparently reoccupied about 1450 B.C. Here again the Late

[1] Addenda p. 342.

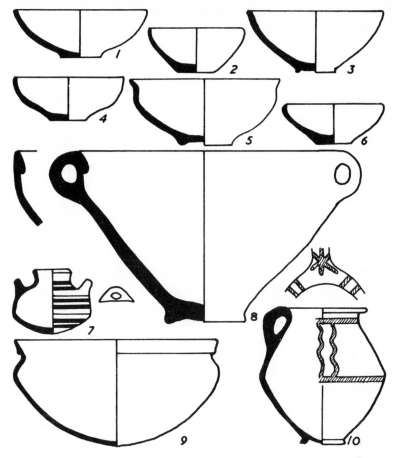

FIG. 50   Pottery of Late Bronze II from Tell Beit Mirsim. $\frac{1}{5}$

Bronze Age occupation is divided into two by a layer of destruction, thick in parts, dating to approximately 1350 B.C. The culture
of the second phase, C2, is typical of the uninspiring civilisation
of L.B. II, which well reflects the unsettled conditions to be
expected when Canaanite culture is struggling against, or
absorbing, wandering bands of the Ḥabiru of the Amarna Letters
or the Hebrews of the Old Testament. Whether the material

remains reflect the decadence of the old inhabitants, or the first stages in the civilisation of the new, it is impossible to say on present evidence.

The crude art of the period is well represented by a stone libation tray (Pl. 43). Almost equally crude are the Astarte plaques which are the most common cult object on almost all sites of the period. That such plaques, with their association with Phoenician religion, are found cannot, however, be taken on any particular site as evidence that it had not yet come under Israelite control, for Tell Beit Mirsim itself provides clear evidence for the occurrence of such plaques or similar figurines right down to the 7th century B.C. The denunciations by the prophets are enough to show that Yahwehism had continuously to struggle with the ancient religion of the land.

The second phase of the Late Bronze Age city at Tell Beit Mirsim ended with another, and very thorough, destruction. This Professor Albright dates to c. 1230 B.C., and considers it to be the work of the Israelites. This is not impossible, but cannot be proved, for there are other historical events which would account for it, namely the raids into Palestine carried out by Merneptah of Egypt about 1230 B.C. or the raids of the Peoples of the Sea about 1200 B.C. The culture of the succeeding level B1 is based on the preceding Late Bronze Age, and neither confirms nor (as suggested above) contradicts the possibility that its inhabitants belonged to a new group.

Tell Duweir is a site in which the Canaanite culture seems to continue uninterrupted until a date late in the 13th century. There, the temple in the Fosse, described earlier in this chapter, was succeeded by an enlarged version about 1400 B.C., and this again was superseded by a third about 1325 B.C. (Pl. 44). The basic plan of the temple remained the same throughout, and the excavators believe that the rebuildings were due not to destructions but to increased prosperity, requiring a more elaborate and larger building. By contrast, the existence of the third temple ends with a tremendous destruction, a fate which soundings showed also overtook the city itself. The most probable date of this is about 1230 B.C. It could again be referred to the effects of Merneptah's punitive campaigns, or, in view of the inclusion of Lachish, with which the site is almost certainly to be identified, in the lists of the places overcome by the Israelites, it might be their work. Again, however, our knowledge of the chronology of the relevant finds, particularly pottery, is not yet sufficiently exact to make a slightly later date impossible, and the alternative that the destruction was carried out by the Peoples of the Sea cannot be excluded.

On historical grounds the evidence for the course of events in the great cities in the north, Beth-shan and Megiddo on the borders of the Plain of Esdraelon, may be expected to be different from those just discussed, since they did not fall into Israelite hands until comparatively late.

At Megiddo, the Late Bronze I city, VIII, probably comes to an end about 1350 B.C. with the inevitable destruction. The succeeding city VII closely follows VIII in plan and the principal buildings uncovered, the temple, the palace and the gate, described above, were reconstructed on very much the same lines. Stratum VII is itself divided into two by a destruction, for which there was stratigraphical and architectural evidence but which did not coincide with any cultural break. The destruction, however, was sufficiently thorough for the ruins of the earlier palace to be covered over by its own débris, and a new one, on very much the same plan, to be built on the filling so formed. This shows that even such a strong site as Megiddo was a victim of the current disturbances, but at the end of the period it did not succumb so immediately to the new perils of the years about 1200 B.C. Stratum VII seems in fact to have lasted down to about 1150 B.C.

In another aspect, Megiddo presents a contrast to the other sites for which we have evidence, for the level of culture here does not seem to reach such a low ebb. The buildings, as far as they have been excavated, have indications of architectural pretensions. The pottery is not so exceedingly uninteresting, for the crude saucer forms found on other sites are hardly present here, and the

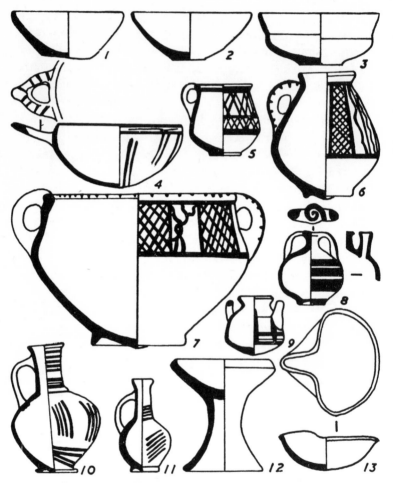

FIG. 51   Pottery of Late Bronze II from Megiddo. $\frac{1}{5}$

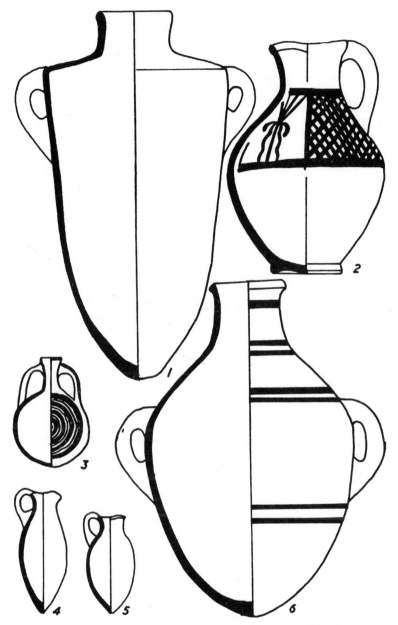

Fig. 52   Pottery of Late Bronze II from Megiddo. $\frac{1}{5}$

217

pottery decoration found during L.B. I has its continuation, though it is less elaborate. Most striking of all is the collection of ivories found in the ruins of the palace of the second phase in VII, which provide an indication of the cultural tastes at least of the ruling classes. These ivories, specimens of which are illustrated on Pls. 45–46, were found in a small room, which it is suggested was a treasury, broken and disordered possibly when articles in precious metals were looted. They must originally have formed the decoration of furniture, but since the room was too small to have contained the furniture they must have been stored for their own sake, as a collection of *objets d'art*. A model pen-case carried a cartouche of Rameses III, which shows that the collection was still being added to in the 12th century B.C., while the oldest object may go back to the 14th century B.C. They represent an art of which specimens are found in Egypt, Cyprus and Phoenicia, and show that Megiddo at least was in contact with the best artistic life of the period. Megiddo, therefore, though it may have had its share in political disturbances, was not submerged in the increasing tide of barbarism.

Beth-shan too may be expected to exhibit a higher degree of civilisation, for it too was a very strong city, and was moreover in close contact with Egypt. Here, however, our knowledge from excavations is confined to a more limited area, that occupied by a succession of temples. The contacts of the city with Egypt, and the control exercised there by that country, are indicated by the finds of scarabs and other objects, dating, in the levels examined, from the time of Thotmes III, and of stelae set up there by Seti I (1320–1301 B.C.) and a statue of Rameses III (1204–1172 B.C.). There are also fairly frequent references to the site in Egyptian texts. The series of temples excavated, moreover, show the increasing influence of Egypt. The earliest, that of Stratum IX, was originally assigned to the period of Thotmes III (1501–1447 B.C.) but must in fact have a terminal date of about 1350 B.C. This is a structure of Canaanite type, with a multiplicity of courts and altars and a rather amorphous plan, and with a *mazzebah* or pillar, which is the Canaanite representation of the deity. The next temple, in Level VII, should be dated *c.* 1300 to 1150 B.C.; it represents a revolution in temple architecture, with a partly roofed forecourt, and a raised sanctuary at the rear; it has been suggested that the plan is reminiscent of small Egyptian shrines of the 14th century B.C., particularly of the Amarna period, but it is not unlike Semitic shrines found elsewhere in Palestine, for instance at Tell el Far'ah.[1] That the basic Canaanite religion was unchanged is shown by the numerous and very interesting cult objects found, indicating that the cult was a fertility one, associated with Ashtoreth and perhaps a storm god Mekal, probably connected with the Syrian Reshef. At Beth-shan there is, within the area excavated, no indication of the destructions which affected the other sites discussed. The Egyptian garrison apparently maintained here at least from the time of Seti I, must have been sufficient to protect the city from the troubles of the time.

The stelae of Seti I set up at Beth-shan provide an interesting record of what was happening. Seti was the first king to restore Egyptian control in Palestine after the disasters of the Amarna period, and he clearly had to deal with a number of marauding and raiding bands. It is recorded in a stela set up at Beth-shan in the first year of his reign (1320–1319 B.C.) that bands from across the Jordan were attacking Beth-shan and neighbouring towns, and his defeat of them is described. In another stela, unfortunately only partly decipherable, the defeat of 'Apiru from the "Mountains of the Jordan" (the last word uncertain) is apparently described. As has already been said, the equation 'Apiru–Ḥabiru–Hebrew is accepted by many scholars, and we here have therefore evidence of bands allied to the Ḥabiru of the Amarna Letters still causing trouble. Whether we have here the other side of the story of the biblical account that the tribe of Manasseh failed to capture Beth-shan there is not yet sufficient evidence to say, but it is not impossible that there is a connection.

The results of the excavations just described have shown the effect on the country of the nomadic invasions of which we have historical evidence from the 14th century onwards. All but the

[1] R.B., LXIV, Fig. 8, p. 575.

very strongest cities suffer from one or more waves of destruction, and whether or not the destructions are followed by the settlement of some of the nomads, prosperity and culture inevitably decline. Egyptian control of the great land route was maintained sufficiently to ensure more settled conditions, and a resulting greater degree of civilisation in the cities along it, and further evidence that even the backward and disturbed conditions of the interior did not prevent trade connections with the Mediterranean area is given by the large amount of imported Cypriot and Syrian pottery found on all sites. Against this background took place the Israelite settlement, sufficiently advanced by c. 1230 B.C. for "the people Israel" to be recorded among those vanquished by Merneptah, but conclusive evidence for the course of the settlement cannot yet be provided by archaeology.

1 The caves in the Wadi Mughara, Mount Carmel (*p. 36*)

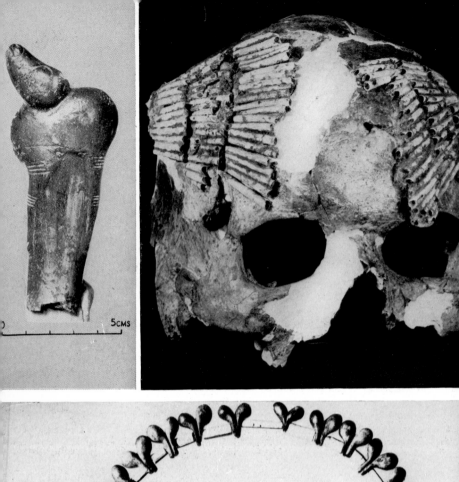

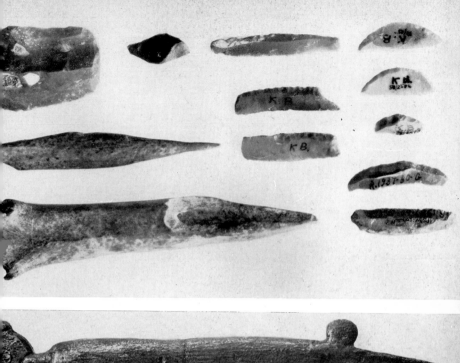

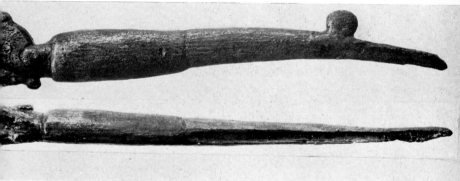

[opposite]

Mesolithic carving of a young deer, from Mugharet el Wad (p. 37)

Skull with crown of *dentalia* shells, from Mugharet el Wad (p. 38)

Necklace of twin pendants carved from bone, Mugharet el Wad (p. 38)

3A   Bone sickle-handle, with animal-head end from Mugharet Kebara (p. 37)

B   Bone and flint implements of the Lower Natufian from Mugharet Kebara (c. 5/6) (p. 36)

4 The mound of ancient Jericho, with modern Jericho beyond (p. 39)

5A A Mesolithic
structure at
Jericho (*p. 41*)

B A house of
Pre-Pottery
Neolithic A
at Jericho (*p. 43*)

[*opposite*]

6A   A house of Pre-Pottery Neolithic A at Jericho (*p. 43*)

B   Steps leading down into a Pre-Pottery Neolithic house at Jericho (*p. 43*)

7   The great stone tower of the Pre-Pottery Neolithic A defences at Jericho (*p. 44*)

8 The defences of
   Jericho in the Pre-
   Pottery Neolithic
   A period (*p. 44*)

[*opposite*]

9A Mesolithic (*top row*) and Proto-Neolithic flint and bone
    implements from Jericho (*c. 5/6*) (*pp. 41, 43*)

B   Pre-Pottery Neolithic A flints from Jericho (*c. 5/6*) (*p. 43*)

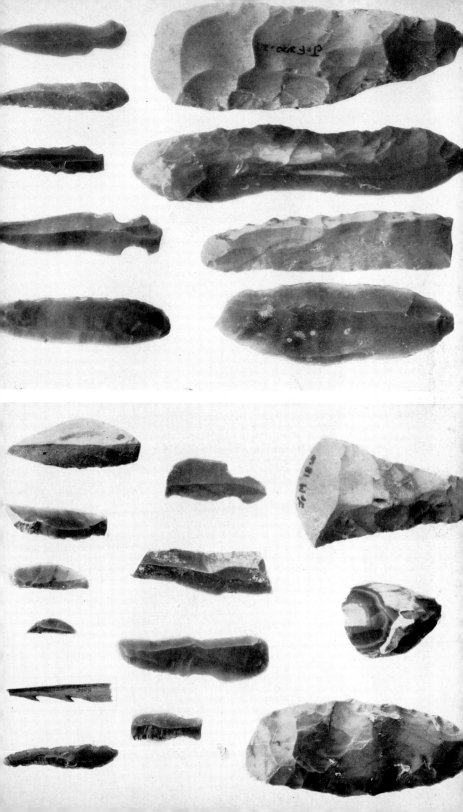

10   Bone tools of the Pre-Pottery Neolithic A
period from Jericho (*c. 5/7*) (*p. 43*)

[opposite]

11   A house of the Pre-Pottery Neolithic B
period at Jericho (*p. 48*)

12A A typical wall of a Pre-Pottery
Neolithic B house at Jericho
(*p. 48*)

B Pre-Pottery Neolithic B flints
and bone tool from Jericho
(*c. 2/3*) (*p. 49*)

15   Front and side view of partly stylised human head in plaster
from Jericho (*p. 54*)

[*opposite*]

14A   Three Neolithic portrait heads from Jericho
(*p. 52*)

B   Completely stylised human head and bust in
plaster from Jericho (*p. 54*)

16 Town wall of Pre-Pottery Neolithic B at Jericho (*p. 55*)

17   Pottery from Sha'ar ha Golan of the Pottery Neolithic B period (*p. 66*)

18 Pebble figurines from Sha'ar ha Golan (*p. 66*)

19A   View of Chalcolithic site in the Wadi Ghazzeh (*p. 77*)
  B   Air view of Megiddo (*p. 92*)

22A   A pottery kiln of the Early Bronze Age at Tell el Farʿah (*p. 110*)

B   Terrace wall of Stratum XVIII at Megiddo (*p. 112*)

23   Altar 4017 at Megiddo (p. 112)

24 View of Beth-shan (*p. 112*)

25 View of Tell Duweir (*p. 118*)

26 Dagger-type tomb of the E.B.-M.B. period at Jericho
(*p. 139*)

[*opposite*]
27 Pottery-type tomb of the E.B.-M.B. period at Jericho (*p. 139*)

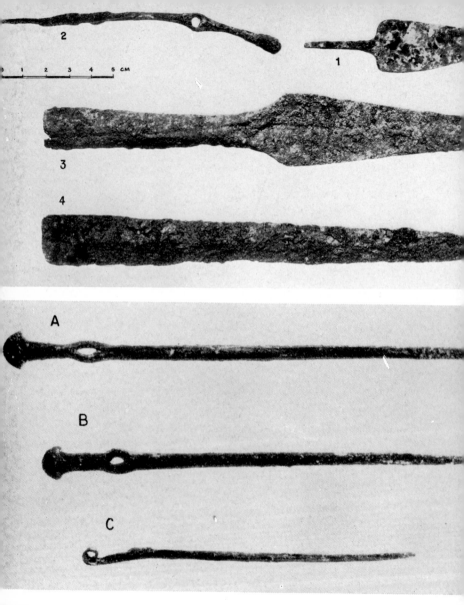

28A   Copper objects from Tomb 1101 B Lower at
       Megiddo (*p. 150*)
  B   Pins from Shaft Tombs at Megiddo (*p. 152*)

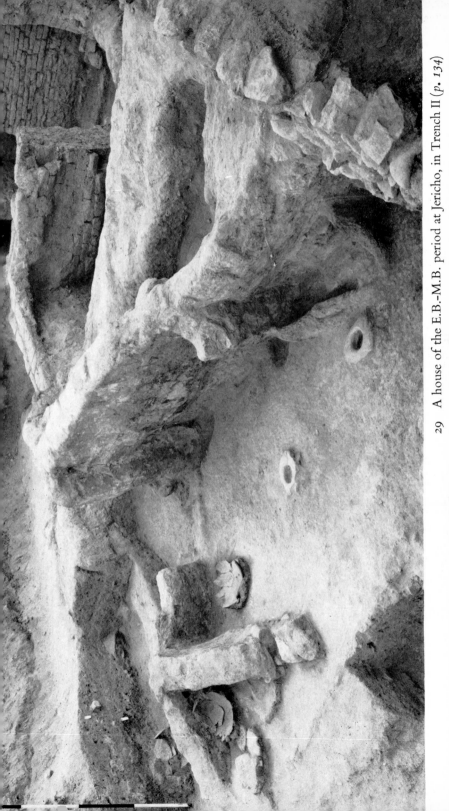

29 A house of the E.B.-M.B. period at Jericho, in Trench II (*p. 134*)

30 Middle Bronze Age plastered rampart at Jericho (*p. 178*)

31   Revetment at base of final Middle Bronze
Age rampart at Jericho (*p. 179*)

32 Middle Bronze
    Age plastered
    rampart at Tell
    Duweir (*p. 180*)

[opposite]
33 Air view of
    Hazor (*p. 181*)

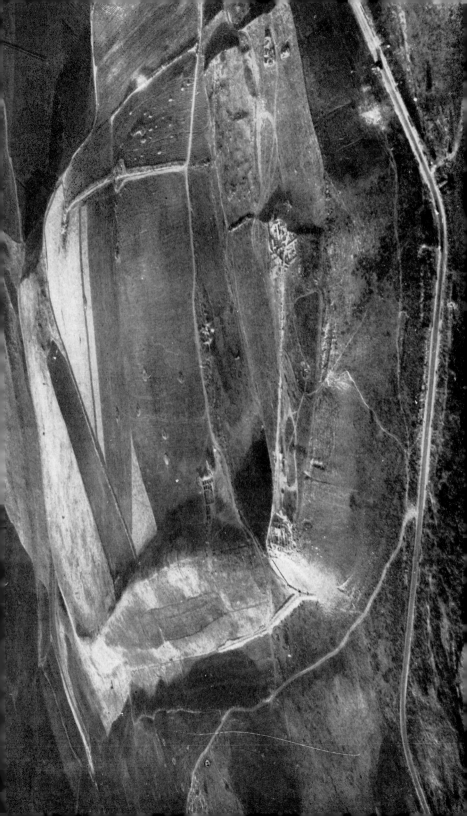

Cm. 1   2   3   4

34A Gaming pieces
     from Tell Beit
     Mirsim (*p. 185*)

B   Part of stela rep-
     resenting a ser-
     pent-god from
     Tell Beit Mirsim
     (*p. 185*)

35 A street in Middle Age Jericho (*p. 187*)

[opposite] The lower part of the Jericho street, with drain beneath (p. 187)

Grain jars in a Middle Bronze Age house at Jericho (p. 187)

37 A typical Middle Bronze Age tomb, G 73, at Jericho (p. 190)

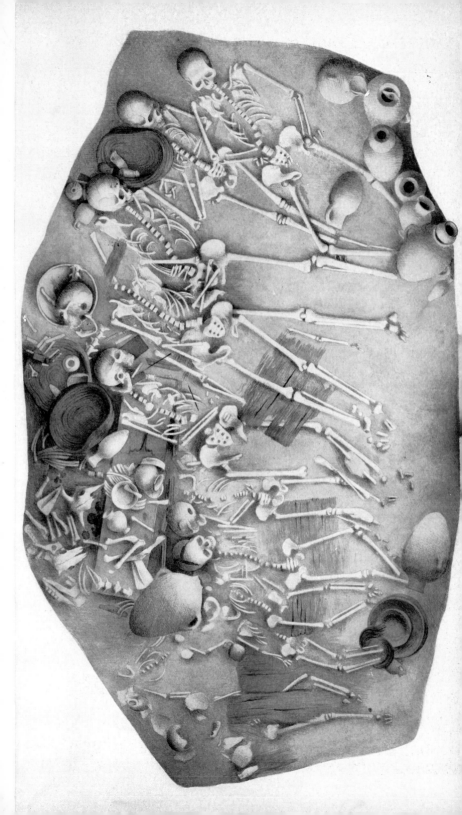

12. Reconstruction of a room in *Middle Bronze Age* ... [*imperial*]

43   Libation tray of limestone from Tell Beit
Mirsim (*p. 214*)

[*opposite*]
42 Fragmentary remains of Late Bronze Age
house at Jericho (*p. 210*)

45 Carved ivory box from Megiddo (*p. 218*)

44 Fosse Temple Structure III at
Tell Duweir (*p. 214*)

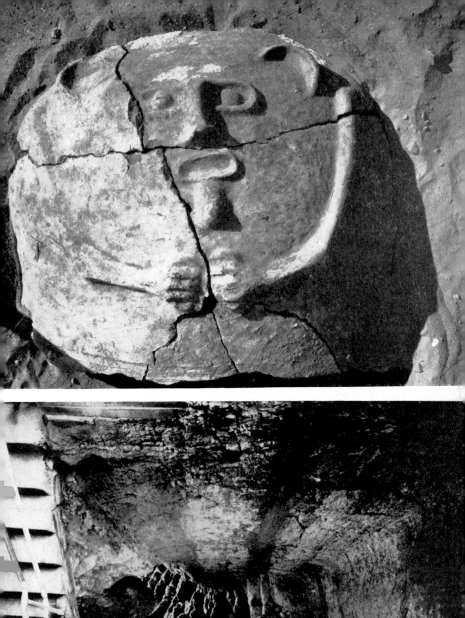

48　The tunnel from the shaft to the spring at Megiddo
(p. 234)

49   The eastern slopes of the earliest Jerusalem. The excavation
trench extends from the post-exilic walls on the crest
of the ridge to the position of the Jebusite and Davidic
walls at the extreme foot of the trench. The position
of the spring which supplied early Jerusalem with its
water is indicated by the lower of the two small
buildings in the right centre.

50A   Air view of the Solomonic gate at Hazor (*p. 248*)

B   Unfinished building of early 9th century B.C. at
Tell el Far‘ah (*p. 261*)

51A The outer enclosure wall of Samaria (*p. 266*)
B The hill of Samaria from the east (*p. 262*)

53A Ivory plaque from Samaria
     (*p. 266*)

   B Ivory plaque representing
     a palm tree, from Samaria
     (*p. 266*)

[*opposite*]
52 The first enclosure
   wall of the royal quarter
   at Samaria (*p. 265*)

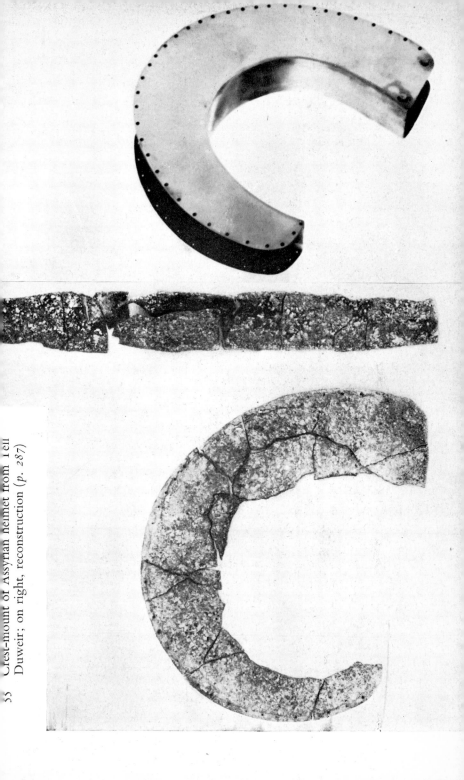

55 Crest-mount of Assyrian helmet from Tell
Duweir; on right, reconstruction (*p. 287*)

★

The Philistines and the Beginning of the Early Iron Age

ABOUT THE year 1200 B.C. there was a catastrophic interruption in the civilisation of the whole of the eastern Mediterranean, producing a Dark Age very like that following the end of the Roman Empire in Europe some sixteen hundred years later, and brought about by similar events, the incursions of barbarian groups. The great empires of the Near East all succumbed to or were severely shaken by these inroads. Palestine did not bear the full brunt, for it was not such a rich prey as the great empires, but its position as part of the land route between Asia Minor, which may have been the home of some of the invaders, and Egypt meant that some of the effects were felt there.

The tale of the attacks of the Peoples of the Sea upon Egypt is graphically described on the monuments of Rameses III. In their final and greatest attack, c. 1196 B.C., they came by land and sea, and were thrown back by the Pharaoh after great battles on both elements. Rameses claimed such a complete victory that he was able to drive through Palestine up into the lands of the Hittites in Syria, for their empire had been disrupted by the new-comers' advance. But in spite of this, he allowed the defeated tribes to settle on the Palestinian and Syrian coast, and it may be doubted if this would have been the case if his victory were as thorough as he claimed. At all events, the failure of the raiders to force their way into Egypt led to the settlement of some at least of them in Palestine.

The Egyptian records make it clear that the Peoples of the Sea

FIG. 53   Representation at Medinet Habu of Egyptians fighting the invading Peoples of the Sea

were a composite group drawn from a number of tribes. The monuments of Rameses III at Medinet Habu (Fig. 53) mention six tribes, the Pulasati or Philistines, the Sherdanu, the Danunu, the Shekelesh, the Zakkala and the Washasha, while other Egyptian lists add some eight more names. Archaeology has so far thrown little unambiguous light on the origins of these groups. Biblical accounts associate the Philistines with Caphtor, which many scholars consider to be the equivalent of the Egyptian Keftiu, and identify as Crete. Philological studies suggest that the homeland of some at least of the groups was in the south-west of Asia Minor, while the equation proposed by some scholars of Danunu with Danaoi and Ekwesh (mentioned in the list of Merneptah) with Achaeans, brings us into contact with the tribes of the Homeric legend. Such archaeological evidence as exists is at least not discordant with such an origin.

It must once more be pointed out that archaeological evidence may in such a case be inadequate, for here again we are dealing with warlike bands. It is true that the Medinet Habu reliefs show the land invaders accompanied by women and children in ox-carts, and they therefore came as intending settlers and not as mere raiders. But even so, their material equipment must have been light, and they would have taken over much from the Canaanites among whom they settled, as indeed archaeological evidence suggests.

There is, however, one class of archaeological material which may reasonably be associated with the newcomers. This is a type of pottery, entirely new to Palestine, decorated with elaborate patterns. The most characteristic elements in the decoration are metopes enclosing stylised birds, very often with back-turned head, friezes of spirals, and groups of interlocking semicircles. The form of the vessels and the elements in the decoration all have their origins in the Late Helladic ceramic art of the Aegean. It has been shown that the closest parallels are in the pottery of Rhodes and Cyprus, but in no case are the Palestine vessels exact copies; the same elements are there, but they are differently combined. The originals from which the Palestinian types

develop can be dated to the late 13th century B.C., while new
fashions which were coming into use about 1200 B.C. are not
represented. In the mixture, too, Egyptian elements are represented,[1] which may be accounted for by the fact that for centuries
Shardans (Sherdanu) and others of the confederates had been in
the habit of serving the Egyptians as mercenaries. The ware of
the vessels does not differ from that of the native Palestinian pots.
The conclusion which is thus suggested is that the newcomers
did not bring this pottery with them, but manufactured it in
Palestine in imitation of the vessels to which they were accus-
tomed in their homeland, which they must have left before the
new 12th century style came into use.

It cannot of course be accepted without question that this
pottery is necessarily associated with the Philistines, but the
evidence does seem to be strongly in favour of this ascription.
It has just been shown that it must be dated to about 1200 B.C.,
while the historical date given for the repulse of the invaders by
Rameses III is c. 1196 B.C. Secondly, the distribution of the pottery
corresponds well with the area occupied by the Philistines. It is
concentrated in the coastal plain and the borders of the hill
country, which was the area of the primary Philistine conquests,
while in the hill country proper it occurs only sporadically.
Finally, archaeological evidence shows that it appears suddenly
at the end of the Late Bronze Age on the coast, but rather later
farther inland.

The archaeological evidence is perhaps best illustrated at
Askelon, which was one of the five chief cities of the Philistines.
The site is a large one, with important Roman buildings in the
upper levels, and for the most part excavation did not penetrate
below these levels. But a cliff face provided a section through
the north edge of the central mound which revealed the strata
belonging to earlier periods, and a cut was made through these
successive strata. This showed a sharp-cut division at the end of
the Late Bronze Age. A continuous layer of ashes, about 50
centimetres thick, indicative of a wholesale destruction, overlay a

[1] T. Dothan, *Antiquity and Survival*, II, pp. 151 ff.

layer which was typical of the cosmopolitan culture of the period in Palestine, with finds showing Cypriot, Mycenaean and Egyptian contacts. Above the ash layer these imports cease, and Philistine pottery and local derivatives appear. It thus seems very probable that the ash layer represents the destruction of the Canaanite town by the Peoples of the Sea, some of whom then settled on the site, and built their own city above the ruins. It is only at Askelon that such good stratigraphical evidence of an important Philistine city has been obtained, but in so far as the other cities, Gaza, Gath, Ashdod and Ekron, have been identified and examined, the evidence produced seems to be similar. In no case do the Philistines seem to have founded new cities; they seized, destroyed (if the history of Askelon is typical) and then occupied towns belonging to their Canaanite predecessors.

Not only did they occupy Canaanite sites, but they seem also to have taken over some part at least of Canaanite culture. The introduction of a distinctive type of pottery has just been described. But associated with it in tomb groups and other deposits are other types which have developed directly from the native Late Bronze Age wares. Even the names of their chief gods, Dagon and Ashtaroth, seem to be Canaanite, but it is very possible that there has been assimilation between these and Aegean deities with similar attributes. It must, however, be admitted that archaeology has not yet given us a clear picture of the Philistines, for none of their important cities has as yet been sufficiently excavated for any generalisations as to Philistine or non-Philistine traits to be made.

Some evidence of their burial customs does exist. At Tell Fara was found a group of five tombs which stand out both in contents and plan from others on the same site.[1] Their contents include some fine pottery vessels with characteristic Philistine decoration, together with many plain vessels of native Late Bronze Age types. There were a number of bronze bowls, while the typical weapons appeared to be daggers and spears. The majority of them was bronze, but there was an iron dagger with a bronze

[1] *Bethpelet*, II, pp. 6 ff.

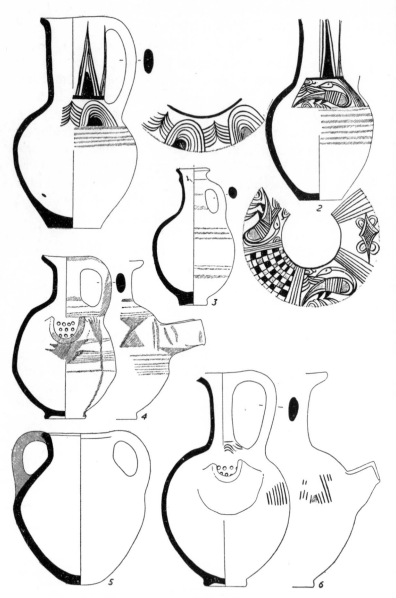

FIG. 54   Pottery from Philistine tombs at Tell Fara. $\frac{1}{5}$

hilt, and a slightly curved iron knife. We thus have here the first appearance of iron in Palestine in well-authenticated associations. In plan, the tombs are consistent. They are approached by a long, narrow, stepped passage or dromos, which enters the base of a trapezoidal-shaped chamber with markedly straight sides. In the centre of the chamber is a sunk well or passage, while round the side benches are left to receive the burials. At the rear of two of the tombs there are subsidiary, smaller chambers, again slightly trapezoidal in plan. The burials appear to have been extended, lying on their backs. These tombs are in strong contrast to the majority of those found in Palestine, which usually consist of one or more irregular rounded chambers. There is thus a suggestion of foreign influence, possibly from the Philistine homelands. Two of the preceding Late Bronze Age tombs at Tell Fara are the only ones which approach them at all nearly in plan and these again are cases in which there appears to be considerable Aegean influence.

Another interesting suggestion of foreign contacts was the discovery in two of these tombs of pottery coffins with anthropoidal lids (Pl. 47A). These coffins are certainly not native to Palestine. They have, however, been also found at Beth-shan, and in Egypt examples are known from a number of sites. At Beth-shan, the dates of the burials of which they formed part appear to belong to Late Bronze II and Early Iron I. In Egypt they range from the time of Thotmes III (1501–1447 B.C.) to as late as 600 B.C. Nearly all, both in Egypt and at Beth-shan, have Aegean and Cypriot objects associated with them. It is known on literary evidence that Shardan mercenaries were employed by the Egyptians, and they are specifically mentioned as forming part of the Egyptian garrison in Palestine at the period of the Amarna Letters. As the Shardans also were one of the tribes making up the Peoples of the Sea defeated by Rameses III, they may well have formed part of the group that settled in Palestine to which the name Philistine was applied by the Israelites, while a related group may have formed part of the Egyptian garrison of Beth-shan.

The area initially settled by the Philistines is difficult to assess

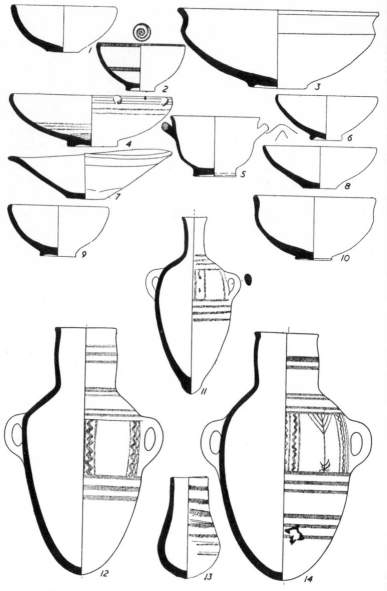

FIG. 55 Pottery from Philistine tombs at Tell Fara. $\frac{1}{5}$

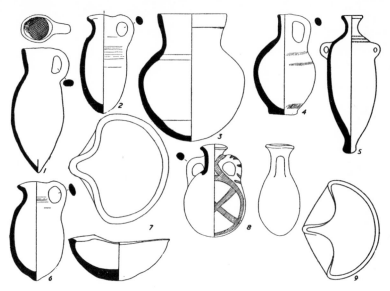

FIG. 56   Pottery from Philistine tombs at Tell Fara. $\frac{1}{5}$

on archaeological evidence. The appearance of a moderate amount of Philistine pottery on a site cannot of course be accepted as evidence of political control, for it might have been acquired in the course of trade. At Megiddo, for instance, a small number of typical sherds occur in both Strata VII and VI, too few, however, to suggest that the Philistines formed any substantial part of the population, for the importance of Megiddo is such that if it had come under their control there would certainly be some literary reference to the fact.

Such exact evidence as there is suggests that an initial settlement on the coast was followed by a more gradual conquest of towns farther inland, up to the edge of the central ridge, which they never settled, though in the 11th century B.C. they exercised some degree of suzerainty over the Israelites there. The evidence comes from the relation of the appearance of the Philistine pottery to the termination of the 13th century Cypriot and Mycenaean imports, which has been described above and which must be

ascribed to the disruption of trade caused by the movements of
the Peoples of the Sea. At the coastal site of Askelon, as we have
seen, the layer in which these Aegean imports occur is separated
from that in which Philistine pottery first appears only by a layer
of burning. Similarly, at Tell Jemmeh, another site near the coast,
the succession again seems to be immediate. In the Shephelah, or
low hill country, there seems, on the other hand, to be an intermediate phase. At Tell Beit Mirsim the typical Late Bronze Age
imports are found in Level C2, destroyed towards the end of the
13th century. This town was immediately succeeded by another,
belonging to Level B1, of which the estimated duration (it is
admittedly only an estimate) was between fifty and a hundred
years. In this level there were no foreign imports at all, and the
pottery represents the development of the native Late Bronze
wares. In the succeeding level, B2, however, there is much
Philistine pottery, and the site must by that time have come under
Philistine control. At Beth Shemesh, again a town of the
Shephelah, Stratum IV, which starts in the 15th century, continues sufficiently late to overlap Tell Beit Mirsim B1. This
stratum is ended by a general destruction of the city, covering the
whole site with a layer of ashes, and in the succeeding Stratum III
much Philistine pottery appears. It may thus be that the expansion
of the Philistines into the Shephelah, which is included in the
biblical land of the Philistines, took some thirty to fifty years.

   Though there is not exact archaeological evidence from a
sufficient number of sites to provide more than a suggestion as
to the process of Philistine expansion, the distribution of sites on
which considerable quantities of their pottery appears does
provide an indication as to their main area of occupation. The
pottery hardly appears at all on the central ridge. It is not found
at Jerusalem, Gibeah or Beth-zur, while there is no more at Tell
Nasbeh, some 9 miles north of Jerusalem, than could be accounted
for by trade. On the coastal plain and in the Shephelah it is found
plentifully as far south as the Wadi Ghazzeh, on which are Tell
Ajjul, Tell Jemmeh and Tell Fara, while the distribution extends
as far north as the neighbourhood of Jaffa, the ancient Joppa. But

even within this area there may have been enclaves which held out. No evidence of the Philistines, for instance, has been found at Tell Duweir and very little at the neighbouring Tell Hesi, but too much weight cannot at present be given to this suggestion since it is not quite certain whether either site was occupied at this period. Farther north, there is no trace of the typical pottery at Dor, in spite of the fact that there is literary evidence that it was occupied by the Sakkala, one of the kindred tribes of the Peoples of the Sea. Similarly, there is no trace of it at Tell Abu Hawam, at the foot of Mount Carmel, while, as has already been mentioned, at Megiddo there is a small amount, probably as a result of trade. At Beth-shan, though it was certainly a Philistine city in the 11th century in the time of Saul, there is none at all.

Thus the area of Philistine occupation was a limited one, though ultimately their political control extended considerably beyond this. For a hundred years or so they lived side by side with their Canaanite and Israelite predecessors. As has already been said, there is no archaeological evidence to decide which sites belong to which of these two groups. It is only on historical grounds, for instance the mention of the people Israel by Merneptah, that we know in fact that the Israelites were by now firmly established in the land, in two groups, divided by the Canaanite wedge round Jerusalem.

Our fullest evidence concerning non-Philistine areas at this period does, however, come from sites which were certainly not Israelite, notably Megiddo. There is actually no mention in the Bible of when this important city came to be part of Israel. It is included in the list of those that remained under the Canaanites in the initial conquest, while it was Israelite by the time of Solomon. It may well be that it came under Israelite control during the 11th century, during much of which period the site was unoccupied, and therefore no particular importance was attached to the fact.

Megiddo does not seem to have suffered immediately from the effects of the raids and settlement of the Peoples of the Sea, no doubt owing to its great strength. Its Late Bronze II Level VII seems to continue down to about 1150 B.C., on the evidence both of the presence of a little Philistine pottery in the layer and of the find of a statue base of Rameses VI, dated to about the middle of the 12th century B.C., apparently in association with a building in Level VII.[1] The period comes to an end with one of the major catastrophes in the history of the site, in which the town was completely destroyed. It was rebuilt immediately, but all the old layout, which had developed, with modifications but no complete break, from the beginning of the Middle Bronze Age, was now completely lost. The substantial well-built structures disappear, to be replaced by much meaner buildings. The sacred area, which may date back even to the third millennium, is obliterated, as is also the great northern gate with its three-pier plan which had retained its Middle Bronze Age form up till now. Even its position is changed, and the new one is some 17 metres farther east; its plan has not been fully recovered, but seems to be quite different. This great destruction may possibly be ascribed to the Philistines, for no reference in the biblical record suggests it was the work of the Israelites. But whoever was responsible, the event does not seem to have affected the culture of the inhabitants. The pottery of the ensuing Stratum VI shows no radical change; the native Late Bronze Age wares continue, as elsewhere, with modifications, and of course without the imports of the earlier period.

There is, however, one significant change, and that is the appearance of iron. An iron knife was found in Stratum VI, and an iron dagger in a tomb which may date to about the middle of the 12th century. Bronze of course continued to be used, and in fact arrowheads, too expendable for the employment of a new and valuable metal, do not appear in iron until about the 10th century B.C. Another innovation which is perhaps suggestive of new contacts is the appearance of fibulae, which in the course of the Early Iron Age entirely superseded the pierced pins developed from Middle Bronze Age types; a change in dress habits is thus suggested.

[1] The excavators' date for the end of Level VII is 1170 B.C., but on these grounds 1150 B.C. seems rather more probable.

The restoration of the city after such a complete destruction is evidence for the vitality of the people of Megiddo. But there is also evidence of a feat which records not only vitality but very great scientific and engineering skill, as well as a strong social organisation. This was the construction of a new water system, which was discovered and re-excavated in 1928.[1] Megiddo is unlike many Palestinian cities in that at no period in its history was it dependent on cisterns for its water supply. There must presumably have been a supply accessible from within the town; otherwise, however strong the walls, it would hardly have held out in time of siege. The original intra-mural supply has not been found, though a depression on the summit, sealed by Iron Age buildings, towards which runs a portion of a channel from a spring to the north, may represent the site of a water-shaft such as existed at Gezer in the Middle Bronze Age.

The system in use throughout the Iron Age, however, dates only from the 12th century B.C. The excavators considered that it was constructed at the end of Period VII. To the present writer the relevant pottery appears to make an association with Stratum VI slightly more probable, but in any case the date would be 12th century and, as evidence of precaution against enemies, would fit in well with that troubled time. The new system drew its water from a spring at the foot of the south-west slopes of the tell. As such, the spring had been used almost throughout the history of the site, successive cleanings-out having gradually cut back into the rock from which it sprang until it became a well within a cave. All this time, access had only been from the foot of the tell, outside the walls, and thus it was presumably useless in the time of war. In the 12th century B.C. it was made accessible from inside the city. It may be conjectured that the arrangements which must have existed earlier for an intra-mural supply had been allowed to fall into disrepair during the long peaceful period represented by Stratum VII. Alternatively, a source of supply used previously may have dried up.

The first means by which the spring was reached from within the city was by a long, sloping, stone-built gallery. At the foot

[1] For pp. 233–5, see Addenda p. 343.

of this, by the spring, was a guard chamber, which was put out
of action when the successor to the gallery was constructed. In
the guard chamber was found the skeleton of a guard killed at
his post, so presumably the arrangement did not prevent surprise
by enemies, and a new method had to be adopted. With the guard
were a number of pottery vessels, which date this phase to the
12th century.

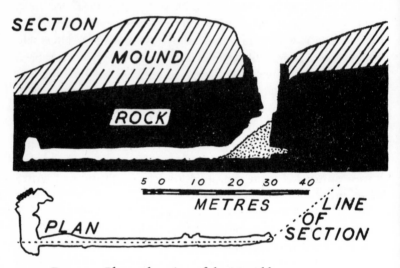

FIG. 57   Plan and section of the Megiddo water system

The succeeding scheme was much more ambitious (Fig. 57). A
great vertical shaft 35 metres deep was sunk from the surface of
the ground, the upper part, through the accumulated occupation
débris, being masonry lined, the lower part through the solid
rock (Pl. 47B). From the foot of this shaft a horizontal gallery 63
metres long was cut to the spring (Pl. 48), to which all access
from outside was then blocked by an enclosing wall. Such an
undertaking would be no light task even today, as the excavators
who had to clear fallen débris from it well realised, and would
have been a much heavier one with the tools and tackle available
in the 12th century B.C. Moreover, its execution demanded a

high degree of skill in planning and surveying, for the necessary levels and direction had to be accurately estimated. The finished work shows how successfully this was done, for the errors that had to be corrected were very slight.

The women of Megiddo were now able to walk down the staircase round the side of the great shaft and along the gallery to fill their jars at the spring in complete safety. It was perhaps because this must have been a laborious task that at a later period the steps were cut out and the floor of the gallery deepened so that the water flowed to the foot of the shaft, which now in fact became a well. But this apparently was not satisfactory, so later again built steps replaced the earlier rock-cut ones, and once more the water-carriers had to descend to the foot of the shaft. With these and other modifications the scheme served to provide Megiddo with water down to the end of its full occupation about 600 B.C.

Stratum VI lasted only until about 1100 B.C. But within this period of about fifty years it was completely destroyed and rebuilt with little reference to the earlier plan. Such a course of events supports the evidence provided by the care lavished on the water supply as to the unsettled state of affairs in the coastal area of Palestine at this period. About 1100 B.C. the city was again destroyed, and this time it was not rebuilt. For about a hundred years it lay unoccupied, probably for the first time in the two thousand years or more of its existence. It is probable that these vicissitudes are due to the activities of the Philistines or the other Peoples of the Sea, for there is no evidence that the Israelites were concerned with them, but at present it can only be a matter for conjecture.

At Beth-shan, as at Megiddo, the Late Bronze II Level VII seems to have lasted until about 1150 B.C.[1] As is the case with the early levels, only the description of the temple area of the succeeding Level VI has been published. This was ascribed by the excavators to the period of Seti I down to the beginning of the reign of Rameses III (1320–1204 B.C.), but should probably be

---

[1] Revised dating, see p. 219.

dated *c.* 1150–1000 B.C. The temple of the preceding Level VII
was destroyed, though whether violently or in order to be
reconstructed is not clear, and its remains were covered with
débris on top of which a new temple was built. This new temple
follows its predecessor closely in plan, with an indirect approach,
a partly roofed court and a raised sanctuary at the rear. The cult
objects indicate that the religion was still the old Canaanite
fertility worship.

All the sites so far described lie outside the area at this period
occupied by the Israelites. It must in fact be admitted that we
know tantalisingly little about the early Israelite settlements. The
reason for this is partly owing to the limitations of archaeological
evidence, partly owing to the limitations of the culture of the
Israelites themselves.

The archaeological limitations arise from the fact that the area
in which these settlements lie is the hill country. Sites in such
districts do not present the same thick deposits of successive
strata as do the sites in the plains. The buildings are naturally
constructed of stone, which is readily available all over the area.
As a result, when buildings of one period decay, their walls are
apt to be dismantled and the stones re-used in their successors.
Thus instead of the ruins being buried intact beneath a mass of
collapsed mud-brick, the usual material for the superstructure in
the plains, they are disturbed and destroyed to the very base of
the walls. The story of the successive phases is thus very much
more difficult to deduce. The excavation of the great site of Gezer,
for instance, carried out before modern refinements of archaeological technique had been introduced, did little to give us a
detailed picture of its history, since the buildings could not be
ascribed to definite periods. The same drawback applies to the
results of the excavation of many other sites in the hill country.

The character of the settlements is the second factor which
limits our information. The period is undoubtedly that in which
the national consciousness of the Israelites is developing greatly.
The biblical narrative shows how the groups were gradually
combining together, with tentative efforts at temporal unification

under the Judges and the stronger spiritual link of a national religion, with the high priest at times exercising temporal power. It is during these centuries that the groups allied by race, but differing in the manner and time of their settlement in Palestine, if the course of events suggested in Chapter 8 is the correct one, must have come to combine their ancestral traditions together under the influence of the Yahwehistic religion, and to believe that all their ancestors took part in the Exodus. The nation was thus emerging, but its culture was as yet primitive. Its settlements were villages, its art crude, and the objects of everyday use homely and utilitarian.

For this reason, excavations on sites such as Shiloh, Bethel and Gibeah, all names famous in biblical history, have produced only the remains of a succession of somewhat rough structures dating to the 13th and 12th centuries B.C. At Bethel the complete destruction described above (p. 212) was followed by a break in occupation, and the succeeding Iron Age structures were much cruder than those of the city destroyed earlier. A second Iron Age level was even more miserable, and it was not until a phase ascribed to the 10th century B.C. that any improvement took place.

Perhaps typical of many villages of the time is the site of Tell el Fûl, lying 5 kilometres north of Jerusalem, and very probably to be identified with the Gibeah which was the home of Saul. Its occupation seems to start at the beginning of the Iron Age, early in the 12th century B.C. It consisted of a village with at its centre a solidly built fortress or tower. The walls of this tower, which was about 15 metres square, were strongly built, but very rough. Much of the superstructure must have been of wood, for when it was destroyed it was covered with a thick layer of ashes and charred timber. It is interesting that the timber employed was cypress and pine, for coniferous trees subsequently disappeared completely from Palestine until modern times, and may in fact have vanished by the time of Gibeah III in the 9th century B.C., when the wood employed was almond. No doubt as settled life in Israel increased, and villages developed into towns, there was increasing deforestation from the need of timber for building.

Gibeah I was completely destroyed, probably in the second half of the 12th century B.C. It is difficult to be certain whether this is to be associated with any event recorded in the Bible. It may be the work of other Israelites, whose vengeance on Gibeah is recorded in Judges xix–xx. On the other hand, warfare with neighbouring tribes was clearly endemic, for the Bible describes "oppressions" by various Eastern neighbours, Moabites, Edomites, Midianites and others, which must belong to this period.

After an interval, a second fortress was built on the ruins of the first, partially incorporating them. This was better constructed than its predecessor, but nothing survived of any architectural pretensions, and its occupants were certainly not acquainted with luxury, to judge from the simple finds. It may be that this was built by the father of Saul, and it may thus illustrate the humble social status from which the leaders of Israel were drawn.

A site about which a little more is known is that of Beth-Shemesh, but it is not clear whether it formed part of Israel at this time. It is referred to in the Bible as a border city of Dan, before that tribe migrated northward, and subsequently as a border city of Israel. Yet to judge from the pottery, the town, which was built about 1150 B.C., was strongly under Philistine influence. It lies in the Shephelah, and must have been somewhere near the border between the Israelites and the Philistines, and the amount of Philistine pottery certainly suggests that it belonged to them, in spite of the biblical references. The remains recovered suggest a fairly large city, though no buildings of any particular merit were found. A principal industry of the town seems to have been bronze-working, for several smelting ovens and fragments of pottery blowpipes were found. Iron was in fairly common use on the site for weapons and jewellery. It is interesting, however, that flints set in wooden hafts continued to be used for sickles until the 10th century B.C. The city was violently destroyed by fire at the end of the 11th century B.C., possibly in Saul's wars with the Philistines.

For something like a hundred years the Philistines and the Israelites lived side by side, the Philistines in the rich coastal plain, the Israelites in the more barren hill country. About 1080 B.C. the Philistines began trying to extend their control over the hill country, and this is the period of oppression by the Philistines of which the Bible gives such a vivid account. The period was one of oppression, but it was also one that gave a stimulus towards nationhood. Saul, leading a revolt which started about 1030 B.C., became the acknowledged leader of the whole country in the struggle, and though his success was varying, and marred by quarrels with the religious leaders and with David, and terminated by defeat on Mount Gilboa, it was on the foundations of the unity that he achieved that David was able to establish the free and united kingdom of Israel.

*

CHAPTER TEN

The United Monarchy

THE UNITED kingdom of Israel had a life span of only three-quarters of a century. It was the only time in which the Jews were an important political power in western Asia. Its glories are triumphantly recorded in the Bible, and the recollection of them profoundly affected Jewish thought and aspirations. Yet the archaeological evidence for the period is meagre in the extreme.

After the disaster on Mount Gilboa, when the bodies of Saul and Jonathan were exhibited as trophies at Beth-shan, the Philistines set up two vassal kingdoms, with David as ruler at Hebron and Ishbaal in the north. In between the two lay Jerusalem, still occupied by the Canaanite tribe of Jebusites. But David, though he had taken refuge with the Philistines when Saul had turned against him, was not prepared to continue as a vassal now that his old leader was dead. He succeeded in defeating Ishbaal, apparently without intervention by the Philistines, thus reuniting the kingdom of Saul, and he threw off the Philistine overlordship. He then achieved the crucial success of capturing Jerusalem.

The control of Jerusalem was essential to the control of a united Palestine, as it lies on the central ridge which is the only convenient route north and south through the hill country. The fact is well illustrated by the dislocation caused by the 1948 frontier between Israel and Jordan, since the natural road between Jerusalem and Bethlehem, 8 kilometres to the south, was cut by a salient of Israel, and the subsequent road connecting the two, in order to keep in Jordan territory, had to make a detour of incredible steepness and engineering difficulty, owing to the valleys running down abruptly from the watershed. From Jerusalem to the east a road runs down to the Jordan Valley near Jericho, across a ford over the Jordan, and up to the rich plateau of Transjordan; while to the west there is a choice of good routes down to the Shephelah and the coastal plain.

The previous lack of cohesion among the Israelites is well illustrated by the fact that this Canaanite enclave had been allowed to persist in their midst for centuries. Without its possession, political unity was impossible. Once it was secured, the great period of Israelite history begins. But the effect of the long division of the Israelites into two groups, added to that of probable difference of origin between the northern and southern tribes, was permanent and contributed to the renewed division into Israel and Judah at the end of the 10th century B.C.

The problems of the archaeology of Jerusalem have attracted investigators ever since exploration in Palestine began. But all the difficulties inherent in dealing with cities in the hill country described in the last chapter are present to a far greater degree in Jerusalem. Occupation here has been more prolonged and on a greater scale than anywhere else in Palestine. Part of Israelite Jerusalem lies under the modern city, and great rubbish deposits and continuous building operations, all tearing up the walls of earlier structures, have profoundly modified the contours of the ground.

The original Canaanite town lay on the hill of Ophel, to the south of the present walled city.[1] This forms a spur slightly below the rest of the ridge, but strength is given by the steep valleys on either side, the Kedron to the east and the Tyropoeon to the west. Most of the latter valley is now imperceptible on the surface, but excavation has shown that the original slope here was nearly as steep as that to the east. Some 20 out of 50 feet of the filling half-way down the valley dates to the period after the destruction of Jerusalem by Titus in A.D. 70, the rest to the period after the end of Byzantine rule. The two valleys converge, and the ancient site was thus strongly defended by nature except on the

[1] See Fig. 67.

neck joining it to the higher ground where modern Jerusalem lies.

It was not only the steep enclosing valleys that caused Ophel to become the site of the original settlement, but the still more important consideration of a perennial water-supply. It was only when lime-mortar came into use (about the end of the second millennium) to provide an impermeable lining for cisterns, that towns could be independent of such a source of water. The source for Jerusalem was the spring Gihon (or the Virgin's Fountain) in the Kedron Valley.

Excavations in Jerusalem began in 1867, the first venture of the newly founded Palestine Exploration Fund. The ensuing three-quarters of a century of excavations made it clear that there was an older Jerusalem stretching south from the present Old City. A line of town wall was traced that ran from the south-east corner of the Old City along the eastern crest of Ophel, across the mouth of the Tyropoeon and round the curve of the Hinnom Valley to join the south-west corner of the Old City. It was generally accepted that this line of wall enclosed Israelite Jerusalem, though there were different theories as to the date at which the expansion from the original settlement on the eastern ridge took place.

A portion of the wall along the eastern crest of Ophel was cleared in excavations between 1923 and 1925, including an imposing stone-built tower. This the excavators ascribed to the work of David and Solomon, and considered it to be an addition to the original Jebusite defences. The weakness in this interpretation, and indeed in the whole identification of the defences on the crest of the ridge as those of the original city, was the relation between the supposed city wall and the water supply in the valley below. The necessity of protected access to water has already been described in connection with Megiddo (pp. 233–5). As was the case at Megiddo, the inhabitants of Jerusalem made provision for such access. Details of a succession of shafts and tunnels connected with the spring, of which the latest and most famous is the Siloam Tunnel (p. 287) were studied by Père Hugues Vincent during cleaning operations carried out by a British expedition in 1909–11. The earliest was a combination of tunnels and a vertical shaft. It was believed that this provided the Jebusites with their access to the water, and it was also suggested that this was the water channel up which Joab and his men crawled to take the defenders in the rear and to enable David to capture the town that the Jebusites believed to be impregnable. Herein lies the weakness in interpretation referred to, for the shaft comes to the surface well outside the line of defences ascribed to David and the Jebusites.

When excavations were resumed at Jerusalem by the British School of Archaeology in 1961, the investigation of this problem was a major objective. It was in fact found that the defences on the crest were late, Post-Exilic and Maccabean, and that the original town wall was 160 feet further east and 83 feet lower on the slope. This wall proved to date from c.1800 B.C., and to have continued in use down to the 8th century B.C. It was thus the wall of the Jebusite town and the wall of the City of David. Of the Middle Bronze Age town to which the wall originally belonged, only slight remains survived the continual process of erosion to which buildings on this steep slope were subjected. There were also some traces of Early Bronze Age occupation and, as already mentioned (p. 90), tombs of the Proto-Urban period have been found in Jerusalem, but there is so far no evidence of a town earlier than 1800 B.C.

[1]David not only took over the defences of the town that he captured, but also a very important element in its lay-out. The Middle Bronze Age town had been built on rock following its steep slope up to the west. In about the 13th century B.C. a great town planning operation was carried out, in which a series of terraces were constructed as a basis for a much more grandiose town. These terraces were taken over and enlarged, and may in fact be the "Millo" (or filling) which David and his successors are said to have built or repaired. A town built on such terraces was much better laid out than one on a steep slope, but the terraces were very liable to collapse, and in fact the only structures that survive on them belong to the last years of the Jewish kingdom in the 7th-6th centuries B.C.

[1] Addenda pp. 343–4.

The capture of Jerusalem is to be dated *c*. 995 B.C. By it, David's position was assured. His growing power inevitably aroused the hostility of the Philistines. Their defeats at Baal-Perazim and Rephaim caused their withdrawal once more to the coastal plain, and they ceased to be a permanent menace. But though David now started on a policy of expansion, he never annexed Philistia. It may be conjectured that Egypt, in spite of its weakness at this time, gave sufficient support to deter him. The coastal plain in fact never became part of the Israelite domain, and the Philistines reappear in the 8th and 7th centuries B.C. as an independent group.

David followed up his success against the Philistines by attacking other ancient enemies. The various "oppressors" were now oppressed in their turn. Moab, Ammon, Edom, were all subjugated, and the most surprising expansion is the defeat of the Aramaeans and the annexation of Damascus. The Israelites thus controlled a large part of the country from the Euphrates to the borders of Egypt, though the Phoenician towns on the Syrian coast remained independent.

This unification and expansion inevitably brought about a revolution in the culture of the country. The people of simple hill villages, united in reality only by religious ties, became part of an organised kingdom. The transfer of the religious centre to Jerusalem established a combined political and religious focus, and strengthened the monarch at the expense of the priesthood. The international contacts of the Israelites were opened up for the first time. Instead of being circumscribed within their limited area, they were brought into touch with the main currents of civilisation of the period. In particular, they were brought into touch with the Phoenicians. Recent archaeological research in Syria and the adjacent countries has shown that Phoenicia at this time had a highly developed civilisation, manifesting itself in fine buildings and a distinctive (though eclectic rather than original) art, and a remarkable development in literature, as well as in the trading and colonising ventures for which they have long been famous. Research in Palestine is beginning to show how strong

Phoenician influence was in the process which began under David, which was in fact the civilising of Israel.

This process was indeed begun under David, but he only provided the groundwork for the great developments under Solomon. There is little in the record, either literary or archaeological, to show that much progress towards civilisation was made during David's reign. For Solomon's reign there is considerable literary evidence, but not much archaeological. Many attempts have been made to reconstruct on paper the Temple Solomon built at Jerusalem on the hill north of Ophel. Finds on other sites make it easier to understand the description and to visualise some of the details, but the area of the Temple and that of the extension of the city under the Israelites lie beneath modern Jerusalem, beyond the reach of the archaeologist's spade.

The site of the Temple lies beneath the Moslem sanctuary, the Haram esh-Sherif, in the centre of which is the Dome of the Rock. It is probable[1] that the axis of the Temple ran east and west, and that the Temple lay to the west of the sacred rock now covered by Abd el Melek's great Dome. The rock may have been the site of the altar of sacrifices. The present enclosure owes its form to Herod's rebuilding of the Temple, begun in 19 B.C. The space for the great courtyard is provided by a terrace supported by massive retaining walls rising in places to at least 130 feet above rock. The layout of Solomon's Temple must also have involved great terracing operations, and Père Vincent believes that portions of the surviving wall at the southern end are actually Solomon's work. This cannot be established with certainty, since the walls were only examined in the pioneer excavations of Sir Charles Warren in 1867–70, before criteria existed for dating different styles of masonry dressing. To the south of the Temple, Solomon built his palace, a great structure with a succession of courts; plans resembling the description given in 1 Kings vi have been found in Mesopotamia. A suggested plan for the whole layout, based by Père Vincent on the biblical description and on comparative archaeological material, is given on Fig. 58.[2]

[1] Vincent et Steve, *Jérusalem de l'Ancien Testament.*   [2] Addenda pp. 344–5.

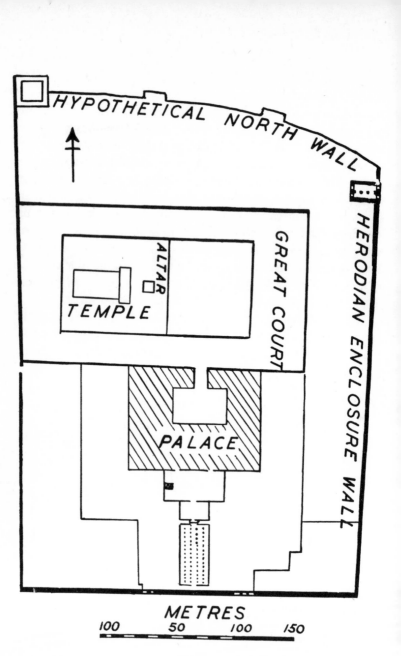

FIG. 58   Suggested plan of Solomon's Temple and Palace

246

But though the site of the Temple itself yields no evidence, it is, however, now clear that Solomon's Temple was wholly Phoenician in character. The most plausible reconstruction makes it a long rectangular building raised on a podium, with a porch leading into an oblong hall lighted by a clerestory, at the back of which a flight of steps led into the Holy of Holies. Surrounding and buttressing the main building were three storeys of small rooms, whose support enabled the walls of the main hall to withstand the thrust of the wide roof. A small temple which reproduces nearly exactly the main features of the central structure has now been excavated at Tell Tainat in Syria, providing valuable evidence of contemporary temple planning in Phoenicia. Archaeological finds, too, have supplied illustrations for the decorations. Fragments of ivory carvings found at Megiddo, Samaria, Arslan Tash in Syria and elsewhere provide many parallels for the carved palm trees, flowers and gold leaf with which it was adorned, and show that the cherubim were almost certainly winged sphinxes. The building methods also were Phoenician, for walls built "with three courses of hewn stone and a course of cedar beams" have been found at Ras Shamra in Syria. Thus, though no remains of the Temple have been found, comparative material does now make it possible to interpret intelligibly the written evidence.

Solomon was thus engaged in decorating his capital with all the luxurious equipment to be found in the most civilised countries of his time. At the same time he was of course profoundly modifying every aspect of his country's culture, including that of its religion. He would appear to have been cosmopolitan in every sense, and to have brought strange gods into the country almost as equals to Yahweh. But of this, unfortunately, archaeology so far has told us nothing.

Most of Solomon's material innovations were no doubt concerned with the rebuilding and beautifying of Jerusalem. The rest of the country may even have been impoverished as a result of exactions to support the luxury of the capital. Excavation has in fact produced little evidence of grandiose building else-where which can be attributed to this period. But in 1 Kings ix. 15, the tax which he levied is said to have been used not only on building the Temple and his palace and the walls of Jerusalem, but also on building Hazor, Megiddo and Gezer. These are all key strategic sites, and attention to them for the security of his kingdom would be reasonable.

The excavations at Hazor[1] suggest that in respect of this site the literary record can be literally interpreted that he founded the town, at least in the sense that the site was not occupied when he began work. Its destruction in the Late Bronze Age, probably at the beginning of the 13th century B.C., has been described in Chapter 8. It does not seem to have been reoccupied until the 10th century B.C. The town then established was insignificant in size compared with its predecessor, enclosing only the western part of the higher area, the tell, in the south-west corner (Pl. 33). This area was enclosed by a casemate wall, a form of defence typical of the period. In 1957 a magnificent gateway was exca-vated near the middle of the east side (Pl. 50A), consisting of an internal entrance passage flanked by four successive guardrooms. The interesting thing is that this gateway can be exactly paralleled in plan, and almost exactly in dimensions, at Gezer and Megiddo.[2] At Gezer, the excavations were carried out at too early a period for the structure to be dated stratigraphically, and the identifica-tion of a part of its plan, associated with a casemate wall similar to that at Hazor, is due to Dr. Yadin. At Megiddo the gateway, here, as probably at Gezer, approached by an oblique sloping ramp with an outer gateway (Fig. 59), is ascribed to Stratum IV. In this stratum there is a group of public buildings which have been attributed to Solomon. They include a number of elaborate stables, and there is no doubt that Solomon added chariots and horsemen to the infantry army of David. His "chariot cities" are mentioned in the Books of Kings and Chronicles (1 Kings ix. 19, x. 26 and 2 Chronicles i. 14) and in one passage (1 Kings ix. 15-19) the building of Megiddo is coupled with a list of the building of

[1] *Hazor*, I.   [2] Y. Yadin, *I.E.J.*, 8.

his store-cities and cities for his chariots and cities for his horse-men, though it is not specifically said that Megiddo is one of these. But, as will be seen (pp. 269 ff.), the published evidence of the pottery and of the architecture shows that these buildings are not earlier than the 9th century B.C. The stratum which on pottery evidence belongs to the Solomonic period is the underlying Stratum V. This was re-founded, after a period of abandonment since c. 1100 B.C., early in the 10th century B.C., and it is possible

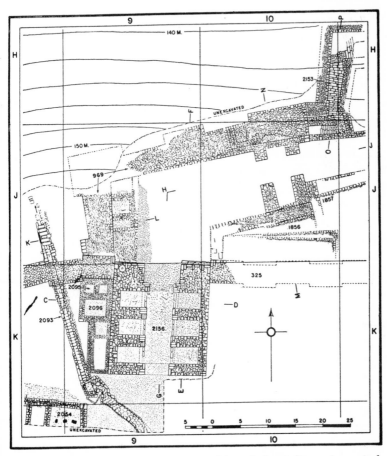

FIG. 59 Gateway of Megiddo, possibly of the Solomonic period

that the re-founding was, as at Hazor, the work of Solomon. The evidence for associating the gate with the stratum is not clear.[1] It is difficult to avoid the conclusion, based on similarity of plan, that it is contemporary with the Hazor gateway, and it may be that in origin it belongs to Stratum V.

The city of Megiddo Stratum VI was destroyed about 1100 B.C., and for an appreciable length of time after that the site was not occupied. It may very possibly have been during this period of desertion that it came under Israelite control, for it is difficult otherwise to account for the fact that there is no mention of its capture by the Israelites. The period of David's expansion to the north may have been the first occasion of its inclusion within the Israelite kingdom. Its rebuilding may date from this time, or else be due to Solomon's interest in foreign trade, for it commands the important route across the Plain of Esdraelon. Archaeological evidence suggests that it was rebuilt early in the 10th century B.C.

The city of Stratum V had certainly no great architectural pretensions. The buildings are mostly small, the walls thin and not particularly well built. The planning agrees well with that of a number of contemporary towns. Round the perimeter, in a band of about 20 metres, the houses are built radially to the edge, while inside that, presumably separated by a ring road, they are uniformly orientated north and south. No city wall was ascribed to the level, and it was suggested that the line of houses on the circumference served the purpose of a wall. This, however, seems unlikely, and as it is recorded that the outside walls had crumbled down the slope, it is possible either that the wall may have done likewise, or may have been destroyed by a later wall.[2] It is particularly unlikely, since to this period is ascribed an elaborate city gate, with a long approach ramp making a right-angled turn to enter the gate. It is suggested above that the remains ascribed to

[1] Indeed in the photograph, *Megiddo*, II, Fig. 108, the masonry underlying the indicated pavement level is not of the type found in foundations at Samaria, and mason's setting-out lines are only found there on the dressed superstructure. Moreover, in *ibid.*, Figs. 89 and 97, the stones of the supposed Stratum V gateway underlying it look much more like the foundation courses of the same wall.

[2] Addenda pp. 345-6.

this period are actually the foundations of the fine superimposed gateway. In any case, they presuppose an associated town wall, though how this is related to that published as belonging to Stratum IV is uncertain.[1] A point of interest is the large number of cult objects recovered (Pl. 49). They included horned altars, incense stands, braziers and chalices, and were found in profusion in so many buildings that it is difficult to deduce that all the find-spots were religious structures. Private chapels in individual houses appear more probable.

Beth-shan also came under Israelite control for the first time at this period. The temple of Level VI appears from the pottery evidence to have continued in use down to the end of the 11th century B.C. In the next level, V, ascribed to the time of Rameses III, but really to be dated to c. 1000–850 B.C., two temples appear, one above the Level VI temple, and one to the north of it. It is possible that these temples were in existence at the time of the battle of Mount Gilboa, since the biblical account refers to a temple of Dagon and a temple of Ashtaroth. They may, however, have been built after the town fell into Israelite hands.

The southern temple was built on top of débris which covered the remains of the previous structure. It represents a revolution in temple planning on the site, for it breaks completely with the plan of the preceding two levels. Its plan in fact resembles that which was suggested above for the Temple at Jerusalem, and is therefore of the Phoenician type. It consists of an entrance, of which the details are somewhat obscure, but which may have taken the form of a porch, a central hall, and a shrine at the rear, unfortunately destroyed by a Hellenistic reservoir. The central hall was flanked by store-rooms, just as was the Temple at Jerusalem. A point of difference is that the central hall is divided by colonnades into aisles and nave, but these are laid out askew to the axis of the building, and based on much slighter founda-

---

[1] A clearance carried out by Yadin in 1959 (Biblical Archaeologist 1960) confirmed this suggestion that a wall belonging to Stratum V is associated with the original gateway, on a plan identical with the Solomonic gateways at Hazor and Gezer.

tions than the other walls; the excavators suggested that they might have been secondary, and they may have been put in because the roof proved unstable, though its span is no greater than that at Jerusalem.

The northern temple was a simple oblong building, with the roof supported by two rows of two columns. These were abolished in a subsequent reconstruction. No traces of a shrine or sanctuary were recovered.

Whether or not these temples were built before the Israelites captured the town, the pottery found in them shows that they certainly continued in use in the Israelite period. The evidence for their use is therefore an interesting commentary on the cosmopolitan religions permitted by Solomon, against which the prophets inveighed so often. The cult in fact differs little from that in preceding periods. There is an even greater profusion of cult objects associated with fertility rites, especially shrine houses, many of them decorated with snakes and doves, and incense stands (like those found at Megiddo). The northern temple seemed to have been used for the worship of Antit-Ashtoreth, and the southern may have been that of a companion male deity, but no definite evidence was found. The cult objects in both were similar.

We have some knowledge of the history of a number of smaller towns at this period. Possibly typical of the layout of such towns is that of Beth-Shemesh II. The preceding town, III, was violently and completely destroyed by fire about 1000 B.C., very probably in David's struggles with the Philistines. Its successor was built on a new plan, and owed little to the earlier layout. The fortifications, which followed the line of the earlier walls and in parts incorporated them, introduced a new principle, which was to become common in Iron Age Palestine. This was that of a double wall connected by cross-walls, and forming a series of casemates. Where the evidence is clear, it is certain that the lower parts of the casemates were filled up solid, the whole in effect forming a very thick wall but with a considerable economy of stone. The outer wall at Beth-Shemesh was c. 1·50 metres thick, the inner 1·10 metres, and the space between c. 1·50, so that the total width of the composite defences was *c.* 4·10 metres, in places thicker.

Stratum II was divided into three phases, of which the first, IIa, is dated 1000–950 B.C. Not a great deal of this phase was recovered, but apparently many of the later buildings were reconstructions of those of this phase, so that the plan of this second Iron Age town was established now. The layout is a very good example of the two-zone type of plan already referred to in connection with Megiddo. At a distance of about 16 metres inside the ramparts was a ring road. The space between this road and the walls was thickly built up with houses arranged radially to the rampart. Inside the ring road the planning is somewhat irregular, but the buildings tend to be orientated north and south.

A number of features characteristic of Iron Age sites in Palestine appear at this stage. One of them is a house plan in which the main block is divided longitudinally by two walls, forming three parallel and approximately equal divisions, while across one end is a room the whole width of the building. It is usually taken that the division formed a four-roomed house, but in none of the examples so far published does there seem to be clear evidence that the longitudinal walls were carried up above ground level; they may therefore be sleeper walls supporting a row of pillars, and the main block may be an aisled hall. Another feature introduced at this time was the use of upright stones up to 1 metre in height. Some of these were incorporated in rubble walls, some free-standing. From the published evidence it is not possible to ascertain where the floor level was in relation to them, and it seems probable that they were at least partially sunk in the ground, and formed bases for wooden pillars supporting the roof. A feature which makes its last appearance at this stage is the presence of round storage silos, stone-lined pits sunk in the ground. Such a method had been in use since the Late Bronze Age, but is not found in Early Iron II.

Stratum IIa is marked by the disappearance of Philistine wares. No doubt, with the driving back of the Philistines to the coastal plain, their cultural influence diminished, but at this period, even in Philistia, the typical pottery dies out, and its place is taken by derivative forms in a new technique. The new technique, which appears early in the 11th century B.C. and becomes dominant in the 10th, is the use of a dark red haematite slip, almost invariably hand-burnished. The effect is often really beautiful. It is a curious reversion to a practice of the Middle Bronze Age, which had died out completely in the interval.

The Early Iron I town at Tell Beit Mirsim duplicates many of the features of Beth-Shemesh. This stratum, B, was divided into three phases, of which the third, B3, is dated c. 1000–930 B.C., and therefore corresponds to Beth-Shemesh IIa. Here again the wall, apparently built in B3, is of the casemated form, of which the overall width was 3·75 metres. There is the same band of radial buildings round the walls, separated by a road from the differently orientated ones in the centre of the town. Round silos continue in use, but disappear in Stratum A. The pottery is the same red hand-burnished ware. Here, as at Beth-Shemesh, there was nothing to suggest any high degree of civilisation. The few moulded, carved or painted fragments illustrate only a very crude art. The most interesting objects are the fertility figurines. These are plaques, like the Astarte plaques of the Late Bronze Age, but represent a pregnant woman. The type is confined to Stratum B, but cannot be more closely dated within that phase. They indicate, however, the strength of the old fertility rites, in spite of the precepts of the religion of Israel.

A site which has provided unusually good evidence of house plans of the 10th century B.C. is Tell el Far'ah. Occupation here was continuous from Middle Bronze II down to the Iron Age, but little of the layout of the earlier periods survived. That of Early Iron I was well preserved in all areas excavated, and showed unusually regularly planned houses. The walls are thin, usually only one course of stones in width, sometimes with a strengthening of masonry filling with rough stones in between. The houses are grouped back to back, opening into parallel streets. The plan of the individual house is essentially tripartite (Fig. 60). The door from the street leads into a courtyard flanked by subsidiary

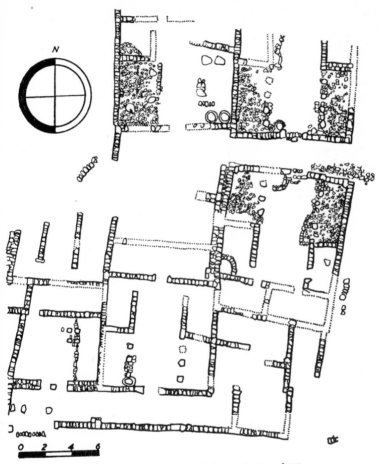

FIG. 60   Plan of Tell el Far'ah Level III

compartments, in part divided from it by pillars and in part by walls. At the end of the courtyard are one or more other rooms. In the courtyard are ovens and other domestic installations. All the houses have a similar plan and roughly the same dimensions. There was obviously very little social inequality.

Archaeology has therefore provided us with little direct evidence of the glories of Solomon's court, and has shown that, away from the capital, the civilisation was not of a very high order, nor are there striking signs of economic prosperity. The country was still one of peasant cultivators, in spite of the cosmopolitan civilisation of the court. The national religion still had as its rival the long-established native fertility rites, stimulated, no doubt, by the acceptance, at the court, of the worship of deities from allied Canaanite cultures.

The sites which have provided the best archaeological evidence, moreover, do little to illustrate another aspect of Solomon's innovations known to us from the Bible, his activities as a merchant prince. Almost no recognisably imported objects have been found in levels of this period in Palestine proper. But excavations in Transjordan have produced evidence of one branch of trade and industry, and have shown that one source of his wealth was the control of copper-working in that district.[1]

Sites giving evidence of copper-working have long been known on either side of the Wadi 'Arabah, the deep cleft continuing the line of the Jordan Valley and the Dead Sea down to the Gulf of 'Aqaba. In the 1930s the American School of Oriental Research in Jerusalem carried out a systematic survey of the area. This has revealed an amazing wealth of sites at which mining and smelting of copper was carried out. The mineral wealth of the district is no doubt one reason for the prolonged struggles between Israel and Edom, for its control was clearly of great economic importance. The most obvious indication of these sites is large heaps of blackened slag. Near them are found surprisingly well-preserved smelting furnaces and the remains of the huts in which the labourers lived. Many of the sites were fortified, and at some are traces of great fortified enclosures, probably serving as compounds in which slave or prisoner labour, on which it is reasonable to suppose that the industry was based, was confined. Much of the mining was open-cast, but at some sites there are caves cut into the sides of the hill, with the roof supported on pillars, from which short tunnels lead farther into the hillside. It appears that the cupriferous rock was mined and taken to near-by centres, at

[1] For pp. 256–8, see Addenda p. 346.

which it was partially smelted or roasted, and then taken else-where for the process to be completed.

The American expedition collected large quantities of pot-sherds from the sites. Some of them belong to the Nabatean period, but a very great number of them belong to the Early Iron Age, and are dated by the finders to the 10th century B.C. Many sites seem to have been occupied solely at that period.

Even without this evidence it would have been not unreason-able to suggest that the most flourishing period of this exploitation was that of the reign of Solomon. The control of mineral resources provides one explanation for his wealth, for its products supplied export goods to be exchanged for the luxuries we know he imported. Moreover, there is almost no other period in Palestinian history when there was a central power able to provide the planning and organisation required. The degree of organisation necessary must have been high. The area is a desolate one, with almost nothing available at hand to support life or industry. Water supplies are scanty, fuel is almost non-existent. Water, food, tools and all other necessities must have been brought by camel or donkey trains, and the only source of the fuel for the smelting that can be suggested is that of the forests of Edom, plentiful till comparatively modern times, from which it must have been brought in the form of charcoal. The caravans which brought these supplies and no doubt carried away with them the partly finished ore, the provision of installations for the final processing and its subsequent marketing all formed part of the organisation required.

One centre, possibly the principal one, for these final stages was also discovered by the American expedition. The site was a small tell, called Tell Kheleifeh, some 500 metres from the present shore of the Gulf of 'Aqaba, and probably on the ancient shore-line. The situation of this settlement is surprising, for the water supply is not nearly as good as farther east, and it receives the full force of the winds blowing down the Arabah. But excavation showed that a large part of it consisted of exceedingly elaborate smelting furnaces, and the situation was undoubtedly selected to obtain the full benefit of the winds to supply the necessary blast for the furnaces.

The first settlement was not a large one, but it was defended by a very strong wall. It was built as a planned whole on virgin soil, and the first stratum was dated by the excavators to the 10th century B.C. on the evidence of the pottery. It thus seems very probable that this was Solomon's port of Ezion-Geber, which must have been somewhere in this neighbourhood, at which his fleet of trading ships was built (it must be remembered that he did not control any ports on the Mediterranean coast), and to which were brought the "gold, silver, ivory, apes, peacocks" from Ophir.

After the time of Solomon, the Israelites controlled the Arabah only intermittently, for it was only during the United Monarchy, or, after the division, when Judah was especially strong, that the Edomites could be kept in subjugation. But whether under Israelites or Edomites, Ezion-Geber remained important as a centre of trade for five centuries. Three rebuildings of the settlement were identified. In the third level was found a jar on which were incised letters of the south Arabian Minaean script, a reminder of the part the port must have played in the trade northwards of south Arabian spices, while in the surface soil were sherds of black-figured Attic ware of the mid-5th century B.C., showing that it also had a place in the trade between the west and the Arabian hinterland.

In the Arabah we thus have evidence of Solomon's position as a great merchant prince which excavations in Palestine have so far failed to produce. It seems clear that his material splendour was concentrated at Jerusalem, where little trace of the period is likely ever to be found. There, Phoenician civilisation must have been firmly established. In lesser towns much of the old simplicity remained. It is true that the remains indicate comparatively orderly towns with a homogeneous type of layout and architecture; for the first time since the Middle Bronze Age there was an appreciable number of true towns, instead of straggling villages, but there can have been few with any pretensions to architectural distinction, and we have no evidence of any particular luxury.

The contrast between the luxury of the capital and the comparative poverty of other districts, to which no doubt exactions to support the royal ambitions contributed materially, was one of the underlying causes of the disintegration of Solomon's kingdom. There is no doubt that the economic basis of the kingdom was unsound, an unsoundness greatly accentuated when Edom, and with it the copper mines, was lost, which apparently happened before the end of Solomon's reign. The other cause, which is the one emphasised in the biblical account, was religious. Solomon's heterodoxy and tolerance of foreign gods aroused fierce opposition from the faithful adherents to the austere religion of Yahweh, and it was they who stimulated the revolt of the northern tribes against Jerusalem. Solomon died c. 935 B.C., and by 930 B.C. Jeroboam had led the northern tribes in revolt against his successor Rehoboam, and the short period of the United Monarchy was at an end.

★

CHAPTER ELEVEN

The Kingdoms of Israel and Judah

THOUGH IT was the revolt of the northern tribes against the luxuries and the religious misdoings of Jerusalem that broke up the United Monarchy, the northern kingdom of Israel was in fact the heir of the civilisation first brought into Palestine by Solomon, while Judah, reacting against the former luxuries of Jerusalem in an attempt to counteract the effects of the schism, regained much of the simplicity and even barbarism of the earlier period.

This was in fact inevitable. Israel was in close geographical contact with Phoenicia and the other civilised countries to the north; Judah was shut in between Israel, with whom she was usually at war, the backward and warlike kingdoms of Transjordan to the east, and the desert to the south.

Fortunately, archaeology has supplied evidence of what is probably the last expression in Palestine of the Phoenician civilisation introduced by Solomon. The evidence for this comes from the site which ultimately became the permanent capital of the Northern Kingdom—Samaria.

In the first years of the divided monarchy, the kings of Israel had no fixed abode. After having been at Shechem the capital was transferred to Tirzah, at least by the time of Baasha, the third king, and possibly earlier. About 885 B.C. Omri laid siege to Tirzah and captured it, and the usurper Zimri perished in the flames of his palace. The recent excavations of the École Biblique make it as certain as archaeological evidence can that Tirzah is to be identified as Tell el Farʿah. The 10th century town at Tell el Farʿah was described in the last chapter. This town was violently destroyed, and the contents of the houses were buried in the débris of the superstructures. In the area excavated, the simple private houses were succeeded by something quite different, a building on a much larger scale and with much more massive walls. But this building was never finished. Its foundations were started from the level of débris within the earlier buildings, above which the stumps of the earlier walls protruded. On the level rested dressed stones intended for the superstructure, but these were never placed in position, and the floor levels which would have buried the tops of the older walls were never laid (Pl. 50B).

In 1 Kings xvi. 23–24 it is recorded "In the thirty and first year of Asa king of Judah began Omri to reign over Israel twelve years: six years reigned he in Tirzah. And he bought the hill of Samaria of Shemer for two talents of silver, and built on the hill, and called the name of the city which he built, after the name of Shemer, owner of the hill, Samaria." This accords remarkably well with the evidence at Tell el Farʿah. Omri's first four years were occupied with struggles with his rival, Tibni. Only then was he free to concentrate on his capital. He began to build, but abandoned his work. On pottery evidence, where Tell el Farʿah stops, Samaria begins. In the pottery of Tell el Farʿah there is a complete absence of the types found in the first two periods at Samaria, while at Samaria the pottery of the preceding stage at Tell el Farʿah is not found. When Omri decided to move to Samaria, he took with him his court, and probably most of the inhabitants of Tirzah. Only at the time of Samaria Period III does some slight occupation reappear at Tell el Farʿah, and only in the time of Samaria Period IV does it become a flourishing town once more.

The reasons for Omri's transfer of the capital were twofold. As the description of his buildings at Samaria will show, he had grandiose ideas about the layout of his capital. For such, an unencumbered site such as Samaria gave him much greater scope. But more important was its strategic position. Though the communications of Tell el Far'ah are good, it looks primarily towards the east. Samaria lies athwart the main north–south route, watchful of any advance up from Judah and in easy contact with Phoenicia, and as the history of Samaria shows, Omri desired intercourse with the cosmopolitan towns of Phoenicia; further evidence of this is his marriage of his son Ahab to Jezebel of Tyre. It was equally important for him to have easy communication to the west, where lay the richest lands of his kingdom. On all counts, Samaria was a much better focus than Tell el Far'ah.

Samaria has the unique interest that it is the only major town founded by the Israelites. Archaeologically it has the importance that, as we have a fixed date for its foundation, we can establish very closely the chronology of the pottery and other objects found associated with its first phase. Culturally it has the importance that we can see how the Israelites, when not hampered by buildings of an earlier stage, set about laying out a city.

The site itself is not a commanding one, but nevertheless has a number of advantages to recommend it. The hill of Samaria (Pl. 51B) is an isolated one, standing in a basin surrounded by higher hills, not, however, sufficiently close to command it, and it rises fairly steeply from the surrounding valleys. The most important fact is that it commands, as does Jerusalem, the great north–south road along the watershed. The modern road passes along its western foot, and the ancient one must have followed approximately the same line. There are reasonably good tracks leading down towards the Jordan on the east, while to the west it looks out towards the coastal plain and the Mediterranean.

Excavation confirms the biblical account that Omri founded his town on a virgin site. A little Proto-Urban pottery was found in pockets in the rock, together with a number of rock-cut pits belonging to the same period. The site was then deserted from at least early in the third millennium until Omri's building operations began. The floor levels associated with his buildings rest directly upon rock. The layout of the town took advantage of the natural shape of the hill. This slopes down from a summit plateau at about 430 metres above sea level to 350 metres at the point enclosed by the city at its greatest extent, in the Roman period, which is still well above the level of the surrounding valleys. The slope from the summit is steep on all sides except to the east. The size of the summit plateau today is *c.* 250 metres from east to west and 160 metres from north to south. A considerable part of this area is, however, due to ancient structures, starting with those of Omri, and the original width from north to south was only about 90 metres.

The whole of this summit plateau was laid out as a royal quarter (Fig. 61). This is a new conception in Palestinian town-planning. No doubt there was a similar layout in Solomon's Jerusalem, but the first concrete evidence for it comes from Samaria. To some extent it corresponds to the acropolis almost invariably associated with Greek towns, but its significance is rather different. The Greek acropolis is the defensible civic centre of a democratic community. The royal quarter at Samaria may have been defensible, for at least in the second phase it was surrounded by a strong wall. That this was not its primary purpose is shown by the fact that the first enclosure wall was not of military character, and what we know of its layout makes it clear that it was in no sense a civic centre, but rather an exclusive enclosure reserved for an autocratic king and his servants. Social development has proceeded a long way from the simple warrior peasants who became the first kings of Israel in the 11th century.

To the first building phase belongs the enclosure of the summit with a wall which, as mentioned above, cannot have been primarily defensive in purpose, since it was only 1·60 metres thick. As well as an enclosure wall, it served as a terrace wall to increase the area of the summit plateau. On the north side it was built where the rock starts to drop steeply, against a prepared scarp about 2 metres high, and the floor level inside the enclosure (destroyed by later structures) must have been at least 4 metres above that on the outside. The wall was everywhere robbed too low for any portion of the interior face to survive, but a few stretches of the outer face were found. Fragmentary as they are,

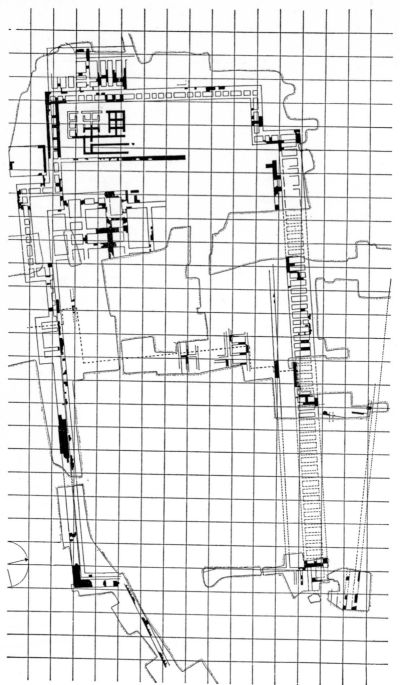

Fig. 61 Plan of the Omri-Ahab Royal Quarter at Samaria

they enable us to obtain an impression of the magnificent masonry of Omri's Samaria. The face is a superb example of the stone-mason's art (Pl. 52). On the rock is a course with the irregular bosses characteristic of foundation work and heavier walls in Israelite Samaria. Above, the stones are dressed flat, and fitted with quite beautiful exactitude.

The line of this magnificent wall was traced all round the summit plateau. The entrance to the enclosure must, from the contours of the ground, have been to the east. Here, the enclosure wall turns forward in a salient, probably leading towards a monumental gateway, but further traces were lost in a later quarry. At the west end of the summit was a building of the same first-rate masonry. Elsewhere within the enclosure only founda-tions survived, but they were sufficient to show that the layout was regular and spacious. Within the area excavated a considerable space was occupied by a great courtyard with a beaten lime floor; the buildings were aligned on the enclosure wall, but set back from it, and the rooms were fairly large.

Such then was Omri's conception of the layout of a royal quarter. To this original plan additions were made within a short period. They might be ascribed to Ahab, who succeeded his father within six years of the transference of the capital to Samaria. One may in fact consider the Omri-Ahab building operations as a continuous process. The principal addition consisted of the extension of the summit plateau by some 15 metres on the north side and some 30 metres on the west. The wall which supported this extension was at the same time clearly defensive in purpose, thus converting the royal quarter into an inner fortress. It was built on the casemate plan which has been shown to be typical of the Iron Age in Palestine. On the north side the overall width was 10 metres while on the other sides it was 5 metres. Like the earlier enclosure wall, the casemate wall turns outwards at the east end towards the presumed entrance. On the north and west sides, the earlier wall continued in use, though partially buried by the fill of the additional terrace, but on the other sides the new wall was built right up against it, and incorporated it.

In addition to the new wall on the summit, there are walls enclosing the middle terraces of the hill which probably belong to this stage, though they replace others presumably belonging to the first stage. They illustrate the other very fine style of Israelite masonry in which the casemates were also built, that with smooth-dressed margins and attractively irregular bosses (Pl. 51A).

These walls, however, do not represent the city walls, and unfortunately little of these has been traced. Remains of what was probably a gate lie beneath the West Gate of the Roman city, and traces of Israelite occupation have been found sufficiently far down the hill to suggest that the Israelite town must have been nearly as large as the Roman one.[1]

Of actual architectural fragments of this period disappointingly little survives. The exception is a number of capitals of pilasters in the proto-Ionic style. These were all found re-used in later walls, but their find-spots at the east end of the summit plateau suggest that they may have formed part of the entrance structure (Fig. 62).

An important indication of the fittings of the buildings survives in the fragments of ivory carvings. Ahab's "house of ivory" is referred to in the Bible, and there can be no doubt that these fragments came from its furniture, though they were recovered from the débris of the destruction caused by the Assyrians in 720 B.C. In these ivories we have striking material evidence, which has hardly survived in any other form, of the artistic tastes of the kings of Israel. The original objects were small in themselves, and many of them much broken, and though some hundreds of fragments were found few of them could be completely restored. This may not seem much from which to deduce the style of decoration of the palace. But it must be remembered that what was recovered was probably only the residue after the palace was looted by the Assyrians. It is therefore fair to suppose that the original decoration must have been very rich, and the use of ivory profuse.

The bulk of the fragments are of plaques, in low or high relief or in openwork (Pls. 53A, B). Very few objects carved in the

[1] Addenda p. 346.

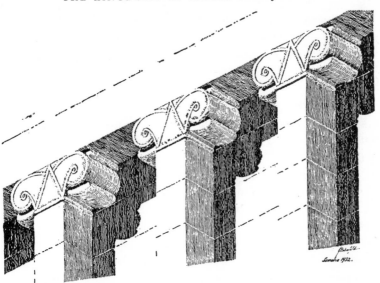

FIG. 62   Restoration of wall of Israelite entrance at Samaria

round were included. The carvings were enriched by gold-foil and
glass and paste insets set in cloisonné work. The majority of the
plaques are Egyptian in subject and basic treatment. But not one
is truly Egyptian; they are the work of men who had seen the
Egyptian originals, but copied them in their own national style.
That the ivories were not made by Egyptians is also shown by
the fact that a number of them had letters in the Hebrew-
Phoenician alphabet carved on their backs. These letters, moreover, provide one of the grounds for assigning the carvings to
the period of Omri and Ahab, for the form of the letters is that
used in the 9th century B.C. The style of the ivories is in fact
Phoenician, an art derivative in its inspiration but with sufficient
life and feeling to make it one of the finest products of a period
not notable for great artistic inspiration.

Further evidence of the origin and date of the ivories comes
from other finds of similar material. There are numerous references to the use of ivory for decorative purposes in Syria. There

are, moreover, two great collections which contain material very comparable to the Samaria ivories. One was discovered in 1928 by a French expedition at Arslan Tash in northern Syria. Many of the objects are almost identical with those from Samaria, but the class with the strongest Egyptian influence is less common. This collection provided important chronological evidence, in that a bed, which was one of the furnishings decorated by the carvings, was inscribed with the name of Hazael of Damascus, who came to the throne in c. 842 B.C. The second collection was found by Layard in 1849 in a palace at Nimrud in Assyria. The palace had been restored by Sargon II and most of the objects in it belong to this period. The ivories are completely un-Assyrian in style. Many of them might have come from the same workshop as those at Samaria, and since they were probably loot or tribute they may well have come from Samaria itself, which was sacked by Sargon in 722 B.C.[1]

The decoration of the palace of Omri and Ahab was thus Phoenician in style. There is little doubt that from the same source came the technique in building already described. As will be seen, other examples of the technique can be found in Palestine. Outside Palestine, it is found at Ras Shamra, dating from the Late Bronze Age, and in the remains of the great port of Tyre. It seems highly probable that Omri imported Phoenician masons, as Solomon had done, for the closeness of his relations with Tyre is shown by the marriage of his son Ahab to Jezebel of Tyre.

Samaria thus was laid out as a new city, dominated by a royal quarter which was beautified by the skill of Phoenician craftsmen. Archaeology has given us tantalisingly brief glimpses of this, for subsequent buildings have destroyed almost everything, but we can in imagination reconstruct some of the setting of the court of Ahab and Jezebel, of which the luxury and evil-doings aroused such wrath in the prophets. Elsewhere on the hill the rest of the

[1] Recently, enormous collections of ivories have been recovered by Professor Mallowan in renewed excavations at Nimrud. They include some close in style to those from Samaria, but their range is very much greater, and is indicative of the rich artistic resources of the lands ruled by the Assyrian kings.

inhabitants of Samaria must have lived, seven thousand of "all the children of Israel," according to the census of Ahab, and possibly many foreigners as well. A hundred and fifty years later, Sargon deported 27,290 persons from the city. So far, the living quarters of the common people have not been excavated, so we cannot tell whether they shared in the greater degree of civilisation of the royal quarter or whether their abodes and their equipment were still simple.

There were some buildings in the same style in Stratum V at Beth-shan, but the site in Palestine which has produced buildings that bear the greatest resemblance to thise phase at Samaria is Megiddo, where Stratum IV both in layout and building style has many similarities. As mentioned in Chapter 10, this stratum was ascribed by the excavators to the period of Solomon. But on the evidence of the plan and masonry and on the independent evidence of the comparison of the pottery of this, the previous and the succeeding periods with that of Samaria, details concerning which were not available when Megiddo was published, it is clear that the buildings of Stratum IV were constructed shortly after Samaria was founded, at about 850 B.C., and continued in use down to about 750 B.C.[1]

In Megiddo V, the summit of the hill was, as has been described (pp. 250–1), occupied by private buildings of an unimpressive character. The builders of Stratum IV swept away all these, and laid out the whole area with large and widely spaced public buildings.[2] The resemblance to the first stage of Samaria is close. The excavators considered that there were two phases in the building operations. The first was the construction of a large palace or residency enclosure, with a smaller building beside it. The enclosure was 57 metres square, with a surface floored with beaten limestone, similar to the courtyard at Samaria. It was entered at one corner by a gateway flanked by towers, and against the far side was a very substantial building, presumably the palace of the governor. The masonry of the gateway (Pl. 54) is strikingly similar to that of the early buildings at Samaria. Almost nothing

[1] *Samaria*, III, pp. 199–204.   [2] Addenda pp. 346–8.

of the superstructure of the palace survives, but the few remaining stones were in the same style. In the gateway were found a number of proto-Ionic pilaster capitals again similar to those at Samaria. The enclosure wall itself was built in a style peculiar to Megiddo at the period. At intervals of 2·50 to 3 metres there were ashlar piers of alternating courses of a stretcher and one or two headers, of which the stones were dressed like those of the gateway. The intervals between the piers were filled with comparatively small and irregular rubble.

After this complex had been in existence for a comparatively short time (there are even some indications that it was never completed in its original form), the buildings of the second phase were put in hand, one of which caused the abolition of part of the house adjoining the palace enclosure. These new structures were in exactly the same style as those already described, and look as though they were put up by the same builders. They involved the laying out of the whole of the rest of the summit (in so far as it has been excavated) with official buildings. One of these was probably another important residence. The rest of the area cleared was occupied by two great stable complexes. The more elaborate of these immediately adjoined the palace. It consisted of a courtyard 55 metres square, flanked on one side by stables and on a second by long buildings which may have housed chariots. In the centre was a water-tank. The stables were made up of five units consisting of a central passage flanked on either side by a row of stables. At the end of each stall was a stone-cut manger and an upright monolith in which there was a tethering-hole. The whole group would have held one hundred and fifty horses. The second group of stables was composed of similar units. There did not in this case appear to be an enclosing court-yard, but the area was not completely excavated. This group may have housed another three hundred horses.

The summit was enclosed by a massive wall, pierced by an elaborate gateway. This consisted of an oblique approach ramp leading up to a double outer gate. Beyond was a courtyard in which a sharp turn was made to the inner gate, an elaborate structure in which four pairs of buttresses provided emplacements for four gates, with three pairs of guardrooms between. The gateway, probably based on that of Stratum V,[1] is in the same building style as the other structures of Stratum V, with ashlar piers and quoins alternating with rubble. This is not, however, the case with the enclosure wall, which was entirely of rather rough rubble. This enclosure wall was built on top of the robbed foundations of the palace belonging to the early phase of Stratum IV. It may in fact be conjectured that this wall is a rebuilding belonging to Stratum III, when it was certainly in use.

Thus, as at Samaria, the summit of the hill at Megiddo was at this stage occupied for official purposes. In spite of the attraction of the theory that the buildings represent one of Solomon's chariot cities, planning, building style and pottery evidence all point to the approximate contemporaneity of this stratum with the first layout of Samaria. Emphasis is, however, on garrison purposes rather than a royal residence, as is natural in view of the strategic importance of the site. As at Samaria, the mass of the population must have lived on the lower slopes, and some traces were observed of an outer city wall.

Samaria and Megiddo stand out from other towns of this period in Palestine of which we have knowledge by reason of this planning with an official quarter dominating the town, though no doubt Jerusalem was similar, and Lachish may have had some features in common with them.

It would seem that at Hazor also there were some major town-planning developments. In Stratum VIII, which is assigned to the period, the defended area was extended to the east end of the tell. The area of the town was thus doubled, though it was still infinitesimal in comparison with the Middle Bronze Age town. At the western tip of the site, a great rectangular citadel was built, so solid that it continued in use down to the Hellenistic period, even when the rest of the site was abandoned. In the centre, across the line of the Solomonic wall, was constructed a massive building divided into aisles by two rows of stone piers 2 metres

[1] See p. 248.

high; it is suggested that this may have been a storehouse. There is therefore much here that is suggestive of a royal quarter.[1]

At Tell el Far'ah an important town again grew up about 800 B.C., with pottery closely similar to that of the Period IV pottery of Samaria. Here, there was not a royal quarter, though an important building immediately inside the gate may have been an administrative centre or governor's residence. In the rest of the town, however, there does seem to have been a marked distinction between a rich quarter and a poor quarter. A group of excellent private houses, built in the same plan as those of the 10th century B.C., with a courtyard flanked on three sides by rooms, is divided by a long straight wall from a quarter in which smaller houses are closely huddled together. This evidence of the growth of social inequality reflects the denunciations of the prophets on the rich for trampling upon the poor.

The other towns excavated show a much simpler plan, and one much closer to those of the preceding period. It so happens that most of our information comes from cities of Judah. Of the sites excavated in the northern kingdom, at Beth-shan clearance was confined almost completely to the temple area, where the two structures of Stratum V (see pp. 251–2) continued in use down to the Persian period, while the fragmentary remains of this period discovered on other sites are insufficient to tell us much about the history or plan of the towns.

On a number of sites a phase of occupation dating from about the beginning of the dual monarchy can be identified. These succeed a violent destruction which may probably be ascribed to the campaign of Shishak I of the Twenty-second Dynasty of Egypt, under whom there was a renaissance of Egyptian power. He appears to have taken advantage of the weakness caused by the secession of the northern tribes to carry out an extensive raid as far north as the Plain of Esdraelon about 926 B.C., and in the process many of the smaller towns no doubt suffered severely. At the foot of Mount Carmel, for instance, Tell Abu Hawam was destroyed and left deserted for several centuries.

It is to Shishak that is ascribed the destruction of the town of

[1] Addenda p. 348.

Tell Beit Mirsim Stratum B. This destruction was very severe. The earlier town was completely obliterated, and its place taken by buildings which owe little in plan to their predecessors. The city wall in the main continued in use, but the casemates were at least partly rebuilt. About one-fifth of the area of the town was excavated. The plan was that which we have already seen established in Iron Age Palestine, including the preceding level on this site, with a ring road separating radially planned houses round the rampart from the central area of the town. The houses are small and irregularly planned. One of the chief interests of the site is the evidence it provides for the great increase in town life compared with the preceding period. In Stratum B, occupation had been comparatively sparse. At least by the end of A, to which most of the structures recovered belong, the town was closely built up, and soundings outside the walls showed that it had spread well beyond them.

Little can be deduced from the plans of the houses, for the space was too cramped in this phase for any regular plan to be followed; any individual house had to accommodate itself to the exigencies of the site available. One characteristic feature was the extensive use of upright stones, already noted as an Iron Age feature (see p. 253). Explanations of the function of these stones are not completely satisfactory, but one suggestion is that in part the free-standing ones were used as uprights for vertical looms. The evidence certainly does suggest that Tell Beit Mirsim was the centre of a textile industry. Many hundreds of loom-weights were found, and scattered all over the area excavated was a surprisingly large number of dyeing plants. It is estimated that there must have been twenty or thirty in the whole town, which was only a small one with a population of two to three thousand persons. Another characteristic of the period is the disappearance of the sunk storage silos, their place being taken by bins on the floors of the houses.

Another site which was violently destroyed in the second half of the 10th century B.C. was Beth-Shemesh, where the buildings of Stratum IIa were covered with a level of ashes from a very fierce fire. The excavators suggest that this occurred about 950 B.C. If so, it must have been due to a chance conflagration, for a destruction by an enemy is improbable at the height of Solomon's power; a destruction by Shishak about 926 B.C. is historically more probable, and the chronological evidence is not so precise as to make this impossible. The rebuilt town of Stratum IIb followed the main lines of that of IIa, described above (p. 253), but here again there is evidence for a considerable growth of town population.

A third small town of which the remains of this period have been excavated is at Tell en Nasbeh. The site may be that of the biblical Mizpah. After occupation in the Early Bronze Age, it was left deserted until the beginning of the Iron Age. The occupation before the end of the 10th century appears to have been slight. It is possible that an early, rather slight, fortification wall may belong to this period. If it is the site of Mizpah, it would seem that in the time of Samuel it was little more than a village, but that would not be out of keeping with what we know of sites mentioned in the records of the time. Mizpah first becomes important with the division into two kingdoms, for it then becomes a frontier post of Judah, and was fortified by Asa of Judah in his struggle with Baasha of Israel. To this period may well belong the very strong defences which succeeded the earlier wall. Unfortunately, the complexity of the stratification resulted in the excavators being unable to establish accurately the date of the walls or that of individual buildings. It is clear, however, that the layout as a whole belongs to the period of the divided monarchy.

The town wall is extremely strong, and illustrates a second type which was in use in the Iron Age in addition to the casemate type. The wall itself was 4 metres thick and was built of heavy rubble. It is interesting that here, as in all the other smaller towns excavated, there is no sign of the Phoenician type of stone-dressing. Projecting from the wall was a series of rectangular towers, irregularly spaced and of varying sizes. The base of the towers and of the walls on the east and west sides of the town was protected by a massive, stone-faced glacis, the base of which was in places as much as 8 metres thick in front of the footings of the wall. The whole constitutes a most formidable defensive system. The single gate was formed by the overlapping for a distance of 14 metres of the two ends of the wall, the outer being strengthened by a massive tower; the gate itself, consisting of double buttresses, with intervening guard-chambers, projecting from the walls, lay at the inner end of the passage so formed.

Inside the walls, the layout shows many of the characteristics of towns of this period. The buildings nearest the walls are radially arranged, with a ring road about 26 metres inside the walls. They are not, however, built right up against the wall; for the most part there is a gap of about 10 metres, in which was a large number of storage silos. Little of the layout of the centre of the town was recovered, owing to the closeness of the rock to the surface. The use of upright stones, in the walls or free-standing, is common, and there are a number of examples of the house plan with one room across the end of a main block divided either into three rooms or three aisles (see p. 253).

Another site connected with the defences of the southern kingdom against the northern is that of Tell el Fûl, identified as Gibeah (Geba). The original fort here, which had been an acropolis for the surrounding village in the period of Saul, had been allowed to fall into ruins in the period of the United Kingdom. It was rebuilt as a fortress serving as an outpost in the defences of Jerusalem at the end of the 10th century B.C. The plan was square, with a massive wall, of which the foot was protected by a thinner wall with an earth filling between the two, and an external stone glacis. The total width of the base of this composite defensive wall was 9 metres. Little of the internal arrangements of the fortress, which enclosed a space *c.* 13 metres square, could be made out, but the internal superstructure was supported on a series of massive piers. If the identifications of Tell el Fûl with Gibeah and Tell en Nasbeh with Mizpah are correct, the two sites may have been fortified at the same time, for it is recorded in

1 Kings xv that when Asa of Judah had persuaded the King of Damascus to attack Baasha of Israel from the north, thus forcing the latter to suspend his campaign against the southern kingdom, Asa destroyed the fort Baasha had built at Ramah, and used the material for the fortification of Gibeah and Mizpah. The association of the fortification of the two sites with this incident is supported by the similarity of the method employed, with the use of the enveloping glacis, and by the employment at Tell el Fûl of re-used stones in the walls.

The fortress at Tell el Fûl did not form part of a town or village, as did its predecessors. It is in fact an example of a fortified tower or *migdal* of which representations appear on Egyptian monuments recording campaigns in Palestine. Such towers may have formed a characteristic part of the defences of Judah at this period, for a number of similar contemporary structures have been identified on the southern borders of the kingdom in the Negeb.

[1]For the two greatest towns of Judah, apart from Jerusalem, our evidence for this period is unfortunately scanty. Gezer was excavated at too early a date for the technique of excavation then in use to make it possible to disentangle the superimposed remains of successive periods. The evidence, however, suggests that there was only slight occupation here between 900 and 500 B.C. The excavation of Tell Duweir, which must be identified as Lachish since there is no other site of sufficient importance in the neighbourhood, had to be suspended before clearance on the hill itself had done more than touch the levels of this period. Lachish is one of the towns included in the biblical list of those fortified by Rehoboam at the time when the division of Solomon's kingdom and the reappearance on the scene of Egypt as a military power under Shishak I again made defence an urgent problem. It is very possible that to Rehoboam should be attributed the fortifications which encircle the site, and which remained in use down to the end of the Israelite period. The method of construction of this wall is interesting. The lowest portion was built of stones on a pronounced batter, forming in fact another example of glacis-

[1] Addenda pp. 348–9.

type defence. Above this there was a section of vertical stone wall
and above this again a section of mud-brick. This illustrates the
way in which stone and mud-brick were combined even on sites
where stone was relatively plentiful. Within the fortifications a
large palace-fortress was identified, with a great open courtyard
in front of it. There may thus have been something in the nature
of an official quarter here, but not enough of the summit was
cleared to determine how it was related to other parts of the
town. The existence of a fairly large official quarter may account
for the fact that the population seems to have overflowed the
walls, for remains of houses of the period were found on the
slopes outside.

Excavation has thus shown us that town life was flourishing
in the period of the dual monarchy. The towns were well
populated, and there seems to have been a certain amount of
specialisation in crafts; at Tell Beit Mirsim there were many
textile workers and at Beth-Shemesh there was a concentration
on the olive oil and wine industry. There are clearly two types
of town, those which are dominated by a large and exclusive
official quarter, and those which seem to be occupied entirely
by private buildings, in the layout and house plan of which there
are many common characteristics. The towns are all walled, and
there appear to be two main types of fortification, the casemate
type and the type with glacis at the foot.

The great cities of Samaria and Megiddo allow us to get some
glimpse of royal and official luxury. The finds at other sites
suggest fairly general prosperity but little luxury. Very little
has been found that suggests any high degree of artistic skill or
taste. Ornaments, consisting of brooches, rings, ear-rings, beads
and other pendants, are simple, the majority of the metal objects
being in bronze, with a few in silver. Little gold of this period
has been found. Iron is in common use for all types of tools and
weapons; for instance iron sickles displace flint ones about 1000
B.C., and iron arrowheads come into common use about the same
time. Enough examples have been found of all types of iron tools,
woodworking and agricultural, such as ploughshares, to show

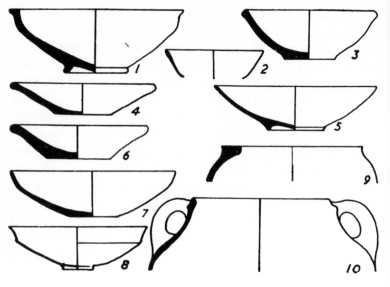

FIG. 63   Pottery of Samaria Period IV $\frac{1}{5}$

that the metal was readily available to everyone. The pottery in use is well made and plentiful, though very little really fine ware has been found. An interesting type of toilet object, suggestive of the fineries of Jezebel and her ladies, is a small limestone palette probably used for mixing cosmetics; examples are found in many sites, so its use was not confined to court circles. Not many cult objects belonging to this period have been found, showing that the religion of Israel had not to face so much competition as previously. An exception, however, is the fertility figurines which are found on many sites in the southern but not the northern kingdom. These are of a type, moulded in the round and not as plaques, which appear first in Early Iron II.

At Samaria the layout of the city with its royal quarter lasted throughout the Israelite period. There is, however, a marked decline in building standards. Within the royal quarter new buildings were put up, to give place to which the earliest very fine enclosure wall was abolished. The new buildings were substantial but the masonry very rough. Later buildings, of irregular plan and alignment, were constructed against the casemated enclosure wall, thus spoiling the original symmetry of the layout. The earliest of these inferior buildings must be dated still within the 9th century B.C., perhaps when Jehu drove out the dynasty of Omri in 841 B.C. About 800 B.C. the casemate enclosure wall had to be at least in part rebuilt after some disaster, and the rebuilt wall, with broken and ill-laid stones, shows none of the fine skill so apparent in the early wall. It is clear that when the Phoenician craftsmen imported by Omri and Ahab were no longer responsible for the work, the Israelites reverted to their old, rough, building technique.

In one of the new buildings in the courtyard was found a large number of ostraca—documents written on potsherds. They represent receipts of taxes collected in kind. The building which contained them may have been a Government storehouse. The structural evidence, and that of the ware of the sherds, suggest a date towards 800 B.C. The receipts range in date from the ninth to the seventeenth year of some king. The political conditions which would best suit are those of the reign of Jehoiahaz, who reigned for seventeen years from 813 to 796 B.C., but during the first eight years of his reign Hazael and Benhadad of Damascus were oppressing Israel. When the Aramaean threat was ended by the invasion of that country by Adadnirari III of Assyria, Jehoiahaz would have been once more in control of the whole kingdom, and able to collect the taxes, thus accounting for the fact that the receipts start only in the ninth year. Archaeological evidence and historical records thus agree well in the dating, and provide an important fixed point in the chronology of Hebrew scripts.

At Megiddo, as at Samaria, the Phoenician building style was short-lived.[1] The great official quarter continued in use for about a century. It was then destroyed, and in the new layout which succeeded it c. 750 B.C. the official quarter was abolished, and its place taken by an ordinary town of private houses. This was fairly

[1] Addenda p. 349.

FIG. 64 Pottery of Samaria Period VI. $\frac{1}{5}$

regularly laid out in insulae divided by well-planned streets, and the buildings were comparatively spacious; it is in this respect quite unlike the earlier towns of this period, and there is no trace of the ring of buildings round the walls. The building, however, reverted to the old rubble-wall technique, with none of the fine ashlar work of the previous stratum.

★

CHAPTER TWELVE

The Fall of the Hebrew Kingdoms and the Post-Exilic Period

LITTLE HAS been said in the previous chapter of the political events affecting the kingdoms of Judah and Israel. The biblical record, supplemented by our present knowledge of the written history of the Near East, makes it clear that peaceful conditions existed only for very short stretches of time throughout the whole period of the dual monarchy. The archaeological record supports that of history. For instance, the fortification of the royal quarter of Samaria may have been caused by the siege of the city by Benhadad II of Damascus at Ahab's accession. The destruction of the fine enclosure wall and its replacement by rougher buildings may have been due to the ravages of Jehu when he exterminated the dynasty of Omri. Rebuildings about the middle of the 8th century B.C. may have been needed after the anarchy that followed the death of Jeroboam II. The end of Stratum IV at Megiddo may have been due to the Assyrian attack on Israel c. 734 B.C., in which most of the northern part of the kingdom was lost. The violent destruction of Stratum V at Hazor is certainly to be ascribed to the same cause. On most sites there is in fact evidence for violent events during this period, but as a rule the archaeological evidence does not provide a sufficiently exact chronology to enable a positive correlation of archaeological and historical events to be made. The general picture is similar, however, and the exact correlation often immaterial.

We know now that behind all the political events in the biblical account lie the vicissitudes in the history of the Assyrian Empire.

After some three centuries in which her history is almost a blank, Assyria became a potent factor again under Ashur-nasi-pal (884–859 B.C.). For the next two and a half centuries she adopted a policy of expansion and conquest, spasmodically interrupted by revolts of the subject peoples, usually at the accession of a new king. Between the Hebrew kingdoms and Assyria lay the Aramaic kingdom of Damascus. When Assyria was weak, Damascus was apt to be a thorn in the flesh of Israel. When Assyria was threatening Damascus, Israel was freed from pressure, and could recover her lost possessions. When Israel was at grips with Damascus, Judah would free herself from Israelite control. When Judah was suffering at the hands of Israel, Edom could revolt from her, and when Israel in turn was weak, the other kingdoms east of the Jordan could likewise break away, or attack in their turn. And so the train of events went on, with now one country and now another in the ascendant.

But with each wave of aggression, the Assyrians pressed farther and farther towards the Mediterranean and to the south. In 734 B.C. Tiglath-pileser III marched right into Palestine. So little did the Hebrews realise the perils involved in dealing with the cruel Mesopotamian power that Ahaz of Judah had appealed to him for help against Israel, and he attacked both Israel and the Philistine cities, which after a long period of quiescence were once more taking advantage of the weakness of Judah. Philistia was annexed by Assyria, and Hosea of Israel was left with only the southern half of his kingdom. Galilee and the territory east of the Jordan were annexed, and the tribes of Reuben, Gad and Manasseh were carried away into captivity. This was in fact the ruthless policy of the Assyrians to control captured territory; whole populations were deported and their place taken by exiles from other parts of the empire. This policy has a singularly modern ring.

This was the beginning of the end for the northern kingdom. In the last stages a new factor appears, the revival of Egypt, which had not intervened in Syrian politics since the time of Shishak I, two centuries earlier. The surviving Syrian kingdoms, relying on help from Egypt, attempted to free themselves from tribute to the Assyrians, but the only result was to hasten the end. In 724 B.C. Shalmaneser V besieged Samaria, which resisted for two years, but fell to his successor Sargon II in 722 B.C. Sargon then advanced right to the Egyptian border and defeated the Egyptians and the Philistines and their other Syrian allies. On his way back in 720 B.C. he carried off the rest of the tribes of Israel into captivity. In their place he settled in Samaria men of Babylon and other foreign cities.

Judah and Phoenicia were the only Syrian kingdoms that survived the great thrust, but future advances were to come. In 705 B.C. Sennacherib once more led the Assyrians south, and much of Judah was ravaged. Lachish was captured and sacked, as were many lesser towns. Jerusalem was besieged, and, though it held out, Hezekiah of Judah had to buy off the Assyrians by paying tribute. Judah survived for another century, but only as a semi-independent vassal. How unreal the independence was is shown in the Assyrian records, where reference is made to a garrison of Philistine mercenaries maintained at Lachish.

On a number of sites archaeological evidence has been found of these events, for their effect was so cataclysmic that there is seldom much doubt in the correlation of the archaeological and historical evidence.

At Samaria the Israelite royal quarter was completely destroyed. In every place where undisturbed levels of the latest Israelite buildings were found, there were thick layers of burnt material. In this débris were found many fragments from the ivory decorations of the palace of Omri and Ahab, and the rest were found in similar débris that had been disturbed in later building operations. Many of the ivories were found completely blackened by fire. Those that were not were found embedded in sticky light-coloured deposits, which clearly represented the mud-brick superstructure of the buildings that had fallen on them in the destruction and thus saved them from being burnt. A period of looting no doubt preceded the firing of the building, and it is tempting to regard the almost identical ivories found in Sargon's palace at Nimrud as the proceeds of this looting. Hardly a wall belonging to the period survives above ground level. It is not always clear how much of this destruction of walls took place at this time, or how much at later periods, when the foundations were dug out for building stone. It is certain that none of the interior buildings survived to any appreciable extent, for their lines are completely ignored by subsequent buildings. The casemate wall round the summit may partly have survived, for its line was followed by the 2nd century Hellenistic fort wall, and it may even have been itself repaired earlier in the Hellenistic period, while the wall on the Middle Terrace certainly was sufficiently intact in the 3rd century B.C. to be strengthened by the great Hellenistic towers. It seems quite reasonable to suppose that the defensive walls were retained and repaired, for Samaria was .made the centre of an administrative district under the Assyrians, while the internal buildings were obliterated. The remnants of the population and the strangers settled there must have lived as best they could in the ruins. Least of all would they have required the great royal buildings of the summit, where no doubt the destruction would have been especially concentrated. The living quarters of the ordinary people, about which we have no evidence, may have suffered less damage, and the inhabitants in their reduced numbers may have lived there.

The evidence for a break in the culture of the site is most striking. From Period I to Period VI of the phases identified in the excavations there is a steady development in the pottery and other finds, but no sudden change and no outside influence. In the layer overlying the destruction, a little of the latest Israelite pottery continues, but together with it appear completely new wares. Noticeable among these are a number of bowls with high flaring rims of very thin fine ware which are quite unlike anything found on the site before, and which have no developments in Palestine. Clearly we have here the pottery imported by some of the new settlers, which dies out after a comparatively short space of time, as the settlers come to use the local pottery.

At Tell el Far'ah an exactly similar course of events can be traced. The buildings of that town which had grown up *c.* 800 B.C. were destroyed by fire. The subsequent occupation is very much poorer and in it appear the same imported types of pottery as at Samaria.

Megiddo was no doubt lost to Israel rather earlier than Samaria, in the annexation of the northern territory in 734 B.C. As has been already suggested, it may have been at this stage that the buildings of Stratum IV were destroyed. The pottery in Stratum III does not show such a sharp break as that at Samaria, but a certain number of new forms, with no obvious local ancestry, do appear. But it may well be that the new layout of Stratum III is due to the Assyrians or to their settlers. The plan with its large, regular, rectangular insulae is quite un-Palestinian. Unfortunately, nothing is known of the Assyrian town sites of the period (only the palaces have been excavated), so one cannot say whether the plan owes anything to direct Assyrian influence, but foreign influence of some sort is strongly suggested.

Though only the northern kingdom was annexed, the towns of the southern kingdom suffered severely in the later Assyrian campaigns. It was probably now that Beth-Shemesh IIb was destroyed by fire. The fortress at Gibeah was destroyed by fire at about the same period. Tell Jemmeh, near Gaza, may have suffered the same fate, and it is interesting that here too foreign pottery appears. There are a few vessels very like those found at Samaria, already mentioned, but most striking of all was a great deposit found together in one pit, which Sir Flinders Petrie called the Dinner Service of the Assyrian governor. A few of the vessels are undoubtedly Assyrian of the late 8th century B.C., small cups of eggshell fineness with high flaring rims, ridiculously small bases, and dimples in the walls. The rest can certainly be called a dinner service; it is not actually Assyrian, but it is a copy of the types found in Assyria in the late 8th century B.C.[1] It consists of scores of plates with peculiar stepped profiles near the base and ridges below the short everted rim. Some are much finer than

---

[1] Material from Professor Mallowan's excavations at Nimrud, not yet published.

others, and of a different ware. They may have been imported by
some officer in the Assyrian army and the rest copied locally to
his direction in imitation of his own native ware.

That Lachish was captured we know from both the biblical
and the Assyrian records. Reliefs found at Nineveh show the siege
in progress. The clearest evidence of this destruction came from
the débris in the lower roadway on which was found the crest of a
bronze helmet identical with those worn by the soldiers depicted
attacking Lachish on the Assyrian reliefs (Pl. 55). Fragments of
some armour and Assyrian weapons were also found. The destruction level of this period within the town, however, has probably
not been reached.[1]

Jerusalem did not fall to the Assyrians, but it was put to desperate straits. In the face of the Assyrian menace, Hezekiah
strengthened the city by carrying out another of those remarkable
feats of engineering in connection with the water supply, of
which examples have already been given. The earlier secret access
to the spring now known as the Virgin's Fountain, described in
Chapter 10, had long been abandoned, and the spring subsequently
used to irrigate gardens on the slopes of Ophel. The older tunnel
was not restored, for the geography of the city had now changed.
Instead, a tunnel was carried right through the hill of Ophel from
the north-east to the south-west slopes, which were at that time
within the walls of the city, and the waters of the spring were
thereby conducted into a pool, the Pool of Siloam of the New
Testament, into which they still run.

The achievements of Hezekiah who "stopped the upper spring
of the waters of Gihon and brought them straight down on the
west side of the city of David" are referred to several times in
2 Kings and 2 Chronicles. The Siloam Tunnel has long been
known, and in 1880 an inscription was discovered on its wall
recording the excitement of the workmen when the two parties

---

[1] To this attack, the destruction of Level III on the summit is also attributed
in *Lachish*, III. But the comparison of the finds from the houses of this phase
with those from other sites suggests that Level III was destroyed in the first
Babylonian campaign of 598 B.C. (see *Samaria*, III, pp. 204–208).

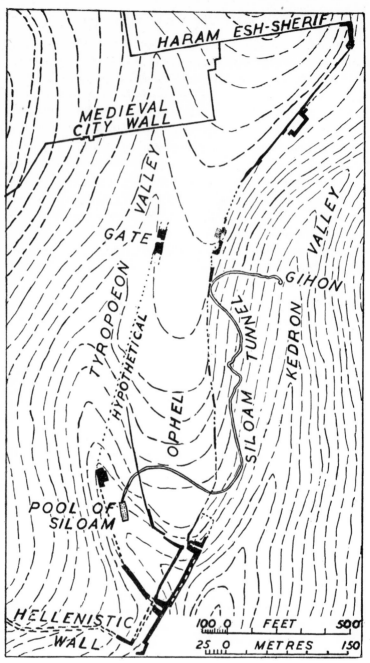

FIG. 65   Plan of the walls of Ophel and the Siloam Tunnel

working from each end met in the heart of the hill. In the excavations of 1909–11 the whole tunnel was cleared out. Archaeological evidence, though it did not provide close confirmation, agreed well with the traditional ascription of this work to Hezekiah, and the meticulous examination carried out at the time by Père Vincent showed how the work was carried out. The line of the tunnel follows a most curiously sinuous course, for which there is no really satisfactory explanation, though it is suggested that it was in part to avoid disturbing ancient royal tombs. The point of junction of the two sections, with frenzied changes of direction hither and thither, gives eloquent illustration to the triumph shown in the inscription. The level of the tunnel was maintained with much more accuracy than was its line, though it too required some adjustment. Père Vincent has shown that this explains why the height of the tunnel varies from as much as 5 metres, at the southern end, to as little as 1·60 metres. Close examination showed that the tunnel as first pierced was in the neighbourhood of 1·60 metres to 2 metres high, but that the slope of the floor was not quite regular. This was adjusted by lowering the floor where necessary, thus forming the higher parts of the tunnel. The resultant level secures a perfect flow from the spring to the pool, with a drop of 2·18 metres in a distance of 512·5 metres. Even though some adjustments were required, it represents an amazing piece of engineering with primitive surveying instruments. No doubt the safe supply of water which the tunnel provided did much to enable the city to withstand the Assyrians' siege.

The kingdom of Judah was not brought to a final end until more than a century after the fall of Israel.[1] There is no doubt that its independence was nominal, and that it was in fact a vassal of Assyria. In 612 B.C. the Assyrian empire gave place to the Babylonian in Mesopotamia, which became heir to the Assyrian dominions and policy. The change in fact made little difference to the Palestinians, and early in the 6th century Nebuchadnezzar took the final step of annexing Judah. This was carried out in two campaigns, in 598 and 589–587 B.C. Of this last century of the existence of the Hebrew kingdom, archaeology has not so far

[1] Addenda pp. 349–50.

produced much evidence. Towns which had been destroyed were in some cases rebuilt. At Beth-Shemesh, for instance, the town of Stratum IIc was built on the ruins of IIb, on approximately the same plan.

It is to this period that Level III of Lachish is probably to be attributed.[1] The town of this period was a large one, probably covering the whole top of the mound and surrounded by a massive wall. The association of the stages in the building of this wall with the Level III houses was not established. The gateway of the period was also not uncovered when excavations had to be suspended; it appears, however, to be similar in plan to that of the overlying one, with the roadway approaching obliquely up a sloping ramp, and then turning to the right through a gateway consisting of a series of brick-built piers on stone foundations. Inside the town, portions of rows of shops fronting on the road leading into the centre of the town from the gate were excavated (Pl. 56). The quarter was certainly a poor one with crowded houses of slight construction. The lower part of the house walls was of stone and the superstructure largely of brick or mud, covered with a layer of mud and chopped straw, and finished with a coat of lime plaster; floors were of cobbles or beaten earth; in the débris of the burning when the town was destroyed were remains of the roofs of timber, brushwood and mud. Similar houses were adjacent to the one imposing building located. This was represented by a great stone-built podium some 35 metres by 78 metres in size, in which there were several structural phases within the Iron Age, the final one possibly belonging to this phase. Nothing of the internal plan could be recovered, but it was presumably a citadel or palace. The evidence from the excavations is therefore meagre, but there is nothing in the buildings or their contents to suggest any great luxury.

Other towns, which had escaped destruction by the Assyrians, continued on the same lines as before. At Tell Beit Mirsim there is no major disturbance to be traced between c. 930 and 588 B.C. At Tell en Nasbeh, likewise, there is continuous occupation. No

[1] See note on p. 287.

doubt the position was the same in many other small towns. The culture remains the same, with perhaps even less to suggest artistic taste than before. Seventh-century pottery can be distinguished from that of the 8th century, but it is a development of it and there is no sharp dividing line. The development is in the direction of dullness and mass production; the pottery of the period is in fact ugly and uninteresting, though technically quite well made. It seems to reflect the low ebb in the political life of the kingdom.

Archaeology fully supports the biblical evidence of the disastrous effect of the Babylonian campaigns which brought this period to a close. Large numbers of towns were destroyed and never occupied again. Of these, Tell Beit Mirsim and Beth-Shemesh are typical examples. There had been periods of intermission of occupation of sites previously, but at no other time had large numbers of sites ceased permanently to be towns. This shows clearly how disastrous an effect the Babylonian policy had on the economy of the country. Probably only a proportion, possibly a quarter, of the population was actually carried into captivity, but the captives included all the leaders, and with it the organisation and trade of the country was broken up. Its economy would no longer support the thickly populated towns of the period of the Jewish kingdoms.

Jerusalem itself was completely sacked and the Temple destroyed. The 1961-67 excavations have uncovered the ruins of the 7th century houses on the eastern slopes destroyed at this time.[1] At Lachish, the evidence of the excavations is probably to be interpreted[2] as showing traces of the two Babylonian campaigns of 596 and 588 B.C. In the first campaign, the town of Level III was utterly destroyed. Perhaps a last effort to prepare the town to withstand the coming assault was the excavation of an enormous rock-cut shaft, rectangular in plan with sides of 80 feet and 70 feet in depth. This colossal undertaking was never finished. The floor was completely irregular, and much lower on the south than on the north. There is no conclusive evidence of its purpose,

[1] Addenda p. 351.   [2] *Samaria*, III, pp. 204-208.

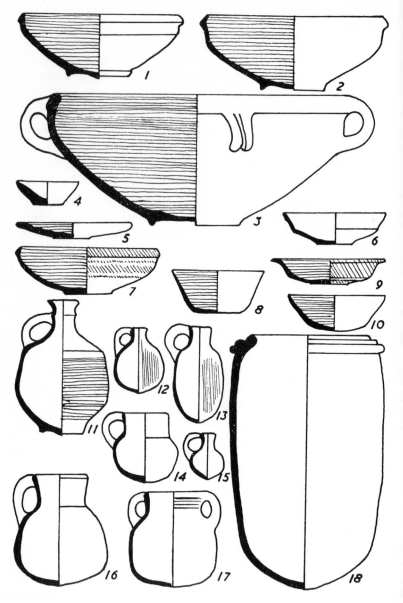

FIG. 66   Pottery of Tell Duweir Level III. $\frac{1}{5}$

but it was probably connected with the water supply, either as a shaft to a spring or as a reservoir. But the Babylonian onslaught must have come before it could be brought into use. Right at the base of the filling are sherds of 6th century pottery, and the hole was left open to fill up gradually in the course of the succeeding centuries.

The débris which overlies the remains of the town of Level III shows the violence and completeness of the destruction. In the gateway, 8 feet of burnt débris separated the floors of this period from their successors. The palace-citadel was completely ruined, and a mass of calcined bricks overlay its stone foundations. Near the palace a row of shops was excavated, one of the few portions of the interior of the city yet cleared. The rooms were found filled with the objects in use at the time of the destruction, which the inhabitants did not have time to rescue, great storage jars for corn, and a weaving establishment, representative of the industries and trade typical of a Palestinian town of the time. Outside the city was found a most extraordinary deposit of some two thousand bodies thrown into an old tomb through a hole in the roof. Some of the bones had been partly calcined, and the bodies must thus have been salvaged from the burnt buildings. J. L. Starkey believed that the remains represent the clearing up of the city after savage slaughter by the Babylonians. Some of the skulls show battle injuries, but the most curious discovery was three skulls which had been trephined. In two cases, a square of bone had been removed by saw cuts. The surgery was very crude, and the patients did not survive. Does this represent experiments carried out by the conquerors on prisoners, in the manner of the Nazis, or the desperate attempts of survivors to save the life of a man injured in battle? Perhaps the second explanation is the more probable, in that in the third case, in which a hole had been made by scraping, the patient had apparently lived long enough for the bone to heal; it must therefore have been an old operation and not the immediate cause of death. Trephining may thus have been a recognised Israelite surgical practice, employed in the other instances on battle casualties.

Above the débris of destruction, the town was rebuilt with a few miserable houses. The incompleted great shaft was left open, to be filled in by gradual accumulation. Only the defences show some thoroughness in rebuilding, with a new gate built on top of the 8 feet of débris covering the ruins of its predecessor. In the final assault of Babylon against Judah, Lachish is listed by Jeremiah together with Jerusalem and Azekah as one of the last strongholds of Judah "for these fenced cities remained of the cities of Judah" (Jer. xxxiv. 7).

But these "fenced cities" soon fell before the Babylonian might. Excavation showed that the restored Lachish was once more destroyed by fire. In a guardroom between the outer and inner gate of the city, in the layer of ashes representing this fire, was found a collection of ostraca, or potsherds used for writing messages. Eighteen ostraca in all were found, of which seven are sufficiently legible to make connected sense, while on the others only isolated sentences and words can be read. The interpretation of the documents is difficult, partly because readings are in places uncertain, and partly because they allude to events and other documents that can only be conjectured. Experts differ both as to the readings and interpretation. But if the interpretation of Professor Torczyner, who was responsible for the full publication, is accepted, the documents are of extraordinary interest from their connection with the biblical account of the last days of the Hebrew kingdom.

The documents are all letters. A number are from a certain Hosha'yahu to his lord Ya'ush, and it is very possible that the less legible ones are part of the same correspondence. Hosha'yahu is apparently the commander of a fortified post and Ya'ush the governor of Lachish. The correspondence may come to a climax in Letter IV, in which Hosha'yahu says "for the signal-stations of Lachish we are watching, according to all the signs which my lord gives, because we do not see [the signals of] Azekah." The mention in Jeremiah of Lachish and Azekah as two of the last surviving cities of Judah has already been quoted. This sentence is most suggestive of impending tragedy; Azekah would appear to have fallen, and Hosha'yahu was dependent on orders getting through to him from the more distant Lachish.

But the documents do not appear to represent a collection of the latest letters received before Lachish fell, as it were the letters in the office filing-basket. In the first place, they seem to deal with events over an appreciable period of time. Secondly, they seem all to be from the same person, being in some cases written on pieces of the same pot, and it would be odd if while one correspondent wrote eighteen letters, no one else wrote any at all. There is, moreover, a theme running through all the intelligible letters, for in each Hosha'yahu seems to be trying to excuse himself and to deny he has committed some crime, which seems to be connected with having read some letters. Professor Torczyner has suggested a most ingenious interpretation, based on another passage, in Letter III, which seems to refer to events recorded in Jeremiah.

The efforts of the military leaders in Jerusalem at the time to oppose the power of Babylon were being greatly hampered by the prophet Jeremiah, who preached submission to Babylon and threatened with the wrath of Yahweh all who fought against its power. Another prophet who preached in the same vein was Urijah. Jeremiah, though often threatened and in peril, managed to escape death as a fifth-columnist. But Urijah was less fortunate. He was warned of impending arrest and fled to Egypt, but "Jehoiakim the king sent men into Egypt, namely Elnathan the son of Achbor, and certain men with him." Urijah was brought back and executed. In Lachish Letter III, in which an unnamed prophet is mentioned, there occurs the passage "Down went the commander of the army [Yi]khbaryahu the son of Elnatan to come to Egypt and . . . his men he sent to take from here," and Professor Torczyner interprets the continuation of the letter to imply that the prophet had written a letter to warn a friend. He considers that the two accounts refer to the same incident, in one of which the general's name and that of his father have been transposed. He suggests that here in fact is the basis of at least one of the charges against Hosha'yahu, that he had improperly read

confidential letters entrusted to him to forward, and had betrayed
to the king or his officers that Urijah had fled to Egypt. This
would imply, of course, that Ya'ush belonged to the party
supporting the prophets Jeremiah and Urijah, and not that of the
court circles. Such an interpretation would also provide an
explanation for the presence of this particular collection of
documents in the guard-chamber. A room at the gate of the city
is traditionally the position of courts of justice in eastern countries.
A court-martial may have been held on Hosha'yahu, to answer a
charge of betraying Urijah, and there are hints in other letters
that military charges may be involved too; the ostraca may have
formed part of the files supplying evidence for the case, the rest
of which may have been on papyrus and thus have been destroyed
in the subsequent fire.

An intelligible explanation of such ancient documents is always
difficult and must be in part conjectural. But whether Professor
Torczyner's deductions are right in every respect or not, the
names used, the language, and many small details reflect the
conditions prevailing at the time at which Jeremiah wrote. They
have also a very human interest. Most of the ancient documents
which have survived are official, religious or business documents.
These are letters dealing with the doings of individuals. Their
association with the last days of the Jewish kingdom is firmly
fixed, for the ashes which covered them represent the final
destruction of Lachish, never again to be occupied as a town,
though it subsequently served as an administrative centre.

The low ebb of civilisation in Palestine, which lasts for the
next three centuries or so, makes it very difficult for archaeology
to recover any evidence. Town life suffered a severe setback, and
such reduced settlements as there were, with little in the way of
substantial buildings, were mostly obliterated by later building
operations.

With the sack of Jerusalem, the administrative centre of the
district, now a Babylonian province, was moved to Mizpah. If
this place is to be identified with Tell en Nasbeh, we can perhaps
see what a very serious blow had been struck at town life in
Palestine. A certain number of objects, notably jar-stamps, have

been found, which must be post-exilic in date, but there is almost nothing in the way of buildings that can be attributed to this period. This is in fact the position on all sites in Palestine which were not completely abandoned. The remnants of the population must have continued to live in such villages as had survived destruction, but contributed little towards their structural history. One reason, no doubt, is that it was mainly the unprogressive peasantry that escaped deportation. Another is that mixed with these Jewish survivors were immigrants from many other lands, brought thither by the Assyrians and Babylonians. The homogeneous Israelite culture was thus broken up, and there was no unifying power to build up a new one in its place.

In 540 B.C. the Babylonian empire was annexed by the Persians under Cyrus. The Persian policy of toleration for the national cultures and religions of their subject races brought about some amelioration in the position of the Jews. During the next hundred years, under successive leaders inspired by religious zeal, parties of Jews returned from Babylonia and attempted to restore Jerusalem. In 520 B.C. Zerubbabel rebuilt the Temple, and in 444 B.C. Nehemiah restored the walls of the city. But the homogeneity of the Jewish people had been too severely disrupted for a new kingdom to grow up round it, even if the Persians would have allowed it. Many Jews preferred to remain among the comforts of civilisation in Babylonia. Those who returned were at continual enmity with the "peoples of the land," whom they despised as being of mixed blood, and each successive group from Babylon made the same accusation against those who had preceded them, whom they denounced as having intermarried with the other inhabitants. These inhabitants in their turn resented the claim of the returned refugees and their descendants to be the only true Jews and the only true followers of the Jewish faith. Quarrels such as these led in time to the Samaritan schism, when Manasseh, the grandson of the High Priest Eliashib, was driven out by Nehemiah, on the grounds of the intermarriage of his family with those of mixed race. Sanballat, governor of Samaria, built for him a temple, as a rival to that of Jerusalem, on Mount Gerizim, and thus to enmity on racial grounds was added a

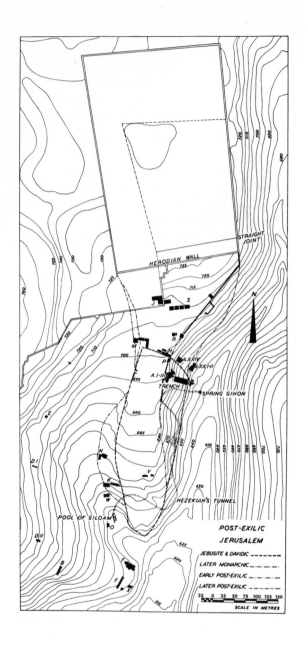

POST-EXILIC
JERUSALEM

JEBUSITE & DAVIDIC — — —
LATER MONARCHIC — · — · —
EARLY POST-EXILIC — · · — · ·
LATER POST-EXILIC — — — —

25 0 25 50 75 100 125 150
SCALE IN METRES

HERODIAN WALL

STRAIGHT
JOINT

SPRING GIHON

HEZEKIAH'S TUNNEL

POOL OF SILOAM

TRENCH I

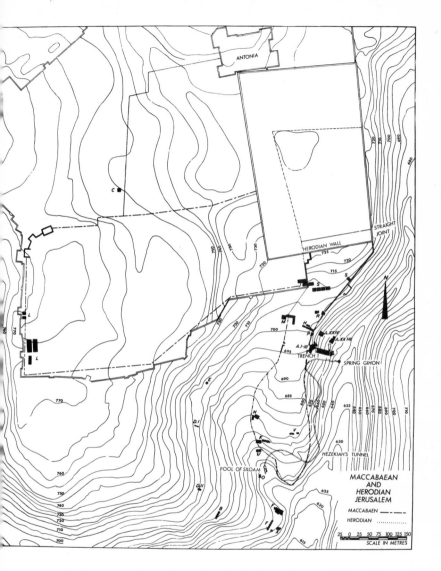

FIG. 67   [and opposite] Plan of Jerusalem in the Maccabean and Herodian
periods. The plan of the Solomonic Temple is presumed to
have continued throughout the Maccabean period. In the
Herodian period, the earlier Temple platform was enveloped
by its larger successor.

conflict of religious centres, which has continued to modern times.

The 1961–7 excavations at Jerusalem have revealed dramatic evidence of the contrast between Jerusalem of the period of the Kingdom of Judah and that of the post-exilic period. Of the temple rebuilt by Zerubbabel no trace has been found,[1] and it will probably always remain inaccessible beneath the great platform built by Herod the Great for his final version of the Temple, now occupied by the glorious Moslem sanctuary of the Dome of the Rock. But the outlines of Nehemiah's town are now beginning to take shape. In the area excavated on the eastern slopes of Ophel, the evidence was clear of the collapse overlying the buildings of the 7th–early 6th centuries B.C., and of the great denudation on the slope that followed the collapse of the terraces on which the houses were built. These were the ruins that confronted Nehemiah in his survey of the city when, wishing to inspect the walls along the eastern valley he says "But there was no room for the beast that was under me to pass" (Nehemiah 2.14). Not only were the ruins daunting, but the town needed for the poor remnant returned from exile was much smaller than that of the period of the monarchy. It was now that the wall on the crest of the hill, for long erroneously ascribed to an earlier period, was constructed, and the excavations proved that against its foot tailed up midden-tips of the 5th–4th centuries B.C.

Post-exilic Jerusalem had therefore shrunk back to the summit of the eastern ridge, and there it remained, for the tower previously ascribed to the time of David is now known to be an addition of the Maccabean period, when the Hasmonean rulers were striving to create a new Jewish kingdom, to the walls of Nehemiah. The position of the defences on the western side of the ridge is probably indicated by the massive gateway found in the 1927 excavations, which was certainly in use in Maccabean times (Fig. 65). The 1961–7 excavations have made it quite clear that the wall enclosing the two ridges (p. 242) did not exist either in the period of the monarchy or in the post-exilic period. It dates only to the period of Herod Agrippa (c. A.D. 40–44), and no occupation on the southern end of the western ridge has been found earlier

[1] Addenda p. 351.

than this date. The northern end of the western ridge was however included within the city during the Maccabean period.

Over the rest of the country, all that we have is a few buildings connected with the administration of the country by the Babylonians and Persians. Presumably only such buildings were sufficiently substantial to survive subsequent disturbances.

The best preserved of such buildings is at Lachish. It was built above the ruins of the palace-fort of the Jewish period; the earlier building had itself been raised on a podium above the contemporary level, and this elevated position was accentuated by the later structure, which was surrounded by an earth ramp. The plan is symptomatic of the new influences in Palestine, for it is quite unlike previous official buildings in that country. It consists of a great courtyard, surrounded on two sides by rows of rooms and on the other two by porticoes. The deeper of these porticoes, raised above the level of the court, leads to a great hall stretching across the width of the courtyard, at the rear of which doorways lead to private rooms and domestic offices. The great hall no doubt served for public audiences, the rooms round the court may have been administrative offices, and those at the rear of the hall the living quarters of the governor. One interesting structural feature is that the rooms were vaulted, in contrast to the pre-exilic buildings, in which, as far as our evidence goes, the ceilings were flat. In some rooms portions of the fallen roof were recovered as they had fallen, showing that the vaults had been formed by voussoirs laid diagonally. The best parallel to this type of building comes from Arslan Tash in northern Syria. It is an illustration of the cosmopolitan character of the Persian empire.

The history of Lachish is probably representative of that of Palestinian towns. For a century or so after its destruction by the Babylonians it had lain in ruins. Then the fortifications were repaired, and it was made an administrative centre, with the necessary official buildings, but apparently little in the way of houses for the ordinary people. Moreover, it was an administrative centre not in Judah, but in the new province of Idumaea, an illustration of the way the Edomites and other semi-nomadic peoples had pushed into Palestine during its weakness.

A possibly similar building, though not identical in plan, of the same general post-exilic period, has been found at Tell Jemmeh, where the latest building is a very massive structure on three sides of a long narrow court. Again there appear to be no contemporary private houses.

In the northern province of Samaria, the successor of the Kingdom of Israel, a building at Megiddo very similar to that at Tell Jemmeh is attributed to Strata II and I. Unfortunately, the uppermost levels were very much denuded, and their exact dating is uncertain. But it is probable that associated with this fortress or residency was a town, covering only part of the area of the old city, of small and ill-built houses. The regularly laid-out insulae which have been attributed to the Assyrian period have disappeared, and the site is in fact a village rather than a town. Its occupation may have lasted down to the middle of the 4th century B.C., but before the beginning of the Hellenistic period even this occupation had ceased, and the history of Megiddo had come to an end.

At Samaria, too, the decline of town life is well illustrated. The site remained an administrative centre, but no official buildings of the period have been discovered in the area excavated. There are traces of a few insignificant buildings on the summit, which must be dated to the 7th and 6th centuries, and more may have been destroyed by subsequent building operations. The clearest evidence that the site was not closely built up comes from probably early in the 5th century, when an area of about 50 metres by 45 metres on the summit was apparently converted into an elaborate garden. Over this area all earlier walls were systematic-ally rooted out and their contemporary floor levels pulled into the resultant holes and levelled over. On top of this make-up, thus carefully cleared of stones and débris, was laid a band, 25 centimetres thick, of sticky chocolate-coloured soil. This type of soil is found in crevices in the rock at Samaria and on the surrounding hills, and must have been especially collected for this purpose. It was recognised by the workmen employed on the excavations as extremely fertile, and was carried away by them for their own gardens. The only explanation for this enclosure seems to be that it was for use as a garden or orchard, which may have been associated with a residence of a Persian governor, lying in the unexcavated area to the east.

Traces of occupation for the whole pre-Hellenistic period at Samaria are very scanty. Only nine coins prior to 300 B.C. were recovered in seven seasons of excavation. Pottery and other finds of the period were equally rare, and only a few isolated groups of buildings could be attributed to it. The finds were sufficient to show that the site was occupied, but their proportion compared with those of earlier and later periods emphasises how slight this occupation was.

The great cities of the Israelite period therefore play little part in the life of the country under the Babylonians and the succeeding Persian empire. The slight glimpses we get of the culture of Palestine come largely from unimportant sites. It is perhaps significant that most of them come from the coastal belt. The Persian empire had reunited the eastern Mediterranean lands to a degree unknown since the Late Bronze Age, and once more one finds in Palestine and Syria pottery and other objects identical with finds in Egypt, Cyprus and Greece. Coastal Palestine thus once more was in the current of eastern Mediterranean trade, while the hill country was a backwater.

Tell Abu Hawam at the foot of Carmel, abandoned since its destruction in the late 10th century B.C., was once more occupied. The architectural remains are unimpressive, and it was nothing more than a village, yet in it appear Corinthian and Attic vases dated from the 6th to the early 4th century. Some of the coarse pottery has Phoenician affinities, and these Greek and Phoenician finds emphasise two of the elements found in the cosmopolitan culture of the period.

At 'Athlit, near Haifa, beneath the Crusader castle, have been found tombs dating to the 5th and 4th centuries B.C. In them were Phoenician coins and scarabs, and much Greek pottery, but there was a predominance of the third element in contemporary culture, namely scarabs and ornaments of Egyptian type. At Tell Jemmeh, Greek pottery of the 6th and 5th centuries B.C. has been found in sufficient quantities to suggest a Greek colony, and other fragments have been found at Askelon and Tanturah on the coast.

At Tell Fara a tomb was discovered which throws interesting light on the contacts with other parts of the Persian empire, and has also produced objects of artistic merit.[1] These consist of the framework of a bronze couch and stool, and a silver bowl and dipper. Representations of similar couches and stools appear on Greek vases of the 6th and 5th centuries while the fact that they were manufactured for the Syrian market is shown that as a guide to their assembly the different components are marked with Hebrew letters of 5th century script. The dipper is Syrian in style, and close parallels for the bowl have been found in the Egyptian Delta and at Susa in Mesopotamia. Tombs belonging to this same period, and producing objects illustrating the same cultural affinities, have also been found at Gezer.

The preceding paragraphs will have shown something of the character of the culture of post-exilic and pre-Hellenistic Palestine. The Jewish civilisation, of no great artistic merit, but homogeneous and with a vigorous town life, has been completely disrupted. The only architectural remains belong to official buildings presumably associated with the Persian administration, and the few rich burials probably belong to members of the official hierarchy. The administrative centres seem to have no large towns associated with them. The few town and village sites which can be ascribed to this period have only mean structures. But nevertheless in the coastal area we have evidence that Palestine was once more in trade relations with the adjacent Mediterranean countries. In particular, we see the increasing contacts with Greece, which paved the way for the inclusion of western Asia in the Hellenistic empire, under which once again town life begins to prosper.

[1] The tomb, No. 650, was dated by the excavator to 850 B.C., but has been shown by J. H. Iliffe (Q.D.A.P., IV) to belong to the 5th or 4th centuries B.C.

★

Excavated Sites and Bibliography

THE MAJORITY of sites to which reference is made in the body of the text have produced evidence concerning the remains of several or many different periods. A brief description of the various excavations can therefore best be given as an appendix. In the main, only excavations subsequent to 1920 are described, since from them most of the evidence is derived.

ABBREVIATIONS

A.J.S.L.L.	*American Journal of Semitic Languages and Literature.*
A.A.S.O.R.	*Annual of the American Schools of Oriental Research.*
A.D.A.J.	*Annual of the Department of Antiquities of Jordan.* Amman.
A.P.E.F.	*Annual of the Palestine Exploration Fund.* London.
B.A.S.O.R.	*Bulletin of the American Schools of Oriental Research.* New Haven, Connecticut.
Eretz Israel	Annual of the Israel Exploration Society. Jerusalem, Israel.
I.E.J.	*Israel Exploration Journal.* Jerusalem, Israel.
J.P.O.S.	*Journal of the Palestine Oriental Society.* Jerusalem, Palestine.
L.A.A.A.	*Liverpool Annals of Art and Archaeology.* University of Liverpool.
O.I.P.	*Oriental Institute Publications.* University of Chicago.
P.E.F.Q.S.	*Palestine Exploration Fund Quarterly Statement.* London.
P.E.Q.	*Palestine Exploration Quarterly.* London.
Q.D.A.P.	*Quarterly of the Department of Antiquities of Palestine.* Jerusalem.
R.B.	*Revue Biblique.* École Biblique et Archéologique de Saint Étienne, Jerusalem, Jordan.

S.A.O.C.   *Studies in Ancient Oriental Civilization*. University of
        Chicago.

(*Note: Tell* and *Wadi* are ignored in the alphabetic order.)

TELL ABU HAWAM

The site is a small mound on the coastal plain, at the foot of Mount
Carmel. It was excavated in 1932–33 by Mr. R. W. Hamilton of the
Palestine Department of Antiquities. The earliest occupation dated to
Late Bronze II, and lasted without any long break until the end of the
10th century B.C. After an interval, it was reoccupied from the 7th
to the 5th centuries B.C.

Bibliography
Q.D.A.P., IV.

TELL ABU MATAR

The site lies 1·5 kilometres south-east of Beersheba, occupying a
mound of loess covered by alluvial loam. It was excavated in 1954 by
M. Jean Perrot. The remains belong to one cultural phase only, the
Chalcolithic, and consist of dwellings which in the earlier stages were
subterranean, cut into the loam and sometimes into the underlying rock
to varying depths. Four main phases could be identified, in the last of
which the subterranean dwellings were succeeded by surface structures.
The culture of the inhabitants can be linked with that of Ghassul.

Bibliography
I.E.J., 5, 6.

'AI

Excavations at 'Ai were carried out by Mme Judith Marquet-Krause
between 1933 and 1935 with funds provided by Baron Edmond de
Rothschild. The main circuit of the Early Bronze Age walls was
traced, and within the town work was concentrated on the area adjoining a great tower on the walls, a large building which may be a palace
or temple, a sanctuary showing a triple succession of rooms, and a small
area of houses. Tombs show that the site was already occupied in the
Proto-Urban phase. Mme Marquet-Krause died in 1936, when only
preliminary reports had been issued, and the material has been published
from her records by her husband, but consists of only her preliminary
reports and a transcription of her field register.

Bibliography
Les Fouilles de 'Ay (Et-Tell), 1933–35. Y. Marquet. 1949. Institut Français d'Archéologie de Beyrouth.

TELL AJJUL

Tell el 'Ajjul was excavated by the British School of Archaeology in Egypt under Sir Flinders Petrie between 1930 and 1934. It lies at the mouth of the Wadi Ghazzeh, some 6 miles south of the modern town of Gaza. The earliest remains excavated on the tell consisted of a cemetery belonging to Middle Bronze I. This lay beneath a large building, called by Petrie a palace, belonging to Middle Bronze II, which was succeeded in turn by four other large buildings, the latest dating probably to the beginning of the Iron Age. Portions of the dwelling-houses of corresponding periods were also excavated. The maximum expansion of the town was apparently in the Middle Bronze Age, when it was defended by a great fosse of the type ascribed to the Hyksos. Occupation of the site must, however, date from an earlier period than that of the town levels excavated, for tombs with the typical pottery and weapons of the Intermediate Early Bronze–Middle Bronze phase were found.

Bibliography
Ancient Gaza, I–IV. Flinders Petrie. British School of Archaeology in Egypt and Bernard Quaritch, 1931–34.
A.D.A.J., III. Tombs of the Intermediate Early Bronze–Middle Bronze Age at Tell Ajjul. K. M. Kenyon.
A.J.S.L.L., 1938. The Chronology of a South Palestinian City. W. J. Albright.

ASKELON

Excavations at the coastal site of Askelon were carried out on behalf of the Palestine Exploration Fund by Professor Garstang in 1920 and 1921. Excavations on the summit cleared only remains of the Roman period, but sections were cut in the face of the mound, which revealed the succession of occupation. The most important result was evidence of a complete break between the end of the Late Bronze Age and the beginning of the Early Iron Age, which can probably be attributed to the Philistine invasion.

Bibliography
P.E.F.Q.S., 1921, 1923.

TELL BEIT MIRSIM

For four seasons between 1926 and 1932 excavations were carried out at Tell Beit Mirsim by the American School of Oriental Research in Jerusalem, under the direction of Professor W. F. Albright. The tell, for which the identification with Kirjath-sepher has been suggested, is a comparatively small mound in the low hill country south-west of Hebron. The importance of the excavations is derived not from the intrinsic merits of the remains revealed, but in the successive layers of occupation dating from late in the third millennium to 6th century B.C., and in the thoroughness with which the objects recovered, especially the pottery, were studied and published. The earliest occupation belongs to a late and decadent phase of Early Bronze III, followed by the Intermediate Early Bronze–Middle Bronze stage (designated Middle Bronze I by Professor Albright), and a series of Middle Bronze Age levels. At the end of the Middle Bronze Age there is a destruction followed by abandonment, and occupation is resumed in the second half of the 15th century B.C. Between the Late Bronze Age and Early Iron Age levels is a destruction, but no appreciable interval in the occupation. The site was finally abandoned after the Babylonian destruction in 588 B.C.

Bibliography
The Archaeology of Palestine and the Bible. W. F. Albright.
Tell Beit Mirsim I: The Pottery of the First Three Campaigns. *A.A.S.O.R.*, XII.
Tell Beit Mirsim Ia: The Bronze Age Pottery of the Fourth Campaign. *A.A.S.O.R.*, XIII.
Tell Beit Mirsim II: The Bronze Age. *A.A.S.O.R.*, XVII.
Tell Beit Mirsim III: The Iron Age. *A.A.S.O.R.*, XXI–XXII.

BETHEL

The site of Bethel has been identified as the modern village of Beitin, a little north-east of Ramullah. A small area was excavated by Professor W. F. Albright in 1934 on behalf of the American School of Oriental Research in Jerusalem. Occupation of the site seems to begin in the Early Bronze–Middle Bronze period, and to continue till near the end of the Late Bronze Age. Professor Albright suggests that the occupation of Bethel was complementary to that of 'Ai, 2 miles away, for the two sites seem rarely to have been occupied at the same time.

The town of the Late Bronze Age was particularly well built. The period comes to an end with a great destruction by fire, probably early in the 13th century B.C., and Professor Albright considers that the destruction was the work of the Israelites. When occupation was renewed, there was a complete break, with a much poorer culture. The site was finally destroyed in the 6th century B.C.

Bibliography

B.A.S.O.R., 56, 57.

BETH-SHAN

Like that of Megiddo, the excavation of Beth-shan by the University of Pennsylvania was planned on a large scale, which likewise could not be carried out. The work was under the direction of Mr. Alan Rowe. The lowest level to be reached on the summit was IX, dating probably from the 14th century B.C. Most of the work was concentrated in an area in which there was a series of superimposed temples, lasting from that date well into the Early Iron Age, and succeeded by a Hellenistic temple and a Byzantine church. The lowest levels were penetrated in a sounding; the dwellings seemed to be in pits comparable to those of Tell Abu Matar, and to be of the Chalcolithic period, succeeded by phases belonging to the Proto-Urban period and the Early Bronze Age. A large number of tombs of all periods from the Early Bronze Age to the Byzantine period were also excavated. The material has been only partially published. Interim reports described the progress of the excavations, and Mr. G. M. Fitzgerald described in detail the pottery of the Chalcolithic to Early Bronze Age, but the final report only deals with the later periods, the Temple buildings from Level IX onwards and the pottery from Level VIII. It is generally agreed that the dates assigned to the levels by the excavators must be drastically lowered; it seems probable that the chronology is approximately: Level VIII, 1350 B.C.; Level VII, 1300 B.C.; Level VI, 1150 B.C.; Level V, 1000 B.C.

Bibliography

Beth-shan I: *The Topography and History of Beth-shan*. A. Rowe. 1930.
Beth-shan II.i: *The Four Canaanite Temples of Beth-shan*. A. Rowe. 1940.
Beth-shan II.ii: *The Four Canaanite Temples of Beth-shan. The Pottery*. G. M. Fitzgerald. 1930.

Beth-shan III: *Beth-shan Excavations 1921–23. The Arab and Byzantine Levels.* G. M. Fitzgerald. 1931.
Beth-shan IV: *A Sixth Century Monastery at Beth-shan.* G. M. Fitzgerald. 1931.
(All published for the University Museum by the University of Pennsylvania Press.)
P.E.F.Q.S., 1927, 1928, 1929, 1931, 1932, 1934.
The Museum Journal, Philadelphia, XXIV. *The Earliest Pottery of Beth-shan.* G. M. Fitzgerald.

BETH-SHEMESH

The tell of 'Ain Shems, lying almost due west of Jerusalem, where the important Wadi Sorek emerges from the hill country of Judah into the Shephelah, was first excavated for the Palestine Exploration Fund in 1911–12. Between 1928 and 1931, extensive excavations were carried out there by the Pacific School of Religion and the American School of Oriental Research in Jerusalem, under Professor Elihu Grant. The earliest remains belong to the Middle Bronze Age. A good succession of levels from the Late Bronze Age to the end of Early Iron II were uncovered. The evidence of a typical town plan in the Iron Age is particularly useful.

Bibliography
A.P.E.F., I and II: Duncan Mackenzie.
Ain Shems I: *Ain Shems Excavations.* E. Grant. 1931.
Ain Shems II: *Ain Shems Excavations.* E. Grant. 1932.
Ain Shems III: *Rumeilah.* E. Grant. 1934.
Ain Shems IV: *Ain Shems Excavations (Pottery).* Text. E. Grant and G. E. Wright. 1939.
(All published at Haverford.)

TELL DU WEIR

The great mound of Tell ed Duweir lies in the low hills west of Hebron. Its identification as the site of Lachish is generally accepted. The excavations were initiated by Sir Henry Wellcome, and subsequently supported by Sir Charles Marston. Work began in 1932, and it was intended to excavate the whole mound through all the stages of occupation, but the work was brought to an end by the political troubles in 1937–38, in which the Director, Mr. J. L. Starkey, was tragically murdered by bandits. The excavation of the town levels, of which the latest belonged to the Hellenistic and Persian periods, only reached the town of Early Iron II. Evidence for occupation at earlier periods comes from caves and tombs, from a section cut in the edge of the mound, and from clearance of areas for dumping. The earliest occupation, in caves in the neighbourhood of the later tell, belongs to the Chalcolithic period. Caves were still used as habitations during the Early Bronze Age, but towards the end of the period occupation of the town site began, and the caves were used for burials. Numerous tombs belonging to the Early Bronze–Middle Bronze period and to the Middle and Late Bronze Ages were found. A massive Middle Bronze Age bank was traced round the town. After it went out of use, a temple was built at its foot, of which the three structural phases lasted from early in the 15th century to the end of the 13th century B.C. The main period of occupation of the town came to an end with its destruction by the Babylonians in 588 B.C., and in the débris of the destruction were found potsherds on which letters had been written during the last months of the existence of the Jewish Kingdom.

Bibliography

Lachish I: *The Lachish Letters.* H. Torczyner, G. L. Harding, A. Lewis, J. L. Starkey. Oxford University Press. 1938.

Lachish II: *The Fosse Temple.* O. Tufnell, C. H. Inge, G. L. Harding. Oxford University Press. 1940.

Lachish III: *The Iron Age.* O. Tufnell, with contributions by Margaret A. Murray and David Diringer. Oxford University Press. 1953.

Lachish IV: *The Bronze Age.* O. Tufnell. Oxford University Press. 1957.

In *Samaria* III (q.v.), pp. 204–208, it is suggested that the destruction of Level III should be dated to 596 B.C. rather than 700 B.C. For a reply to this, see *P.E.Q.* 1960.

TELL FARA

Tell el Far'a lies some 14 miles above Tell el 'Ajjul on the Wadi Ghazzeh, at the point where the wadi debouches into the coastal plain. Like Tell Ajjul, it was excavated by Sir Flinders Petrie for the British School of Archaeology in Egypt, between 1928 and 1930. City levels from Middle Bronze II down to the Iron Age were excavated, and a great wealth of material of the same periods was also recovered from tombs. Among the most important of these were five tombs with rich Philistine pottery. Excavations were also carried out in a number of prehistoric occupation sites in the neighbourhood of the tell. The majority of these belonged to the Chalcolithic period, and pottery, stone artifacts and other objects similar to those from Ghassul were found; other sites belonged to the Early Bronze Age.

Bibliography
Beth-pelet (*Tell Fara*), I-II. Flinders Petrie. British School of Archaeology in Egypt and Bernard Quaritch. 1930 and 1932.

TELL EL FAR'AH

The northern Tell el Far'ah is situated near the head of the important Wadi Far'ah, which provides a highway from the Jordan Valley into hill country. Excavations have been in progress there since 1946, directed by Père R. de Vaux on behalf of the Dominican École Biblique de St. Étienne. Occupation on the site has been traced back to the Chalcolithic, though no structures of this period have been found. The succeeding Proto-Urban period is represented by a number of large tomb groups, of which the pottery shows a mingling of Proto-Urban A and C. The first structures on the town site belong to early in the Early Bronze Age. In E.B. II, massive town walls were built and five successive phases within the Early Bronze Age have been so far identified. Occupation of the site, however, seems to come to an end in E.B. II. From that period there was a gap in occupation until Middle Bronze II. The site continued to be important until early in the 9th century B.C. A break then, with an unfinished building, confirms the identification of the site with Tirzah, the capital of Omri before he moved to Samaria. Occupation begins again on a small scale in the second half of the 9th century, and continues until the town was destroyed by the Assyrians in 722 B.C. Some occupation continued till 600 B.C., when the site was abandoned.

Bibliography
R.B., LIV, LV, LVI, LVIII, LIX, LXII, LXIV, LXVIII, LXIX.
P.E.Q., 1956.

GEZER

Gezer is one of the most important sites on the western fringes of the hill country. It was excavated for the Palestine Exploration Fund in

1902–05 and 1907–09 by Professor R. A. S. Macalister. Though the material was studied and published with the most exemplary care, the excavation methods and lack of knowledge of the pottery at the time rendered the very complicated history of the site difficult of interpretation. Some small-scale excavations were also carried out by Mr. Alan Rowe in 1934. The published material shows that the site was continuously occupied from the Chalcolithic to the Early Iron Age, and perhaps on into Roman and Byzantine times.

Bibliography
The Excavations of Gezer. Vols. I–III. R. A. S. Macalister. London, 1912.
P.E.Q., 1935.

GHASSUL

The excavations at Teleilat Ghassul were carried out between 1930 and 1938 by the Pontifical Biblical Institute. The site consisted of a group of very low mounds in the Jordan Valley, on two of which excavations were carried out. It was ascertained that there were four main levels of occupation, but most of the work was confined to the top stratum IV, which was subdivided into two stages. The whole range of occupation appeared to lie within the Chalcolithic period.

Bibliography
Teleilāt Ghassul I: A. Mallon, R. Koeppel, R. Neuville. 1934.
Teleilāt Ghassul II: R. Koeppel. 1940.
        (Published at Rome, by the Pontifical Biblical Institute.)

GIBEAH

The site of Tell el Fûl, 3 miles north of Jerusalem, was excavated in 1922 by the American School of Oriental Research in Jerusalem, under Professor W. F. Albright. The site was dominated by a fort-like building, in which four stages, all belonging to the Early Iron Age, were identified. The earlier were surrounded by a small village, but the latest was apparently an isolated watch tower.

Bibliography
A.A.S.O.R., IV.

HAZOR

The very large and important site of Hazor lies in the Jordan Valley between Lake Huleh and the Sea of Galilee. It was excavated by the

Israel Exploration Fund between 1955 and 1958, under the direction
of Dr. Y. Yadin. It consists of two parts, a tell at the south-west
corner and a great defended plateau to the north. Occupation on the
tell began in the Early Bronze Age, and lasted down to the Hellenistic
period. The plateau area, defended by a massive bank, was added in
Middle Bronze II, and continued to be occupied down to the early
13th century B.C., when the site was probably captured by the Israelites.
The tell was an important place in the Early Iron Age, and was
probably fortified by Solomon. It was destroyed by the Assyrians in
730 B.C., but the citadel continued to be used down to the Hellenistic
period.

Bibliography
Hazor I and II. Y. Yadin.
I.E.J., 6, 7, 8, 9.

Hederah

The site lies in the Plain of Sharon. The finds were made in a cave
excavated by Professor E. L. Sukenik. They were of the Chalcolithic
period, with affinities to the finds of Ghassul. The most interesting were
unique pottery ossuaries made in the form of houses.

Bibliography
J.P.O.S., XVII.

Tell Hesi

Tell el Hesi lies on the edge of the coastal plain, due west of Hebron.
It was first excavated by Sir Flinders Petrie in 1890 and at this site
Petrie made the first beginnings of stratigraphical excavation in
Palestine and the first beginnings of linking strata with pottery. He
recorded his finds in feet above sea level and observed the changing
pottery types in the different levels. By observing the levels at which
recognisable Egyptian objects were found, he made a start in establishing the chronology of Palestinian sites by linking them with Egypt;
upon this link with Egypt Palestinian chronology is mainly dependent.
Since his dating of the earlier Egyptian dynasties was too high the
actual chronology he suggested for Tell Hesi has had to be revised,
and his identification of the site as Lachish is not now accepted, but his
work here was revolutionary in its importance.

The excavations were continued in 1892 by F. J. Bliss, by the same methods. In the lowest level of occupation was found an important group of copper weapons. A crescentic axehead is almost exactly paralleled by one found in an Early Bronze III tomb at Jericho, thus dating the first occupation of the site to *c.* 2600 B.C.

Bibliography
Tell el Hesy (Lachish). W. Flinders Petrie. London, 1891.
A Mound of Many Cities. F. J. Bliss. London, 1894.
Eleventh Annual Report of the Institute of Archaeology, University of London. K. M. Kenyon. A Crescentic Axehead from Jericho, and a Group of Weapons from Tell el Hesi.

TELL JEMMEH

Tell Jemmeh was the first site to be excavated, in 1926–27, by Sir Flinders Petrie, after the transference to Palestine of the activities of the British School of Archaeology in Egypt. The importance of the excavations lies not in the remains uncovered, but in the continuous succession of strata from the 13th to the 5th century B.C.

Bibliography
Gerar. Flinders Petrie. British School of Archaeology in Egypt and Bernard Quaritch. 1928.

JERICHO

Jericho was first investigated by the Palestine Fund in 1873, but this work was on a small scale. The first major excavations were those carried out between 1907 and 1909 by a joint Austrian-German mission under Sellin and Watzinger. These excavations showed the great potentialities of the site, but the developments made in the study of Palestinian pottery after the first war made a revision of the suggested datings essential. Further excavations were therefore undertaken by Professor John Garstang between 1930 and 1936, with an expedition sponsored by the Institute of Archaeology of the University of Liverpool, and financed by a number of museums and individuals, chief among the latter being Sir Charles Marston and Lord Melchett. Further excavations were undertaken between 1952 and 1958 by an expedition sponsored by the British School of Archaeology in Jerusalem, the Palestine Exploration Fund and the British Academy, in collaboration with the American School of Oriental Research in Jerusalem and the Royal Ontario Museum, under the direction of the author. The last expedition showed that almost all traces of the Late Bronze Age town of the time of Joshua had been destroyed by erosion, and that the identification of one of the lines of town walls as belonging to this period was mistaken. Occupation of the site started in the Mesolithic, c. 9000 B.C., and there was a continuous development from that stage into a town of the Pre-Pottery Neolithic period, c. 8000 B.C., successively occupied by two different groups of people. Thereafter there was a very much lesser occupation by Neolithic people with pottery, but it is not yet clear whether there was a gap before these arrived, and again before the arrival of the Proto-Urban groups. From that time, late in the fourth millennium, there was continuous occupation until the town was destroyed c. 1580 B.C. It was probably reoccupied c. 1400 B.C., but of the town of this period almost nothing remains.

Bibliography
Jericho. E. Sellin and C. Watzinger. Leipzig, 1913.
L.A.A.A., XIX, XX, XXI, XXII.
P.E.F.Q.S., 1930, 1931, 1935, 1936.
The Story of Jericho. J. Garstang and J. B. E. Garstang. London, 1948.
P.E.Q., 1951, 1952, 1953, 1954, 1955, 1956, 1957.
Excavations at Jericho, Vols. I and II. K. M. Kenyon. London, 1960 and 1965.

JERUSALEM

Innumerable expeditions have investigated the problems of the archaeology of Jerusalem, but the continuous occupation of the site for thousands of years has rendered excavation very difficult and most of the results have been inconclusive. Much of the site lies beneath the present walled city and in those parts which are outside the walls successive phases of occupation have made the earlier remains very fragmentary. The first major excavations were undertaken on behalf of the Palestine Exploration Fund by Captain (later Sir Charles) Warren in 1864–67; Warren accomplished an amazing amount in investigating the walls of the Temple area, and his results were beautifully recorded. Between 1894 and 1897 F. J. Bliss and A. C. Dickie carried out widespread excavations in the area to the south of the walled city, again on behalf of the Fund. Both these excavations were admirably carried out for their period, and excellently recorded, but at that stage stratigraphical methods and pottery chronology had not been developed to assist in dating strata, so ascriptions of structures to periods could only be theories, and these theories have since been proved to be wrong.

In 1909 and 1911 the Parker Mission carried out many soundings and tunnellings on Ophel, the south-eastern spur of Jerusalem, generally accepted as the site of the original settlement, in search of David's tomb. The main result was to uncover a series of water channels in connection with the Virgin's Fountain. In 1913–14, R. Weill, on behalf of Baron Edmond de Rothschild, conducted excavations on the southern tip of Ophel, in which fragments of a complicated series of fortifications were uncovered. The interpretation of the results of both these expeditions owes much to the constant interest of Père Hugues Vincent of the Dominican École Biblique. In 1923 the Palestine Exploration Fund renewed its attack on the problems of the history of the city, with excavations on the hill of Ophel, outside the walls of medieval and modern Jerusalem. From 1923 to 1925 they were directed by Professor R. A. S. Macalister, and in 1927 by Mr. J. W. Crowfoot. The site was very much disturbed, and only fragmentary remains were recovered. Attention was mainly directed to the recovery of evidence concerning the Jebusite and early Israelite defences. In the 1927 excavations an imposing gateway was found well up the inner side of the Ophel ridge, which was in use in the Maccabean period, and evidence was provided that the southern end of the Tyropoeon Valley dividing Ophel from the western ridge was not occupied until that period. In excavations carried out at the present citadel between 1934 and 1948 on behalf of the Department of Antiquities of Palestine, Mr. C. N. Johns was able to date stratigraphically the older lines of wall there (at the north-west corner of the early city) and to show that the earliest line of wall crossing the Tyropoeon Valley and connecting the points of the western and eastern ridges was not earlier than the Hellenistic period. Further excavations on behalf of the Department by Mr. R. W. Hamilton against the north wall of the present city provided dating for the expansion of the town to the north in Herodian and Roman times, which falls outside the scope of the present volume. In 1961 the British School of Archaeology, in collaboration with the École Biblique and the Royal Ontario Museum, began a large scale excavation in all areas of ancient Jerusalem completed in 1967.

The outline of the history of the city emerging from these excavations may be given briefly. The original settlement was on the eastern of the two ridges which compose the site. There was some occupation in the fourth millennia, but the remains are fragmentary. The earliest town wall found is Middle Bronze Age, but little survives of the town of the period. In the Late Bronze Age, it was a Jebusite stronghold, so strong that it long defied Israelite capture, of which the surviving structures consist of terraces to support houses on the steep eastern slope. About 1000 B.C. Jerusalem was at last captured by the Israelites under David. His city was that of the preceding Jebusites, whose walls he rebuilt. Under Solomon, the Temple was built on the northern part of the eastern ridge, and presumably the town was extended to the north to join the site of the Temple. As far as present evidence goes, the city was limited to the eastern ridge throughout the period of the Monarchy. Very little of the internal structures have survived, and indeed little to indicate the culture of the inhabitants. The latest excavations have made it clear that the southern part of the western ridge was only occupied and enclosed by a wall by Herod Agrippa c. A.D. 40–44; whether expansion to the northern end of the ridge took place before the time of Herod the Great is as yet uncertain. In 587 B.C. the city fell to the Babylonians, and was destroyed and depopulated. In 538 B.C. Cyrus allowed some of the exiles to return and to rebuild the Temple. The walls, however, were not rebuilt until the governor-ship of Nehemiah, probably 445–433 B.C. In his rebuilding, the lower slopes of the eastern ridge were abandoned, and the wall followed the crest. The position of the west wall at this period, just below the western crest of the eastern ridge, is indicated by the gate found in 1927. The elongated town on the eastern ridge remained the main part of Jerusalem until the ambitious expansion of Herod Agrippa in the 1st century A.D., though at some stage, probably late Maccabean or Herodian, there had been an extension to the northern end of the western ridge.

Bibliography

The Survey of Western Palestine. Jerusalem. C. Warren and E. R. Conder.

Excavations at Jerusalem 1894–1897. F. J. Bliss and A. C. Dickie.

Jérusalem sous Terre. H. V(incent). London, 1911.

La Cité de David, I and II. R. Weill. Paris, 1920 and 1947.

A.P.E.F., IV. *Excavations on the Hill of Ophel, Jerusalem, 1923–5.* R. A. S. Macalister and J. G. Duncan. London, 1926.

A.P.E.F., V. *Excavations in the Tyropoeon Valley, Jerusalem, 1927.* J. W. Crowfoot. London, 1929.

P.E.Q., 1962, 1963, 1964, 1965, 1966, 1967, 1968. Interim reports on Excavations 1961–67. K. M. Kenyon.

MEGIDDO

The prime instigator of the great excavations carried out at Megiddo between 1925 and 1939 by the Oriental Institute of Chicago was Professor James Breasted. The work was directed in turn by Dr. C. S. Fisher (1925–27), Mr. P. L. O. Guy (1927–35) and Mr. G. Loud (1935–39). The excavations were on the most monumental scale of any carried out in Palestine. The whole mound was acquired by the Oriental Institute, and the original intention was to excavate it layer by layer in its entirety. Such a scheme proved beyond the resources even of the Oriental Institute. Strata I to V (numbering from the top downwards), dating from approximately 350 B.C. to 1000 B.C. (excavators' date 1060 B.C.), were completely cleared. Excavation on the tell itself was carried beyond that stage only in four areas and only in one was bed-rock reached, in an area approximately 40 metres by 25 metres. In addition to work on the tell itself, a large area was cleared on the lower slopes of the hill, for the purpose of freeing space for dumping. In this was found a further sequence of the earliest periods of occupation, dating from the beginning of the Early Bronze Age to the end of the third millennium, and also a large number of tombs of all periods.

Bibliography

Megiddo I: Seasons of 1925–34. Strata I–V. R. S. Lamon and G. M. Shipton. 1939. *O.I.P.* XLII.

Megiddo II: Seasons of 1935–39. (1 vol. text, 1 plates) G. Loud. 1948. *O.I.P.* LXII.

The Megiddo Water System. R. S. Lamon. 1935. *O.I.P.* XXXII.

Material Remains of the Megiddo Cult. H. G. May. 1935. *O.I.P.* XXVI.

Megiddo Tombs. P. L. O. Guy and R. M. Engberg. 1938. *O.I.P.* XXXIII.

Notes on the Chalcolithic and Early Bronze Age Pottery of Megiddo. R. M. Engberg and G. M. Shipton. 1934. *S.A.O.C.* 10.

The Pottery of Megiddo Strata VI to XX. G. M. Shipton. *S.A.O.C.* 17.
    (All published by the University of Chicago Press.)

Eretz Israel V. Some notes on the Early and Middle Bronze Age strata of Megiddo. K. M. Kenyon.

WADI EL MUGHARA

In the Wadi el Mughara, running from the Carmel ridge down to the Mediterranean, are a number of caves that were excavated between

1929 and 1934 by Professor Dorothy Garrod, on behalf of the American School of Prehistoric Research and the British School of Archaeology in Jerusalem. The caves provided overlapping sequences of deposits from the Middle Palaeolithic to the Mesolithic. For the period covered by the present volume, the important part of the series is the Mesolithic. A rich series of deposits, with accompanying burials, belonged to the Lower Natufian, the Mesolithic of Palestine. They indicated the possibility that incipient agriculture was being practised. They were succeeded by Middle and Upper Natufian deposits; in the Middle Natufian there was evidence that the dog had been domesticated. The Natufian deposits link with the Mesolithic of Jericho.

Bibliography
The Stone Age of Mount Carmel, I. D. A. E. Garrod and D. N. A. Bate, Clarendon Press, Oxford. 1937.
Proceedings of the British Academy, XLIII. The Natufian Culture. D. A. E. Garrod.

TELL NASBEH

Tell en Nasbeh lies beside the main route between Judah and Israel, near the boundary between the two kingdoms, some 8 miles north of Jerusalem. It was completely excavated between 1926 and 1935 by Dr. W. F. Badé for the Palestine Institute of the Pacific School of Religion, Berkeley, California. Structural remains earlier than the Early Iron Age were scanty, but tombs belonging to the Proto-Urban period were found. The main occupation of the site does not start until the 11th century B.C., and continued throughout the period of the Jewish Kingdom, with remains of decreasing importance in the Post-Exilic period.

Bibliography
Tell en Nasbeh I: *Archaeological and Historical Results*. C. C. McCown.
Tell en Nasbeh II: *The Pottery*. J. C. Wampler. Palestine Institute of the Pacific School of Religion and American School of Oriental Research, Berkeley and Newhaven.

SAMARIA

The town of Samaria lies on a low hill beside the main north–south route through Palestine, some 10 miles north-west of the pass between

Mount Gerizim and Mount Ebal, and overlooking the broad Wadi esh Sha'ir running down to the coastal plain. The first excavations were carried out on behalf of Harvard University by Professor G. A. Reisner from 1908 to 1910. From 1931 to 1935 further excavations were directed by Mr. J. W. Crowfoot on behalf of a joint expedition sponsored by Harvard University, the Hebrew University in Jerusalem, the Palestine Exploration Fund, the British Academy and the British School of Archaeology in Jerusalem. The results of the work of the two expeditions provided good evidence for the complete history of the site. Although some sporadic occupation had existed on the hill in the Proto-Urban period, the foundation of the city dated only from the 9th century B.C., but it had a continuous existence thereafter until the Byzantine period. The history of the royal quarter of the Israelite city was traced in detail, and also that of the Hellenistic fort and Roman temple which succeeded it on the summit of the hill. The most important finds were a group of ostraca of the time of Jeroboam II and a collection of ivory carvings probably from the palace of Ahab.

Bibliography

Harvard Excavations at Samaria. G. A. Reisner, C. S. Fisher, D. G. Lyon. Cambridge, Mass., 1924.

Samaria-Sebaste I: The Buildings. J. W. Crowfoot, K. M. Kenyon, E. L. Sukenik. Palestine Exploration Fund. 1942.

Samaria-Sebaste II: Early Ivories from Samaria. J. W. and G. M. Crowfoot. Palestine Exploration Fund. 1938.

Samaria-Sebaste III: The Objects. J. W. Crowfoot, G. M. Crowfoot, K. M. Kenyon. Palestine Exploration Fund. 1957.

Additions to Excavated Sites and Bibliography

Archaeology	Archaeological Institute of Samaria. Cambridge, Mass.
Atiqot	Journal of the Israel Department of Antiquities. Jerusalem, Israel.
B.A.	*The Biblical Archaeologist*. American Schools of Oriental Research. Cambridge, Mass.
C.A.H.	*Cambridge Ancient History*. Revised edition, at present only issued in fascicules.

'AI

Excavations were resumed at 'Ai by an expedition sponsored by the Southern Baptist Theological Seminary and other American institutions, under the direction of Professor J. A. Callaway. It proved possible to give chronological precision to the defences of the Early Bronze Age, and to the sanctuary. The Iron Age settlement was shown to consist of an undefended village of less than 3 acres, with two Iron Age I phases dating from the 12th century. Professor Callaway suggests that it is the capture of this village which is reflected in Joshua 8 1–28.

Bibliography
The 1964 'Ai (Et Tell) Excavations. J. A. Callaway. *B.A.S.O.R.*, no. 178.
Journal of Biblical Literature. J. A. Callaway.
Pottery from the Tombs at 'Ai (Et-Tell). J. A. Callaway. Monograph of the Colt Archaeological Institute. London, 1964.

TELL AJJUL

Bibliography
The Courtyard Cemetery at Tell el-Ajjul, Palestine. O. Tufnell. *Bulletin of the University of London Institute of Archaeology III.*

ARAD

The excavations of Arad, the largest and most important tell in the eastern Negeb, were begun in 1962. The site, situated 20 miles slightly north of east of Beersheba, proved to consist of two quite separate elements. An original Chalcolithic settlement was succeeded by an Early Bronze Age town, of which the walls enclosed an area of 25 acres. This was abandoned at the end of Early Bronze II. The next occupation belongs at earliest to the 10th century B.C., and was concentrated on a mound in the north-east corner of the earlier site. It consisted of a citadel, with which was associated a most interesting sanctuary, that lasted down to the end of the Kingdom of Judah, and was succeeded by similar frontier posts in the Hellenistic and Roman periods and an Arab *khan.*

Bibliography
I.E.J., 14, 15, 16, 17.

Archaeology, 17.
Ancient Arad. Guide to exhibition in the Israel Museum 1917.

Beth-shan

Bibliography
The Iron Age of Beth Shan. Francis W. James. Museum Monographs
of the University Museum. Pennsylvania, 1966.

Bab edh-Dhrā

Attention was attracted to the area of Bab edh-Dhrā, to the east of the
Dead Sea adjoining the Lisan, the tongue of land that projects into the
Dead Sea,[1] by the rich finds appearing in the hands of antiquities
dealers in Jerusalem. Excavations were conducted there by Dr. Paul
Lapp on behalf of the American School of Oriental Research in 1965.
The large Early Bronze Age town apparently came to an end with the
arrival of the E.B.-M.B. invaders, but hardly any investigation of the
town has taken place. Adjacent to it was a most imposing and important cemetery. The earliest tombs belonged to the Proto-Urban period,
and were shaft tombs in which a number of chambers opened out of a
single shaft. It was calculated that there may be as many as 20,000
chambers in the whole cemetery.

The bodies in the tombs excavated were mostly disarticulated and
were accompanied by a lavish number of pottery vessels. In the Early
Bronze Age there were some shaft tombs, but most of the bodies
were deposited in a disarticulated mass in charnel houses, which at
least in some instances had an upper storey. There were also tombs of
the E.B.-M.B. period, in which intact bodies were buried in a narrow
grave, above which was a small tumulus of stones.

Bibliography
R.B., LXXIII.
Archaeology, 19.

Dhahr Mirzbaneh

In 1963, a cemetery of the E.B.-M.B. period was located in the
neighbourhood of 'Ain es-Samiyeh, about seven miles north-east of
Beitin, and was excavated by Dr. Paul Lapp. There was evidence of an

---

[1] The position is given in the *Oxford Bible Atlas*, p. 96.

adjacent camping site, and it is suggested that it was occupied seasonally by a group of fifty to one hundred individuals.

Bibliography
The Dhahr Mirzbaneh Tombs. P.W. Lapp. American Schools of Oriental Research. 1966.

GEZER

New large-scale excavations were begun in Gezer in 1964 by the Hebrew Union College Biblical and Archaeological School in Jerusalem, which will allow the history of the site to be established much more exactly. Already evidence has appeared concerning the Middle Bronze Age defences with a plastered bank resembling that of Jericho. A number of studies have also been made of the published evidence.

Bibliography
B.A., XXX.
The Gezer Crematorium Re-examined. J. A. Callaway. *P.E.Q.*, 1962.
Solomon's City Wall and Gate at Gezer. Y. Yadin. *I.E.J.*, 8.

GHASSUL

Excavations at Ghassul were resumed in 1960 by the Pontifical Biblical Institute, under the direction of Father Robert North, and in 1967 by the British School of Archaeology in Jerusalem, under the direction of Dr. J. B. Hennessy. These later excavations provide great hope of establishing a more exact stratification and chronology of the site.

Bibliography
Analecta Biblica, 1960. Rome.
Levant, I.

GIBEON

The site of el-Jib, convincingly identified with the Biblical Gibeon, was excavated between 1956 and 1962 by the University of Pennsylvania under the direction of Dr. J. B. Pritchard. Tombs proved occupation in the Proto-Urban period, providing material comparable with that at Tell Nasbeh, and the Early Bronze-Middle Bronze period, with material comparable with Dhahr Mirbaneh. The earliest occupation found on the tell belongs to Middle Bronze II, and the relatively rich material of this period from tombs is comparable with that of

Jericho phases II and III; no tombs seem as late as Jericho IV and V, suggesting that the Middle Bronze town may have come to an end earlier than that of Jericho. Only a few tombs provide evidence for the Late Bronze Age, and the bigger groups certainly come late in the period, possibly 13th century B.C. The earliest town wall found is dated to the 12th century and the later one to the 10th, but there is not much evidence. The most striking remains of Iron Age date are the water systems. One is an enormous shaft, with steps circling down round its wall, comparable with the shaft at Megiddo, but not associated with a tunnel at its base, and it is therefore considered as a pool. The filling showed that it went out of use in the 7th-6th century B.C. A staircase and tunnel to a spring outside the town are considered to be later, but there was no dating evidence. A very large number of stamped jar-handles of 7th-early 6th century dates and a number of rock cuttings are considered as evidence of a wine-making industry.

Bibliography
Museum Monographs of the University of Pennsylvania Museum:
  Hebrew Inscriptions and Stamps from Gibeon. J. B. Pritchard. 1959.
  The Water System of Gibeon. J. B. Pritchard. 1961.
  The Bronze Age Cemetery at Gibeon. J. B. Pritchard. 1963.
  Winery, Defenses and Soundings at Gibeon. J. B. Pritchard. 1964.

MEGIDDO.

In 1960, Professor Y. Yadin began, on behalf of the Hebrew University, a series of small scale excavations to investigate conclusions by the earlier excavators that appeared puzzling in the light of subsequent research. The most important results were to establish with some certainty the buildings that belonged to the Solomonic period and to the mid 9th century. A considerable amount of additional research has also been done on various aspects of the published evidence.

Bibliography
New Light on Solomon's Megiddo. Y. Yadin. *B.A.*, XXIII.
I.E.J., 1966, 1967.
Megiddo, Hazor, Samaria and Chronology. K. M. Kenyon. *Bulletin No. 4 of the University of London Institute of Archaeology.*
The Middle and Late Bronze Age Strata at Megiddo. K. M. Kenyon. *Levant*, I.

An Interpretation of the Megiddo Sacred Area during Middle Bronze II.
  C. Epstein.
I.E.J., 15.
King Solomon's Palace and Building 1723 in Megiddo. D. Ussishkin.
  I.E.J., 16.

SAMARIA

In 1967 the British School of Archaeology in Jerusalem recommenced excavations at Samaria under the direction of Dr. J. B. Hennessy. The purpose of the excavation was to investigate the occupation on the lower slopes of the hill around the area of the royal quarter. The results so far have had the surprising result of showing that to the north-west of the summit plateau immediately outside the royal quarter, there was no occupation until at earliest the 5th century B.C. It is very probable that this conclusion involves the whole of the western slopes of the hill. If there was a lower town, occupied by the ordinary population, it is likely to lie to the east, and this still remains to be investigated.

SHECHEM

The site of the Biblical Shechem can be identified at Balata at the northern end of the pass between Mount Gerizim and Mount Ebal. The site was excavated at intervals between 1913 and 1934 by Dr. E. Sellin and, in the later seasons, Dr. G. Welter. Very little has been published concerning the results of these excavations. Work was resumed between 1956 and 1964 by the Drew-McCormick Expedition under the direction of Dr. G. E. Wright. There was some occupation in the Pre-Pottery Neolithic period, but the first town belongs only to the Middle Bronze Age, M.B. I to early M.B. II. A free-standing town wall was succeeded by an earth rampart of the usual type, which was in turn succeeded by a wall of cyclopean masonry associated with a fine triple-buttress gateway. On the fill behind the wall was a building interpreted as a temple. The town was destroyed at the end of the Middle Bronze Age, and deserted till at least the end of the 16th century B.C. Shechem appears prominently in the Amarna Letters. Little of the interior of the Late Bronze Age town has been excavated. It seems probable that a gateway built with magnificent orthostats belongs to this period, though this was not the opinion of the excavators. The Late Bronze town was destroyed in the 12th century B.C.,

and the site was only re-occupied in the 10th century B.C. Like Samaria
and T. el Far'ah, Israelite Shechem was destroyed by the Assyrians
c. 720 B.C., and in the slight occupation of the succeeding period
imported Assyrian pottery appears. There was a gap in occupation
between c. 475 B.C. and c. 331 B.C., when the Samaritans re-occupied
it down to its final destruction in 101 B.C.

Bibliography
Shechem. *The Biography of a Biblical City.* G. E. Wright. McGraw-Hill
   Book Company. New York, 1964.

Brief Bibliography of articles bearing on the problems discussed

Athlit: "Phoenician Tombs." C. N. Johns. *Q.D.A.P.,* VI.
Copper Mining in the 'Arabah: N. Glueck. *B.A.S.O.R.*
The Exodus: *From Joseph to Joshua.* H. H. Rowley, Schweich Lectures.
   British Academy, 1948.
Habiru, etc.: "Ethnic Studies in the Near East." E. A. Speiser.
   A.A.S.O.R.
   "Habiru and Hebrew." H. H. Rowley. *P.E.Q.,* 1942.
   "The Habiru, the Hebrews and the Arabs." A. Guillaume. *P.E.Q.,*
   1940.
   "New Light on the Habiru-Hebrew Question." J. W. Jack. *P.E.Q.,*
   1940.
The Hyksos: *The Hyksos Reconsidered.* R. M. Engberg. *O.I.P.*
Jerusalem: "King Solomon's Temple and other buildings and works
   of art." J. L. Myres. *P.E.Q.,* 1948.
   "Tell Tainat." C. C. McCown, *American Journal of Archaeology.* 1937.
The Philistines: *The Philistines.* R. A. S. Macalister. Schweich Lectures.
   British Academy, 1911.
Pottery: *The Pottery of Palestine from the Earliest Times to the end of the
   Early Bronze Age.* G. E. Wright.
   "A Palestine Potter." W. A. Heurtley. *Q.D.A.P.*

Addenda to Brief Bibliography of Articles and Monography

Amorites and Canaanites. K. M. Kenyon. British Academy Schweich Lectures. Oxford University Press. London. 1966.

Early Bronze Age.
The Foreign Relations of Palestine During the Early Bronze Age. J. B. Hennessy. Colt Archaeological Institute Publications. London. 1967.

Les Hurrites de l'Histoire et les Horites de la Bible. R. de Vaux. *R.B.,* LXXIV.
Oxford Bible Atlas. Edited by H. G. May, R.W. Hamilton, G. N. S. Hunt. Oxford University Press. London. 1962.
Palestinian Bichrome Ware. C. M. Epstein. Leiden. 1966.

Revision and Addenda

pp. 20–22.   In the ten years since this book was prepared for printing, very great progress has been made in the study of the beginnings of the Neolithic in Western Asia. Numerous excavations have been carried out, and much attention has been paid to the environmental studies that throw light on the beginnings of agriculture and the domestication of animals.

We now have a fairly clear picture of the distribution of the wild wheats and barleys that were the ancestors of the cultivated varieties.[1] The important early wheats were emmer, *triticum dicoccum*, which was considerably the more important, and einkorn, *triticum monoccum*. The wild ancestor of emmer, *triticum dicoccoides*, has a limited distribution, in the mountains of the Syro-Palestinian coast and the hill slopes of north-eastern Iraq. Since its cultivated descendant had such preponderant importance, it must be accepted that this area played an important part in the genesis of agriculture. *Triticum aegilopoides*, the ancestor of einkorn, had a wider distribution, covering the same area and most of Asia Minor. The wild ancestor of barley, *hordeum spontaneum*, is again found in this area, but its extension is even wider, in a broad band stretching to the region south and east of the Caspian. Since the wheats, emmer and einkorn, and barley are the basis of cultivated grains, it is reasonable to deduce especial importance in the beginnings of agriculture for the area in which all these are found.

The first food animals to be domesticated were goats and sheep. Their natural habitat corresponds closely with that described for the first grain-producing plants. There is considerable difficulty in deciding at what point domestication has taken place. Ultimately, the domesticated animals become smaller than their wild progenitors. But it

[1] See especially Helbaek, *Science*, Vol. 130, no. 3372.

requires many generations for morphological changes resulting from domestication to be reflected in the skeletons, which are in any case usually only fragmentarily recovered in excavations.

The ecological background to the beginnings of settlement is thus beginning to take shape. At the same time the excavation of a number of new sites has high-lighted the diversity of origins in the development in the area which environmental studies pin-point as the focus of progress. The most important sites are in Anatolia, Hacilar and Catal Hüyük. At the latter site there are remarkable developments towards town life by *c.* 6500 B.C. on Carbon-14 dating. The Neolithic culture there is not identical with either of the well-defined stages at Jericho. But there are suggestive contacts, especially in the practice of covering the walls and floors with a continuous surface of burnished plaster, that suggest that the Neolithic of Catal Hüyük and the second stages of the Pre-Pottery Neolithic at Jericho had a common ancestor, perhaps in the archaeologically *terra incognita* of northern Syria. This brand of early Neolithic culture was certainly secondary in Palestine, though probably, primary in Anatolia. The probable interpretation is that a primary northern culture supervened on a primary southern culture in Palestine.

There is still much to be done in tracing the links between the sites and stages of the first evolution of settled life, which is the basis of all progress towards civilisation. The one fact that seems clear is that there is no one centre from which all progress spread, but a number of centres in which the same environmental peculiarities gave an impetus to further progress, in a period perhaps of the ninth to sixth millennia B.C. An amalgam of all these tributaries produced the main stream of progress towards the next step in human organisation.

CHAPTER 2   *The Beginnings of Settled Life*

p. 42. The Carbon-14 dating given in the text is the first that was available. Since then other datings have been provided. A corrected date from the same apparatus (the Royal Institution in collaboration with Professor F. E. Zeuner) gives 8840 B.C. $\pm$ 180, and dates from Philadelphia give a date of 9216 B.C. $\pm$ 103 based on a half-life of 5568 or 9687 B.C. $\pm$ 107, based on a half-life of 5800. Archaeologists must await the resolution by the scientists of the discrepancies between the different techniques. But it would seem reasonable to adopt a date of *c.* 9000 B.C. as a minimum for this phase.

p. 44. Subsequent Carbon-14 datings also suggest an earlier date for Pre-Pottery Neolithic A. An occupation layer soon after the construction of the first phase of the defences is dated by Philadelphia 7825 B.C. $+$ 110 based on a half-life of 5598, or 8232 B.C. $+$ 114 based on a half-life of 5800 B.C. A destruction layer late in the life of the second stage of defences is dated 8340 B.C. $+$ 200 by the British Museum, and the two Philadelphia dates are on two separate runs 7677 B.C. $+$ 104, or 7734 B.C. $+$ 232, and 8076 B.C. $+$ 108, or 8136 B.C. $+$ 242. A deposit contemporary with the construction of the final stage of the wall and tower is dated by the British Museum 8290 B.C. $+$ 200. It would seem that the construction of the defences must date back to about 8000 B.C. and possibly a few hundred years earlier.

p. 45. Examination of the plant evidence has now shown that cultivated grains are found in the Pre-Pottery Neolithic A levels at Jericho, though the number of all specimens recovered from this period is small. Examples of emmer wheat, *triticum dicoccum*, and two-row barley, *hordeum distichum*, were found, both of which are cultivated forms. It is interesting that so far examples of the respective wild ancestors, *triticum dicoccoides*, and *hordeum spontaneum*, have not been identified. Both are at home in Palestine, but their usual habitat is in the upland ranges. It would be quite in keeping with the trend of archaeological evidence that the first experiments in agriculture were made by the Neolithic Natufians of, for instance, the Mount Carmel caves, and that the migrants to the Jordan Valley brought with them grain that had already produced the mutations that made it more suitable for agriculture.

p. 46. A further interesting feature in connection with Pre-Pottery Neolithic A Jericho is the evidence that some form of trade had already developed. Progress has recently been made in the identification of the sources of obsidian used for tools on ancient sites. An appreciable quantity was found in Pre-Pottery Neolithic A levels, and the nearest known site for this particular type is near Kayseri, in Anatolia, a distance of some five hundred miles away. So far we have no evidence of how such trade was organised, but the probability is that there were a series of middlemen. It is at least certain that there must have been fairly widespread contacts among groups.

p. 50.   The analysis of the animals' bones now completed does not prove that domestication had taken place. Bones of cattle, goats and pigs were all found. But they are all of large animals, related to the wild species. It is generally accepted that the effect of domestication was to reduce the size of the animal, a thesis fully supported by the evidence from Jericho. None of the characteristics that have been claimed as evidence of domestication has been found in the Pre-Pottery Neolithic A examples. It has however already been pointed out that the reflection of domestication by morphological changes in animal skeletons takes a very long time. All that can be said is that the remains of potentially domesticable animals were found in considerable numbers, but domestication cannot be proved. There is, on the contrary, clear evidence that wild animals provided much of the meat. The bones of gazelle form 36.91 % of the total of the Pre-Pottery Neolithic A examples. Unless Professor Zeuner's theory that gazelle may have been herded can be substantiated, this means that hunting provided most of the food supply, even though arrowheads were not common. Another interesting fact is that at this period carnivores, especially foxes, must have been eaten, for fox bones out-number those of any other species at this period. In the Pre-Pottery Neolithic B period, the proportion was very greatly reduced.

p. 56.   New Carbon-14 dates have also been obtained for Pre-Pottery Neolithic B. In squares E I, II, V, a date for the third building phase from the bottom is given by Philadelphia as 6708 B.C. $\pm$ 96 on the 5568 half-life and 7068 B.C. $\pm$ 100 on 5800 half-life. For occupation levels associated with the sixth building stage, the two Philadelphia dates are 7006 B.C. $\pm$ 98 and 7379 B.C. $\pm$ 102, while the British Museum date for the same level is 7110 B.C. $\pm$ 200. For Trench I the Philadelphia datings for occupation levels associated with the fourth of the Pre-Pottery Neolithic B building stages were 6660 B.C. $\pm$ 69 and 7019 B.C. $\pm$ 72. It would seem on this evidence that the greater part of Pre-Pottery Neolithic B falls within the seventh millennium. One is however still inclined to treat these Carbon-14 dates with caution. There is nothing in itself against accepting the surprisingly great antiquity of Pre-Pottery Neolithic Jericho, but it does stretch out the stages between this and *c.* 3000 B.C. to an uncomfortable extent.

At the time that Jericho was being excavated, its Pre-Pottery Neolithic cultures stood in almost complete isolation. It always seemed unlikely that this was a true picture. In the twelve years since the Jericho excavations were completed, much has been done to show that this isolation was only the accident of discovery. The most important additional discoveries are mainly the work of Miss Diana Kirkbride. Miss Kirkbride's main excavations were at the site of Beidha, a little north of Petra, some 100 miles to the south of Jericho. There she found a Pre-Pottery Neolithic village of very definite permanence and elaboration. Six main levels were identified. In them there is a transition from the round houses to rectilinear houses with plastered floors. The sequence cannot be precisely correlated with those at Jericho, but there are significant links, including the appearance in the later stages of the highly characteristic querns of Jericho Pre-Pottery Neolithic B. Here, too, grains were cultivated, especially the cultivated form of wild barley. Emmer wheat was also found, but not its wild ancestor. Carbon-14 datings for Beidha, done at Copenhagen, range from 6990 B.C. or 6760 B.C. ± 160 for the lowest level, VI, to 6600 B.C. for level II. On present evidence it would therefore seem that chronologically the Beidha occupation equates with Pre-Pottery Neolithic B at Jericho, though there are certainly some links with the previous period. Another important aspect upon which Miss Kirkbride was able to throw light was that there were a number of other sites of the period in the same area. It is probable that a similar intensive search elsewhere would have similar results, and might produce an overall picture of fairly numerous Neolithic villages. What we as yet cannot say is whether any towns on the scale of Jericho lie in the heart of any of the other tells.

CHAPTER 3   *From the First Settlements to the Beginnings of Civilization*

p. 75.   In 1967, further excavations at Ghassul were begun by the British School of Archaeology in Jerusalem. The first results showed that the stratification was extremely complex, with an accumulation of up to five metres of deposit. In this depth, nine successive building stages could be identified, with very many more floor levels. The main complication in interpretation was the presence of many earthquake cracks, which in some instances resulted in a floor level on one side of a crack dropping as much as 60 centimetres in relation to that on the other side. It is for this reason that some of the results from the earlier excavations have proved puzzling, since this feature was not recognised. Preliminary results suggest that there are clear distinctions at least between the lower four stages and the upper five, with less marked ones within the last group. An interesting environmental discovery was that the site was founded on a sand-bank near slow-moving water, possibly an enlarged version of the Jordan.

CHAPTER 4   *The Proto-Urban Period*

p. 82.   Dates for the Beersheba sites of Tell Abu Matar and Safadi have now been given as 3325 B.C. ± 150 and 3460 B.C. ± 350 and 3310 B.C. ± 350. The terminal date for the Ghassulian culture, at which it begins to be succeeded by the Proto-Urban cultures could therefore be *c.* 3300 B.C.

p. 88.   The Proto-Urban tombs published in *Jericho II* have provided further evidence concerning both the burial practices and the differentiation of the groups. It now seems clear that the burial practice was that of multiple successive burials in large communal tombs. As the bodies decayed, the skulls were carefully removed and stacked around the wall of the chamber. It is the care with which the skulls were moved ensuring the preservation of delicate nasal bones, that shows that the skeletons could not have been collected up from primary burials elsewhere and transported to the tombs in which they were found. As the tombs became full, the skulls were carefully removed from the bodies and stacked, and most of the other bones were disposed of, in the case of Tomb A 94 by cremation. A recent study suggests that the same process can be deduced concerning Cave-Tomb 2 I at Gezer.[1] The evidence of the further tombs studied in *Jericho II* shows that successive phases in the Proto-Urban A pottery can be identified. In Tomb K2 the second phase is succeeded by one containing Proto-Urban B pottery, associated with a new burial custom involving the use of stone platforms. Some pottery forms of Proto-Urban A types continued in use, suggesting that there was some mixture of population.

A re-examination has now been made of the allied pottery from

[1] *P.E.Q.*, 1962.

'Ai,[1] which brings additional precision to the pottery typology. These tombs emphasise the Jericho evidence that the stage at which the Proto-Urban B people appeared does not long precede the beginnings of Early Bronze I.

p. 92.   In 1965–67 a large Proto-Urban cemetery at Bab edh-Dhra near the south-east end of the Dead Sea was exacavated by Dr. Paul Lapp. Dr. Lapp is not inclined to accept Proto-Urban C pottery as representing a separate group but rather as a technique for ceramic imitation of stone vessels. This does not seem convincing on present evidence (why should it be done at T. el Alayik and not at Jericho, a mile to the north?), but full consideration must await the publication of the Bab edh-Dhra material.

p. 98.   A further Carbon-14 dating from the upper levels of Safadi, certainly contemporary with the Proto-Urban cultures, is 3160 B.C. ± 310. A study of the connections between Palestine and adjacent countries,[2] has emphasised the length of the Proto-Urban period, especially at Tell Gath, and shown that there is a clear chronological overlap with the First Dynasty of Egypt, certainly to the time of Narmer and probably overlapping that of his successor Menes. On the chronology adopted in the revised version of the Cambridge Ancient History, this would give a terminal date of *c.* 3050 B.C. Other datings would place the end of the period a hundred or two hundred years later, which in many ways would fit the Palestinian evidence better.

CHAPTER 5   *The City States of the Early Bronze Age*

p. 110.   The completion of the excavations at Tell el Far'ah has shown that the original interpretation has to be corrected. It is now clear that the first Early Bronze Age town was in fact defended by a town wall. The wall of Period I was of mud-bricks on stone foundations, and, like the first houses, it was built directly over the remains of the Proto-Urban (or, as Père de Vaux would prefer, Pre-Urban) period. It is to this first stage in the defences that belongs the gateway on the west side, with its two very well-preserved brick-built towers projecting outwards from the wall. The wall has been traced almost the complete

[1] J. A. Callaway, *Pottery of the Tombs at 'Ai (Et-Tell).*
[2] J. B. Hennessy, *The Foreign Relations of Palestine during the Early Bronze Age.*

length of the west edge of the summit plateau, with some evidence
that there was a projecting tower at each extremity. The remains of the
wall peter out at the north end, and the line of the north wall was not
established; it lay however appreciably to the north of the later rampart. To the south it is suggested that no defences were required, owing
to the steepness of the slope, and the eastern perimeter has not been
investigated. These defences date to early in Early Bronze I. It seems
probable that the people who built them came from an area in which
building in rectangular, form-made, mud-bricks was already fully
established. At Far'ah, urbanisation certainly seems to be imposed by
newcomers and not to develop out of the preceding period. The later
stone wall, with which the brick-built gate continued in use, comes at
the beginning of E.B. II. To the north, it was set back from its predecessor, and it was the continuation under it and beyond it to the north
of the earliest houses that led to the original interpretation that the
first town was not defended.

p. 116.   Recent work by Professor J. A. Callaway at 'Ai has given
more precision to the finds from the site. There was some occupation
during E.B. I. The first and innermost phase of the fortifications and
their succeeding strengthening belongs to E.B. II. To this belongs what
was called the citadel, which was actually only a strengthened area of
the defences. Against the inner side of the earliest wall, though
secondary to it, was built the earliest stage of the sanctuary, which had
in fact two and not three stages. This was a simple structure, with two
rooms and a circular altar. To the same period belongs the first stage
of an important building on the summit of the hill, which had
previously been identified alternatively as a palace or temple, but is
now considered to be a citadel within an acropolis with its own independent fortifications. All these structures came to an end in a tremendous fire. The succeeding phase is considered to cover the first
half of E.B. III. To it belongs the massive wall that in one area made
up the outermost of the three juxtaposed defence lines and in the
sanctuary area took the place of the earlier one, with a stone-faced
revetting at its outer foot. The rebuilt wall destroyed the earlier sanctuary, which was replaced by the later one with the different and more
elaborate plan described on p. 116. It is probably not necessary to
suppose that the vessels datable to the Second and Third Egyptian

Dynasties were derived from the earlier sanctuary, for it can be shown[1] that E.B. III in Palestine is likely to overlap the period of the Second Dynasty, and to start c. 2700 B.C. At the same time in the acropolis area, the citadel was almost completely rebuilt as a long oblong room with a central row of columns. The masonry of the walls is exquisite, of hammer-dressed slabs of stone, which it is convincingly suggested imitate mud-bricks and, as with a mud-brick wall, the stones are set in mud mortar and the face was plastered. Professor Callaway sees strong Egyptian influence in the style of construction.

p. 119. A most important addition to knowledge of the Early Bronze Age towns in southern Palestine has been made by the excavations at Arad, a site 20 miles slightly north of east from Beersheba. It is a site in a semi-arid zone, only marginally suitable for agriculture. It appears in the Biblical record, and it is suggested that the site of Solomon's citadel there can be identified. This formed a very small part of the first Arad. There was an original settlement belonging to the Ghassulian culture, comparable with the Beersheba settlements. This was succeeded by an Early Bronze Age town covering an area of 25 acres. By the time of the second of four identified phases, it was surrounded by a stone wall 2.50 metres thick, with projecting semi-circular bastions, which may be compared with an early phase in the Jericho defences (p. 107). A number of houses built against the city wall, and divided by streets have been excavated. In the low-lying central area of the city, a building public in character has been excavated, which it is suggested is a sanctuary. The finds show a firm connection with Egypt. There is evidence to support the theory that Arad may have been an important site on a trade route by which Egypt was supplied with bitumen from the Dead Sea. The Egyptian finds are all related to the First Egyptian Dynasty. The occupation of Arad on this evidence and on that of the indigenous culture thus belongs only to Early Bronze Age I and II, and may have come to an end with a great destruction c. 2700 B.C. The history of Arad is therefore very different from that of the other Palestinian towns, lying to the north and in a marginally more fertile area. It is highly probable that trade with Egypt is the decisive factor in the history of Arad, but the full implications have still to be worked out.

[1] Hennessy, *op. cit.*, pp. 71 and 86–8.

p. 122. In 1959, a sanctuary was identified at Tell el Far'ah. It lasted throughout the Early Bronze Age, but the most convincing remains belong to the first period, early in E.B. I. A large room had an open front at the east end. Its area was divided into two by a somewhat oblique kerb of bricks, on which there stood a rectangular stone structure, perhaps an altar. To the west of this kerb, the walls were flanked by trenches 25 centimetres high, widening into a platform in the north-west corner. It is suggested that this area formed the *cella* of the sanctuary. The plan is clearly very different from that at 'Ai, but we have so little comparative material that we cannot interpret the significance. This sanctuary belonged only to the first period; its successors had less distinctive features, but could also have been sanctuaries.

p. 127. A thorough examination of the contacts between Palestine and Egypt has recently been made.[1] Egyptian objects of the First Dynasty date are found in Palestine both in Proto-Urban and Early Bronze I assemblages. If the Cambridge Ancient History dates for the First Dynasty of 3100–2900 B.C. are accepted (which is unwelcome to Palestinian archaeologists), this would imply an initial date for E.B. I of *c.* 3050 B.C. The whole of E.B. I would seem to come within the period of the First Dynasty, for E.B. II also seems to overlap with that period, and may start *c.* 2950 B.C. E.B. II again covers a comparatively short period, for E.B. III has links with the Second Dynasty (*C.A.H.*, 2900–2686 B.C.), and may start about 2700 B.C. These correlations accord not only with the finds of Egyptian imports, but with the amount of evidence concerning the different periods. There is no doubt that E.B. III is the longest and most important period. Dr. Hennessy's date for its end is 2350 B.C.

CHAPTER 6   *The Arrival of the Amorites*

p. 148. Considerable additional material to the E.B.-M.B. period has accumulated in the last ten years. The most important is perhaps that in the hills to the east and north-east of Jericho, from the crest of the hills to half-way down the arid slopes to the Jordan Valley. Material from Khirbet es-Samiyeh, from early unrecorded excavations and now in the Institute of Archaeology in London, had suggested some of the

[1] J. B. Hennessy, *The Foreign Relations of Palestine during the Early Bronze Age.*

closest parallels to the small jars characteristic of the Jericho Pottery-type tombs (Fig. 25, 1–6), as did vessels also in the Institute described as from "Cave East of Olivet," probably excavated by Warren on the slopes of the Mount of Olives at Jerusalem. There is now additional information about both these areas.

It appears that there is a whole group of cemeteries in the neighbour-hood of 'Ain es-Samiyeh about seven miles north-east of Beitin, in desolate, rocky, hill-country. At one of them, Dhahr Mirzbaneh, Dr. Paul Lapp excavated thirty-six tombs.[1] In plan and section, they are closely similar to the Pottery-type tombs at Jericho. Like these, they contain only disarticulated bones; some even contain none, and it seems more reasonable to interpret them as tombs prepared and not used, than as "burials without bones," which seems a very strange descrip-tion: cenotaphs would be a better one if this interpretation is to be accepted. A difference from Jericho is that four shafts had two distinct chambers at the base, only found in one instance at Jericho in a compo-site-type tomb, and there were no lamp niches. The pottery vessels again are similar but not identical to those of the Jericho Pottery-type tombs. In both, the small jars (Fig. 25, 1–6) and the four-spouted lamps are by far the most common finds, but the Mirzbaneh tombs include the large, flat based jars with flaring rims, to which the nearest Jericho parallels come from the Outsize-type tombs, but more akin to those of the southern sites of T. Ajjul, T. Duweir and T. Neit Mersim. A dagger and a javelin, again not found at Jericho in the Pottery-type tombs, were also included. An interesting point about the Mirzbaneh cemetery was that there was evidence of adjacent camping sites, suggesting seasonal visits of a pastoral community.

Similar tombs, with similar finds were made at el-Jib, near Ramul-lah. There, many of the tombs had been re-used in the Middle Bronze Age, but the contents of those that had not been, and the finds left in the re-used tombs, had just the same range, with large pots distinctly closer to those from the Outsize tombs at Jericho.

Thirdly, eleven tombs were excavated in 1965 on the east side of the Mount of Olives.[2] They introduce a new type—in form of shaft and chamber similar to the Jericho-Dagger-type tombs but somewhat larger, but containing pottery with features of that from Pottery-type tombs but also other forms.

[1] P. W. Lapp, *The Dhahr Mirzbaneh Tombs.*
[2] *P.E.Q.*, 1966.

It can hardly be doubted that these groups are allied to those at Jericho, especially to the group burying there in the Pottery-type tombs. The blurring of the sharpness of the distinctions could again suggest some amalgamation or intermarriage which is one hypothesis put forward in connection with the Ajjul groups (p. 146).

p. 153. It is now possible to amplify the picture of the Megiddo-El Husn group by the evidence from Beth-shan. During the Pennsylvania excavations at this site, a large number of tombs of the E.B.-M.B. period were excavated in the Northern Cemetery. They have not yet been published, but I am indebted for information concerning the records of them to Mrs. Garner James and Mr. E. Oren. Many of the tombs had been re-used in later periods, but there was clear evidence of their original period and plan. The tombs all had rectangular shafts, associated with single, two linearly-arranged or multiple chambers, and the latter are exceedingly close to the Megiddo Shaft-Tomb plans, though somewhat less regular. The contents of all tombs are closely comparable with those of the Megiddo Shaft-Tombs. The Beth-shan evidence, therefore, adds most useful emphasis on the regional distribution of this E.B.-M.B. group. Tombs from Maʿayan Barukh,[1] southeast of Affula, seem to belong to the same northern group on the evidence of both pottery and metal objects, especially pins, though it has its own variants.

p. 155. A further example of the complete destruction of a large Early Bronze Age town by E.B.-M.B. people for whom evidence comes only from burials is at Bab edh-Dhra, on the east side of the Dead Sea, near the Lisan,[2]

p. 159. The identification of the authors of the disturbances as Amorites has been discussed in detail in two studies.[3] A completely different explanation is proposed by Dr. Lapp.[4] Dr. Lapp would identify the newcomers as being the Beaker Folk who appear in Western Europe at about the same time whom he would derive from Soviet Central Asia. He considers they arrived in southern Palestine

[1] Atiqot III.
[2] See P. W. Lapp, *The Dhahr Mirzbaneh Tombs.*
[3] *C.A.H.* Revised edition Vol. I, Chap. XXI; *Amorites and Canaanites.*
[4] op cit., pp. 86ff.

in two waves by sea, the first wave spreading thence to cause the First Intermediate Period in Egypt, the second taking its place and spreading northwards over the whole of Palestine. The argument is an elaborate one, and not at present convincing. The more usual identification of the raiders with the Amorites still seems more plausible.

CHAPTER 7 *The Middle Bronze Age and the Hyksos*

p. 191. The tombs published in Jericho II add a few more examples of beds and stools. A second bed is probably to be identified, again in a tomb of a family of distinction, since the principal body lay on a platform of mud-bricks. Seven additional tombs, and possibly a further two, contained stools. Of the certain examples, three had features marking them as the burial place of important people.

CHAPTER 8 *The Late Bronze Age and the Coming of the Israelites*

p. 197. A re-assessment of the evidence for Megiddo in the Middle and Late Bronze Ages[1] indicates that a considerable revision of the history of the town in the Late Bronze Age is required. The gateway shown on Fig. 46 belongs to the 14th century B.C., and there is no evidence for the 16th century B.C. gateway.

p. 198. It would seem that even at Hazor there was some decline at this period. There was at best a much reduced population in the latter part of the 16th century B.C., and for much of the 15th century, and there may even have been a gap.

p. 203. In the re-assessment of the Megiddo evidence it is suggested[2] that in the later stages of the Middle Bronze Age and at the beginning of the Late Bronze Age, the sacred area was occupied by successors to the E.B.-M.B. temple of which only very scanty remains survive. It would seem that these continue down to the destruction of Megiddo by Thotmes III in 1481 B.C., following which the town lay in ruins for about a hundred years. The temple here described probably only belongs to the beginning of the 14th century B.C.

[1] *Levant* I, pp. 25–60.
[2] ibid., pp. 40–55.

p. 212. Hazor was certainly a much more important town than Jericho. After the period of decline referred to above, there was a large and flourishing town from the late 15th century onwards. Structures and levels dating from then to the 13th century have been found all over the tell and the lower city that was added in M.B. II. The L.B. structures in the lower city, which alone have been fully published, have three main strata, Stratum II, late L.B.I dating to the end of the 15th century, Stratum IB. covering most of the 14th century, and IA belonging to the early 13th century. The most interesting structures are two sanctuaries. One, on a small scale, is cut back into the inner side of the great bank built as the M.B. defences of the area, furnished with a row of miniature stele, some bearing cult symbols. The second was at the extreme north end of the lower town, and in its developed form was tripartite, with a porch flanked by pillars and lions carved on orthostats, a central room and an inner Holy of Holies. In the latter many cult vessels and furnishings were found—impressive stone and pottery vessels, altars and so on. In the tripartite plan and linear arrangement of the chambers, the sanctuary foreshadows the Jerusalem temple, though the proportions of the components are very different. In both sanctuaries, as in other structures (the domestic buildings are not very impressive), there is a simpler stage in Stratum II, followed by the most imposing stage in IB and a poorer reconstruction after a destruction in IA. Precision is given to the dating by a richly furnished tomb with a number of Mycenaean vessels. The finds are typical of Stratum IB. Some of the finds, including a scarab of Thotmes IV (1412–1403) may go back to the beginning of the 14th century B.C. The Mycenaean pottery is all to be classified as Mycenaean IIIA.2, most of it late in the period, which ends *c.* 1304 B.C. Stratum IB therefore comes to an end at that point. Professor Yadin suggests that it was destroyed by Seti I *c.* 1318 B.C., which is a reasonable hypothesis. Stratum IA immediately follows the destruction. In general, the finds are close to those from IB. Some Mycenaean IIIB pottery is however found. This could possibly be as late as 1230 B.C. But the poorness of the remains and the closeness of the finds to those of IB argue strongly for an early stage in the use of Mycenaean IIIB. The end of Stratum IA was violent and long-lasting. It marked the end of occupation in the lower town, and an interruption of the occupation of the tell, until about the time of Solomon. On present evidence, there is no reason to put the end of Stratum IA later than the first quarter of the 13th century B.C. It would thus fall between one and two generations after the destruction of Jericho at the date here suggested. If both destructions are to be attributed to the invading Israelites, which is at least possible, it would measure this expansion rate in quite reasonable terms.

A third site that, with Jericho and Hazor, appears dramatically in the conquests of Joshua is 'Ai (Joshua 8. 1–29). The site is with great probability to be identified with et-Tell, some ten miles north of Jerusalem. The excavations carried out here between 1933 and 1935 provided a serious problem for archaeologists, for the main city proved to belong to the Early Bronze Age (see pp. 115 ff and 306) and the site was unoccupied during the usually accepted period of the entry of the Israelites in the Late Bronze Age. More recent excavations have defined an Iron Age occupation as belonging to Iron Age I and dating to the 12th century B.C. It is suggested that it is the capture of the 'Ai of this period that is reflected in the Book of Joshua. It is true that it was a village of less than 3 acres and apparently without town walls. However, neither the small size of the settlement nor the comparatively late date would conflict with a picture of the entry of the Israelites as a gradual infiltration over a long period by a number of separate groups.

CHAPTER 9   *The Philistines and the Beginning of the Early Iron Age*

pp. 233–5. A recent re-examination by Professor Yadin of the evidence concerning the Megiddo water system has shown that the first access to the spring, the sloping gallery, is to be dated to the time of Solomon, and the succeeding shaft and tunnel is not likely to be earlier than the time of Ahab. The evidence for this is described below, in notes on p. 345.

CHAPTER 10   *The United Monarchy*

p. 243. The east wall of the Jebusite-Davidic town was therefore well down the east slope, at a point strategically low enough to deny attackers access to the spring, but not so low that it was commanded by an enemy on the other side of the valley. The line from the identified point has not been further traced, but may be presumed to follow about the same contour to the southern tip of the ridge. The west wall seems to run north from this point along the edge of the summit of the ridge, for areas below this line were shown by excavation to be outside the Iron Age town. The northern wall can be shown to have crossed the ridge at a distance c. 200 metres south of the present south wall of the Haram.[1] The area enclosed by the walls was 10·87 acres.

p. 245. Some little additional evidence has now been secured concerning Solomonic Jerusalem. The site of the Temple lies some 200 metres north of the north wall of the Jebusite-Davidic town. It was linked to it by a wall that was not a prolongation of the earlier east wall, low on the slope, but by one following the crest of the hill. On the west side it is possible that the wall followed the line of the projecting salient in the present wall of the Old City. The plan is shown on Fig. 58.

It has become regrettably clear that, though the lines of the enclosure walls can be suggested, virtually nothing has survived of the interior of the city of Solomon or of its predecessor and successors. A considerable part of the surface of the ridge has been excavated during the past fifty years, and it is now clear that these excavations, especially those of M. Weill in 1913–14, must be interpreted as showing that the surface of the rock has been extensively quarried, and the overlying buildings therefore destroyed. Much of this quarrying took place when Aelia Capitolina succeeded Jerusalem, leaving the area of the original city outside the wall, but some quarrying had already taken place in the time of Herod the Great.

It is now possible to suggest the limits of the platform of Solomon's Temple. Clearance outside the south-east angle of Herod's platform has revealed a straight joint between Herod's masonry to the south and earlier masonry to the north at a distance of 32·72 metres from the present south-east corner. The style of the earlier stone-work suggests comparisons with structures of the Persian period in Syria, especially at Eshmoun,[2] near Sidon, and Byblos.[3] It is very tempting to associate it with the reconstruction of the Temple by Zerubbabel c. 516 B.C., when the Persian successors to the Babylonians allowed the exiles to return to Jerusalem. It is very unlikely that Zerubbabel would have enlarged Solomon's Temple, and it is reasonable to suggest that beneath this angle lies the angle of Solomon's platform. No corresponding break is to be found on the west side of Herod's platform. It is to be presumed that the earlier west wall lies further east, within the

[1] P.E.Q., 1969.
[2] *Bulletin du Musée de Beyrouth,* XVIII, XIX.
[3] ibid., XIX.

core of the platform, and it can very tentatively be suggested that the
line of the existing salient was directed towards it.

p. 250. Excavations by Professor Yadin in 1960,[1] 1966[2] and 1967[3]
produced most satisfactory evidence about the defences of Solomonic
Megiddo and of some of the buildings. On the Megiddo Stratum IV
plan a solid wall built with a series of offsets and insets is shown
associated with the gateway which on plan is so close to the Solomonic
Gate at Hazor (see p. 248 and Fig. 59). An excavation in the north-east
sector of the site[4] showed that beneath the offsets and insets wall was a
casemate wall. This wall was associated with a large scale building
in the courtyard constructed of the ashlar blocks found in the gateway
and also in the "palace" building found on the south side of the mound[5]
(see pp. 264–70). The new "palace" or "fortress", moreover, lies
beneath one of the stable buildings of Stratum IV. Though no junction
of the casemate wall with the gateway has been established, on the
Hazor parallel we can say with some certainty that they belong
together. The elements of the plan of Solomonic Megiddo are therefore beginning to emerge. The summit of the mound was surrounded
by a casemate wall with the elaborate gateway shown on Fig. 59. The
lay-out of this town included at least two important buildings of
official character, of which the outer wall formed part of the defences.
With the southern one went an adjacent building. This had had to be
explained as an earlier phase, destroyed when the stables were built
(see p. 270), but now that it can be accepted that the "palace" is Solomonic, it falls into place as part of the original plan. The courtyard wall
of the southern "palace" is certainly a rebuild, but there may have been
an earlier one, for an entrance into the enclosure seems to be original.
The rest of the summit seems to have been occupied by the unimpressive private houses ascribed to Stratum V.

An additional feature that can now be shown to be Solomonic is the
first stage of the water system. This consisted of a gallery cut into the
surface of the mound sloping down to the foot near the source of the
spring[6] (see pp. 233–4). This was earlier than the offsets and insets wall,
which crossed its top. The guard-chamber that seemed to protect
access from it to the spring was apparently abandoned in the 12th

---

[1] *Biblical Archaeologist*, 1960.   [2] *I.E.J.* 16, pp. 227 ff.   [3] *I.E.J.* 17, pp. 119 ff.
[4] *M.I.*, Fig. 119.   [5] ibid., Fig. 12.
[6] See R. S. Lamon, *Megiddo Water System.*

century B.C. (see p. 234) and this was considered to date the gallery. However, the excavations in 1966 showed that the gallery was cut through the remains of Stratum VI, here claimed to end *c.* 1100 B.C., and of Stratum VB, which may belong to the time of David. It thus seems very probable that the gallery, which is built in good ashlar, belongs to the time of Solomon.

pp. 256–8. Subsequent exploration, mainly by B. Rothenberg, has shown that it is not possible to associate the mining sites in the 'Arabah with Solomon. Various periods of mining are proved, from the Chalcolithic onwards, and the technological evidence of the processes is most interesting. Mining in the Early Iron Age, however, can be dated as not later than the 11th century B.C. It was carried out by the Edomites, and may even have been brought to an end by David's conquests.[1] The copper for the fitments of bronze of Solomon's temple, the pillars and basins, must have come from Cyprus or some site on the mainland, such as Sinai, not yet identified.

CHAPTER 11   *The Kingdoms of Israel and Judah*

p. 266. Further excavations at Samaria in 1968 showed that there were no buildings earlier than the 6th–5th centuries B.C. on the terrace immediately below the summit to the north-west. It may therefore be that the town did not extend to the west slopes of the hill, and that the lower town that is presumed to have existed outside the royal quarter lay on the gentler slope to the east, beneath the forum of the Roman period and the modern village east of it. Further excavation is required.

p. 269. The elucidation of the Solomonic period at Megiddo now makes the position of the main Stratum IV buildings there much clearer. The discovery of a northern "palace" or fortress beneath one of the stable buildings has already been described. This enables one to place the original construction of the "palace" also into the Solomonic period, and makes it no longer necessary to suggest that the important official building 1482 to its west[2] was truncated immediately after its construction by the main Stratum IV lay-out of the stables. The

[1] *Bulletin of the Museum Haaretz, Tel Aviv*, No. 7, 1965.
[2] M.I., Fig. 12.

Solomonic buildings are related to those of Samaria since Solomon and Omri both employed Phoenician masons.

One can thus see two important and quite distinct phases in the lay-out of Megiddo. To the Solomonic period belong the gateway (Fig. 59), the casemate wall (see p. 249), two forts or palaces and building 1482 adjoining the southern palace. The southern palace was associated with a large courtyard, on the evidence that the gateway (p. 54) is built in the authentic ashlar style. The rest of the summit was occupied by ordinary and unimpressive private dwellings. The second phase is a revolutionary development that transformed the summit into a reserved royal quarter on the lines of that established by Omri at Samaria in 880 B.C. To this belong the stables which, with the court-yard of the southern "palace" take up so much of the area that has been excavated. The construction of the stables involved the abolition of the northern "fortress" and of part of building 1482 adjoining the southern "palace". To this phase can now be ascribed the great water-shaft and tunnel, described on pp. 233–5. It is certainly later than the Solomonic gallery, and though no new dating evidence has so far been found, the probability is very high that it belongs to this phase of great public buildings.

The date of the Stratum IV buildings at Megiddo is probably soon after 850 B.C.[1] They could belong to the time of Ahab, or to early in the time of Jehu, who in 841 B.C. drove out the dynasty of Omri. The former is perhaps more likely. But it is equally clear that it is unlikely that this "royal quarter" at Megiddo comes early in the time of Ahab, both on the pottery evidence and that of architecture.

The peculiar structure of the stables and the enclosure wall of the palace courtyard, with piers of ashlar blocks at intervals in walls mainly built of rubble, is mentioned on p. 271. An examination of the ashlar blocks in these piers shows that the stones are certainly re-used.[2] These walls are therefore distinct from those of the "palace," the adja-cent building 1482, the northern fortress, and also the gateway into the courtyard of the "palace." It can be deduced that the ashlar blocks were robbed from the earlier buildings, and the walls of the northern fortress were in fact found in places to have been robbed to the base of their foundations. The walls of the "palace" courtyard apparently had to be rebuilt. It would seem that by the time the Megiddo Stratum IV

[1] *Samaria III*, pp. 199–204; *Megiddo, Hazor, Samaria and Chronology*, p. 151.
[2] *Megiddo, Hazor, Samaria and Chronology*, p. 149.

royal quarter was laid out, Phoenician masons were no longer available. The transformation of the whole summit of the hill in this way is nevertheless impressive evidence of royal power.

p. 272. The latest discoveries at Hazor show that here too at this period a grandiose water system was established. The excavation is not yet (1969) complete, but the upper part consists of a great shaft with steps descending its sides, very closely similar to that at Megiddo. Its relation to earlier structures proved that it belonged to this stage, which at Megiddo can so far only be surmised.

p. 276. The recent excavations of Arad show that the site performed a function on the southern frontiers of Judah somewhat similar to that of Tell el Fûl on the north. The extensive town of the Early Bronze Age has already been described. The north-east corner of the site stands up as a tell high above the level of the rest of the site, for on it was constructed a citadel, founded directly on the final Early Bronze II remains. It was certainly a citadel throughout the life of the kingdom of Judah, with later stages in the Hellenistic, Roman and Arab periods. Its earliest stage may even belong to the time of Solomon, though the evidence for this has still to be presented. The plan throughout the Iron Age was basically the same, with enclosing walls about 50 metres on each side, the earliest of casemate form, the later built on the offsets and insets plan, and a central courtyard surrounded by buildings on three sides. Some were certainly administrative, for a number of ostraca almost certainly belonging to official archives have been found. One complex is of especial interest, since it was certainly a sanctuary. In a large courtyard was a massive altar 2·5 metres square, standing high above the floor level, and built of mud and undressed stones. At the west end of the courtyard was a wide room, entered on one of its long sides, with the entrance flanked by two pillars that recall the pillars Jachin and Boaz of Solomon's Temple. Against the wall of this sanctuary were two benches. In the long side opposite the entrance a very small room projects to the west, plausibly identified as a Holy of Holies. In or near it were found in various strata two small stone altars and a mazzebah or cult stone. The excavators' claim that this is certainly a sanctuary of Yahweh, on the grounds that it complies with Biblical ritual laws and that it was part of an official citadel, is not completely convincing. The plan certainly bears no relation to that of

Solomon's Temple, for it is planned on a broad and not longitudinal axis, and it can only be called tripartite if part of the courtyard is arbitrarily divided off and called a porch. The impossibility of an unorthodox sanctuary being included within a distant official frontier post is not supported by the evidence of considerable heterodoxy in the highest circles. Moreover, it does not now seem likely that the sanctuary was abolished during Josiah's reforms, for the later citadel wall that destroyed it probably belongs to the Hellenistic period.[1] Even if the implications of evidence of official cult centres of Yahweh outside Jerusalem are not accepted, the site remains of very great interest for the organisation of the kingdom of Judah.

p. 279. As described above, it is now clear that the Phoenician-style masonry at Megiddo has already disappeared in Stratum IV. It is in fact likely that the Stratum IV buildings were destroyed in the Assyrian complex of the town in 734 B.C. and that the new lay-out belongs to the time of the Assyrian domination of this area of the kingdom of Israel.

CHAPTER *12   The Fall of the Hebrew Kingdoms and the Post-Exilic Period*

p. 289. The few surviving domestic buildings in Jerusalem found by the 1961–7 expedition belong to this final century of the kingdom of Judah. They survive at the summit of the eastern slope above the spring Gihon. They are constructed directly on the terraces that were the Jebusite contribution to the planning of Jerusalem (see p. 243), and which were repaired by David and his successors. The terraces were precarious structures, dependent on retaining walls, each bounding a terrace and each supported by terraces lower down the hill. The frequent catastrophes, from natural agencies or human destruction, are proved by the fact that though the original terraces were certainly Jebusite, and some repairing can be attributed to the early stages of the Monarchy, the only houses actually to survive on them belong to the 7th century B.C. They consist of domestic buildings of unimpressive character. The walls are of very roughly dressed stones, only roughly coursed, set in mud-mortar and originally traced with a covering of mud-mortar. Most of the rooms were small, and the planning was

[1] *I.E.J.,* 15.

only roughly rectangular. One room only was of larger size of the tripartite plan found at Tell Nasbeh, in which a central area is divided from two side areas by rows of monolithic piers; only one of these rows was found, as the easternmost had collapsed down the hill in the erosion following the Babylonian destruction. The basically domestic use is shown by the plan and by the find of a characteristic domed clay oven. In one area, the find of forty-one stone weights, some of them inscribed with their denomination, suggests the abode of a shopkeeper or craftsman.

To a period that may just precede this final century in the history of Monarchic Jerusalem or may belong to its beginning, belongs one of the most interesting finds of the 1961-7 excavations; the question of whether it is to be ascribed to the end of the 8th century or the early part of the 7th has still to be established by a detailed analysis of the finds. It consisted of structures low on the eastern slope, outside the contemporary walls. One complex consisted of a shallow cave surrounded by massive walls, in which there was a large deposit of pottery. Adjoining it was a small room in which there were two standing stones, certainly to be interpreted as mazzeboth, or cult symbols. On the rock scarp above was a small rectangular structure that could well be an altar. It is reasonably certain that the complex is to be interpreted as a sanctuary, in which the cave served the function of a *favissa*, a repository of vessels offered in the sanctuary, which would not thereafter be returned to profane use. Ten metres to the south was a larger cave, containing a much larger deposit of objects, mainly pottery vessels, but including a fine incense burner and a large number of figurines, female figures of the fertility-goddess type, and animals including horses with disks on their foreheads, possibly associated with the "horses of the sun." This cave must also have been a *favissa* of the same or an adjacent sanctuary. The complex must be interpreted as an extra-mural sanctuary of an unorthodox cult. The denunciations of the prophets prepare one for such sanctuaries, but it is a surprise to find this evidence within 300 metres of the Temple of Yahweh. It is tempting to see in the great accumulation of objects, some 1,300 in all in the larger cave, evidence of the cleansing of all unorthodox sanctuaries by Josiah c. 750 B.C. The stratification makes it difficult to accept a date as late as this, and full interpretation must wait until the analysis of the finds has been completed.

p. 291. The houses on the crest of the eastern slope described above (p. 39) show the violence of the destruction. The surviving floors are covered with great piles of stones from the collapsed upper parts of the walls. More disastrous still was the collapse of the retaining walls that supported the terraces on which the houses on the eastern slope were built. The whole structure on the slope was an interlocking one, each terrace being partly supported by that lower down the slope, with the lowest supported by the town wall. When the lowest walls were breached, as must clearly have been the case in the Babylonian destruction, the next terraces up the hill would be weakened, and the collapse would have spread cumulatively back up the hill behind each breach in the town wall. The effect would not be instantaneous, but a single hard winter's rains would complete it. The surviving remains on the eastern slope show the result. Low down the slope only substructures and what are probably to be interpreted as basements survive. At the summit there are the remains of houses already described. Their outer edge has however collapsed, with the retaining wall that supported them. This is clearest in the large room, originally tripartite with the plan, that can be presumed from parallels, of a central hall divided from side aisles by two lines of monolithic piers. At just the point at which the easternmost line should have been found, steep lines of erosion cut down across the floor, and the rest of the building has disappeared. The cumulative collapse created the tumble of stones that confronted the excavators in 1961–7, and which had also confronted Nehemiah when he came to rebuild the city walls.

p. 300. Reference has already been made (p. 344) to the evidence provided by the straight joint against which the Herodian addition to the Temple platform was made. An earlier boundary of the Temple platform 32·72 metres north of the present south wall is certain. This corner of the platform must therefore be at least as early as the pre-Herodian Maccabean period. There is visual evidence of at least three reconstructions in the surviving masonry, and this in itself could carry the first visible stage back to the time when Zerubbabel completed the rebuilding of the Temple *c.* 516 B.C. under the aegis of the Persian successors to the Babylonians. This ascription is supported by a comparison of the masonry with that of known Persian structures in Syria, that of the great temples of Eshmoun[1] near Sidon, dated to the late 6th–early 5th century B.C. and the rather later Persian structures at Byblos. The suggestion that this Persian-style platform corresponds in outline with that of the Solomonic period is discussed above (p. 344).

[1] *Bulletin du Musée de Beyrouth*, XVIII, XIX.

Index

[N.B. *The Revision and Addenda section has not been indexed, but cross-references will be found throughout the text.*]

Index

Abraham, 183, 194
Abu Hawam, Tell, 231, 272, 301, 306
Abu Matar, Tell, 77 ff., 306
'Affuleh, 77, 81, 96
Agriculture:
  Neolithic, 20, 37, 42, 45
  Chalcolithic, 79
  Early Bronze Age, 108, 134
  Iron Age, 277
Ahab, 262, 265, 282
'Ai, 88, 97, 99, 113, 115–7, 122, 130, 306
'Ain Mallaha, 38
Ajjul, Tell, 119, 135, 143, 153, 154,
  164, 165, 180, 188, 192, 230, 307
Albright, Professor W. F., 114, 160,
  166n, 212, 214
Amarna age, 185, 202, 219
Amarna letters, 182, 206, 207, 209,
  219, 227
American School of Oriental Research
  in Jerusalem, 256
Amorites, 136, 159–60, 207
'Arabah, Wadi, 256
Arabs, 27
Archaeology, what it can do, and its
  limitations, 22 ff.
  Methods, 31 ff.
Architecture:
  Iron Age, 265–6, 270
Arslan Tash, 247, 268, 298
Askelon, 224, 230, 301, 305
Assyrians, 266, 282–3, 285, 286 ff., 297
'Athlit, 302
Azekah, 294

Babylonians, 289, 291, 294, 297–8, 300
Beit Mirsim, Tell, 308
  Early Bronze Age, 119

Beit Mirsim, Tell (cont'd.)
  E.B.–M.B., 152, 153, 154
  Middle Bronze Age, 166, 176, 181,
    185, 194, 197
  Late Bronze Age, 212–4
  Iron Age, 230, 254, 273, 290, 291
Beth-shan: 83, 84, 103, 309
  Chalcolithic, 96
  Proto-Urban, 96
  Early Bronze Age, 112–4, 127
  E.B.–M.B., 152, 153
  Late Bronze Age, 215, 218–9, 227
  Iron Age, 227, 231, 235–6, 240, 269,
    272
Beth Shemesh, 230, 238, 252–4, 273–4,
  286, 290, 291, 310
Beth-zur, 230
Bethel, 115, 212, 237, 308
Bible, 17, 18
Brak, 152, 158
Bricks, mud:
  Pre-Pottery Neolithic A, 43
  Pre-Pottery Neolithic B, 48
  Pottery Neolithic, 65
  Early Bronze Age, 105
Bronze, 164, 238
Bronze Age, 20
Burial customs:
  Mesolithic, 37–8
  Pre-Pottery Neolithic, 53, 85
  Pottery Neolithic, 85
  Ghassulian, 85
  Proto-Urban, 84–8
  Early Bronze Age, 122–3
  E.B.–M.B., 137 ff.
  Middle Bronze Age, 167, 189 ff.
  Iron Age, 227
Byblos, 22, 34, 58, 66–7, 121, 160, 161,
  163–4, 169, 193

355

*Printed in Great Britain
by The Garden City Press Limited
Letchworth, Hertfordshire*